CAMBRIDGE STUDIES IN MEDIEVAL LITERATURE 6

The *Cantar de mio Cid*

This book, the first to accord full treatment to the important thematic complex of the acquisition and distribution of wealth, interprets the *Cantar de mio Cid* as a work that transmutes moral values first into the economic values of a gift economy, then into genealogical values. In disproving the legend of the hero's bastardy, the poet echoes the concerns of the Castilian court of Alfonso VIII and reaffirms the dignity of the Cid's progeny and relatives, who included the king and the Lara family of Molina. Considering the poem's distortions of history more significant than its retention of historical features, Joseph Duggan ascribes its depiction of the penurious hero who acquires wealth, power, and kinship alliances to the Castilian monarchy's preoccupations with furthering the Reconquest in the dark period between the defeat of Alarcos and the victory of Las Navas de Tolosa. He posits that the *Cantar de mio Cid* was composed around the year 1200 in substantially the form in which we have it, in the course of a singer's performance. The occasion on which it was performed may have been Alfonso VIII's meeting in that year with Pedro II of Aragon at Ariza in the valley of the Jalón river, in which much of the poem's action takes place.

Arguing against a number of recent tendencies in *Cid* scholarship, he denies the necessity of assuming that the poet was a man of learning, that he was directly influenced by French literature, or that he was familiar with written law. This ground-breaking monograph provides a major contribution to medieval Hispanic studies.

CAMBRIDGE STUDIES IN MEDIEVAL LITERATURE

General Editor: Professor Alastair Minnis, Professor of Medieval Literature, University of York

Editorial Board
Professor Piero Boitani (Professor of English, Rome)
Professor Patrick Boyde (Serena Professor of Italian, Cambridge)
Professor John Burrow, FBA (Winterstoke Professor of English, Bristol)
Peter Dronke, FBA (Reader in Medieval Latin Literature, Cambridge)
Professor John Freccero (Rosina Pierotti Professor of Italian, Stanford)
Tony Hunt (Reader in French, St Andrews)
Dr Nigel Palmer (Lecturer in Medieval German, Oxford)
Professor Winthrop Wetherbee (Professor of English, Cornell)

This new series of critical books seeks to cover the whole area of literature written in the major medieval languages – the main European vernaculars, and Medieval Latin and Greek – during the period c. 1100–c. 1500. Its chief aim is to publish and stimulate fresh scholarship and criticism on medieval literature, special emphasis being placed on understanding major works of poetry, prose and drama in relation to the contemporary cultures and learning which fostered them. It will accommodate studies which bring a special expertise or neglected body of knowledge to bear on the interpretative problems of important texts. Texts, genres and literary conventions which, while significant in their own times and places and of considerable value to the medievalist, have been undervalued or misrepresented in modern times, fall within its range; and it will give space to innovative critical approaches to medieval texts of all types.

Titles published
Dante's Inferno: *Difficulty and Dead Poetry*, by Robin Kirkpatrick
Dante and Difference: Writing in the Commedia, by Jeremy Tambling
Troubadours and Irony, by Simon Gaunt
Piers Plowman *and the New Anticlericalism*, by Wendy Scase
The Medieval Greek Romance, by Roderick Beaton
The Cantar de mio Cid*: Poetic Creation in its Economic and Social Contexts*, by Joseph J. Duggan

Other titles in preparation
The Genesis of Piers Plowman, by Charlotte Brewer
Literary Theory in the German Middle Ages, by Walter Haug
(translated from the German)
Reformist Apocalypticism and Piers Plowman, by Kathryn Kerby-Fulton
The Divine Comedy *and the Medieval Other World*, by Alison Morgan

The *Cantar de mio Cid*

Poetic Creation in its Economic and Social Contexts

JOSEPH J. DUGGAN

Professor of French, Comparative
Literature, and Romance Philology,
University of California, Berkeley

CAMBRIDGE UNIVERSITY PRESS

Cambridge
New York   New Rochelle
Melbourne   Sydney

Published by the Press Syndicate of the University of Cambridge
The Pitt Building, Trumpington Street, Cambridge CB2 1RP
32 East 57th Street, New York, NY 10022, USA
10 Stamford Road, Oakleigh, Melbourne 3166, Australia

© Cambridge University Press 1989

First published 1989

Printed in Great Britain at
the University Press, Cambridge

British Library cataloguing in publication data
Duggan, Joseph J.
The cantar de mio Cid: poetic creation in
its economic and social contexts. –
(Cambridge studies in medieval literature: 6)
1. Poetry in Spanish. Cid (Poem)
I. Title
861.'1

Library of Congress cataloguing in publication data
Duggan, Joseph J.
The Cantar de mio Cid: poetic creation in its economic and social
contexts/Joseph J. Duggan.
p.   cm. – (Cambridge studies in medieval literature: 6)
Bibliography.
Includes index.
ISBN 0–521–36194–X
1. Cantar de mio Cid. 2. Wealth in literature. 3. Social status
in literature. I. Title
PQ6380.D8   1989
861'.1–dc 19   88–39532   CIP

ISBN 0 521 36194 X

FP

For Annalee

Contents

Acknowledgments	*page* viii
Modern equivalents to names in the maps	ix
Maps	x
1 Historical and theoretical framework	1
2 The acquisition of wealth	16
3 Economy and gift-giving	30
4 Social status, legitimacy, and inherited worth	43
5 The poet's milieu	58
6 Geography and history	82
7 The *Cantar de mio Cid* and the French epic tradition	108
8 Mode of composition	124
9 Conclusion	143
Notes	149
List of references	157
Index	168

Acknowledgments

The idea of writing a study of the economic and social aspects of the *Cantar de mio Cid* first came to me in 1977; I returned to the project sporadically, while working on others, over a ten-year period. About half of the typescript was written by the summer of 1986, and I completed the other half during a sabbatical leave taken with the generous support of a Humanities Research Fellowship from the University of California, Berkeley. My early study of the poem was subsidized by a grant from the National Endowment for the Humanities, and a large portion of the research was carried out in 1980–81 during my tenure as a Guggenheim Fellow. I would like also to acknowledge the help of the Committee on Research of the University of California, Berkeley, which provided funds for research assistance and various other expenses.

The onerous tasks of finding and fetching the works listed in the bibliography would have been substantially more time-consuming and exasperating without the aid of the Library Delivery Service of the Doe Library, University of California, Berkeley, and particularly of its director, Gregory Olin, and of Bruce Webb. My research assistant Karen Akiyama also provided cheerful and efficient help at critical points.

A number of friends and colleagues gave generously of their time and expertise to answer queries, contribute bibliographical references, and read sections of the book, among them Thomas Bisson, Anthony Cascardi, Charles B. Faulhaber, Ira Lapidus, and Thomas G. Rosenmeyer. Samuel G. Armistead, Jerry R. Craddock, Alan Deyermond, Michael Harney, Joan Ramon Resina, and Thomas J. Walsh read most of the typescript and gave me many invaluable suggestions. They should not, of course, be held responsible for the author's ideas, nor for any errors that remain.

Modern equivalents to names in the maps

Alcala = Alcalá de Henares
Las Alcarrias = La Alcarria
Alcobiella = Alcubilla del Marqués
Alfama = Alhama
Anquita = Anguita
Arbuxuelo = El valle de Arbujuelo
Atienza = Atienza
Bovierca = Bubierca
Calatayut = Calatayud
Castejon = Castejón de Henares
Çelfa la de Canal = Cella
Çetina = Cetina
Çorita = Zorita
Daroca = Daroca
Fariza = Ariza
Fita = Hita
Frontael = Bronchales
Guadalfajara = Guadalajara
Huesa = Huesa
Luzon = Luzón
Medina = Medinaceli
Miedes = Miedes de Atienza
Molina = Molina de Aragón
Mont Alvan = Montalbán
Mont Real = Monreal del Campo
Navas de Palos = Navapalos
El Poyo de mio Çid = El Poyo
Rio Fenares = Río Henares
Rio Siloca = Río Jiloca
Rio Salon = Río Jalón
Rio Tajo = Río Tajo
Sancta Maria d'Alvarracin = Albarracín
Sant Estevan = San Esteban de Gormaz
Teca = Ateca
Teruel = Teruel
Torançio = Campo Taranz
La Torre de doña Urraca = La Torre

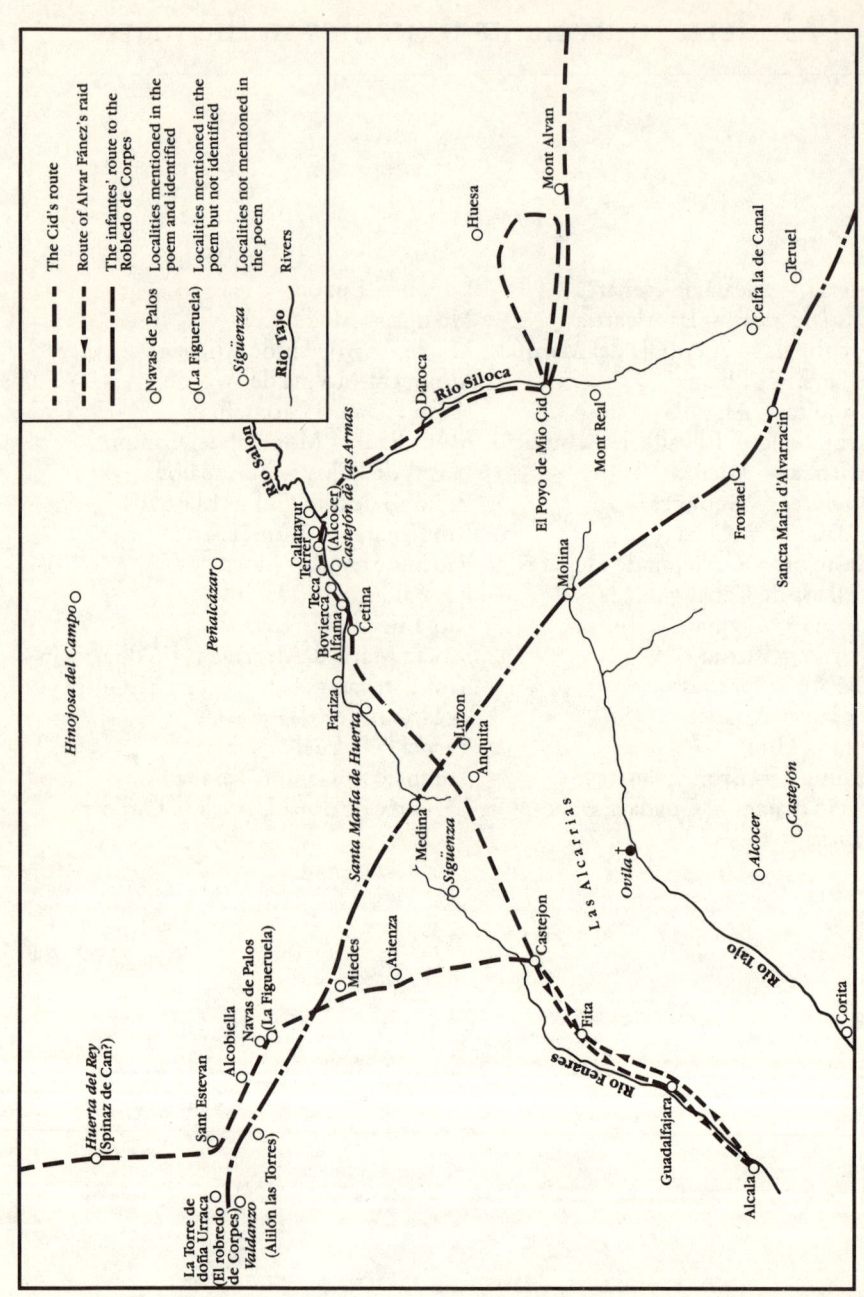

Map 1. The routes followed in the poem

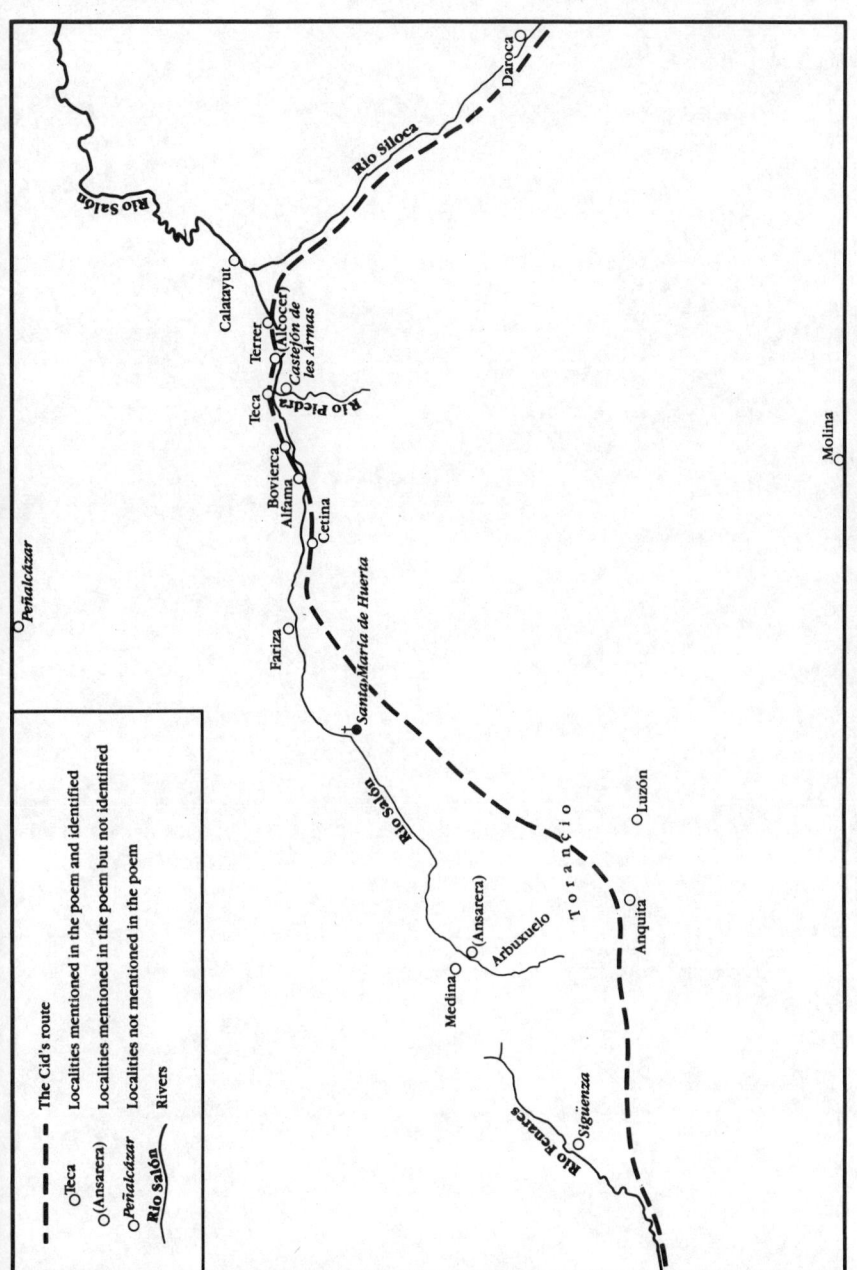

Map 2. The poetic Cid's route in the valley of the Jalón

I

Historical and theoretical framework

When one approaches a literary text, the experience is accompanied by a set of expectations about its nature that typically concern its aesthetic and moral qualities, its entertainment value, the functions and characteristics associated with genres, its usefulness, and perhaps, on a more sophisticated level, preconceptions about its situation in history and within the general framework of a literary tradition. Readers coming upon the same text will read it differently according to what they expect of it. Likewise, those encountering the same pieces of extratextual information relevant to their reading may interpret them variously according to their model of the text's functions – a model that is in turn the product of their anticipations.

As reading proceeds, the expectations evolve: new information leads to an adjustment in the model. Even in the case of a text that one has read many times, it is not unusual to find aspects that take hold in one's consciousness for the first time, impress us unexpectedly with their importance, charm or intrigue or disgust us in new ways, strike a chord with notes with which they could not harmonize before because the instrument had not been tuned for them, as the effects of experience, with the consequent appropriation of new ideas and perhaps even new affective states, allow us to respond to its richness in previously unattainable ways. Although as a comparatist and philologist trained in the Romance languages and literatures I had read and taught the *Cantar de mio Cid* many times, I was blind to the significance of the role that economic and social elements play in it until a day about a decade ago when I discussed with my colleague Howard Bloch the interpretation of the medieval European economy that the historian Georges Duby had formulated. It immediately became apparent to me that the obsessiveness of the poem's economic themes must be linked in a significant way to the milieu in which it was composed.

This idea was reinforced by comparisons and contrasts with epic poems composed in French and Occitan as well as in other languages outside the Romance family. I would certainly never have written this book were it not for my experiences as a teacher and scholar in the field of Comparative Literature.

The formulation of a model of the text's functions that is adequate for an informed reading includes in the current instance the conceptualization of mental structures both medieval and modern and an awareness of the distinctions between them. Hypotheses need to be scrutinized to establish that they do not presuppose the existence in the Middle Ages of abstractions that are actually shaped by modern notions. It serves no purpose to insist that every step in a chain of reasoning rest upon an element of factual data when the concepts that the data supposedly inform are anachronistic. The concepts of the legal profession, of the economic and social values of the nobility, and of literary artistry that have been introduced into the debates over the *Cid* poet and his intentions during the past three decades frequently betray an insufficient sensitivity to the differences that separate the medieval civilization from the modern.

Inescapably, of course, one always works within the parameters of one's own system of values, which leads sometimes to new insights into the text but no doubt just as often to the blocking of vision and the denial of what to readers and listeners in other times and places was obvious. This book shares with a number of its predecessors a bipartite quality: it is an attempt to read the *Cantar de mio Cid* in ways in which it was perceived by its first audiences; and it is an essay in the history of scholarship, dealing, although at times obliquely, with the perceptions (and occasionally the intellectual myopia as well) of those who have contributed to formulating the expectations with which we come to the poem today.

Among the major literary genres, the epic has been the most readily affected by nationalistic tendencies in scholarship, since traditionally it has figured the most prominently in the consciousness that a people has of its own past. In a number of European literatures the first text of substantial length is an epic poem that, even when it did not recount the founding of the nation, came to serve as a basis for the cohesiveness of the notion of national identity in the consciousness of the people with whom it was linked. Most often the historical consciousness of the nation has singled out an appropriate text to fill a need in accord with the image it wished to project of the national past. In the case of Castilian Spain the choice was not difficult, the accidents of history having eliminated the quasi totality of medieval Castilian epic

The nationalistic imperative exerts enormous pressure on the model of how the chosen epic text ought to function. Its Spanish manifestation at the turn of the nineteenth century accounts in part not only for the particular interpretations that Ramón Menéndez Pidal, the most influential of *Cid* scholars, imposed on the text, but also, and perhaps more importantly, for the fact that Menéndez Pidal did *not* see in it certain features that seem to cry out for elucidation: its preoccupation with economic detail, its egregious distortion of history, and its suggestion that the hero's ancestry was subject to question. I believe that Leo Spitzer's ascription (1948) of some aspects of Menéndez Pidal's view to his position as a member of the Generation of 1898 is essentially correct.

The poem's representation of Rodrigo Díaz of Vivar as a man whose status was measured by the economic value of the booty he acquired through violent means and who was constrained to defend himself against a charge of bastardy

Historical and theoretical framework

is surely at variance with the position the Cid has come to occupy in the Spanish public's notion of the Reconquest, that crucible of national identity. While the principal designer of that notion, Menéndez Pidal, was undoubtedly ill prepared for a venture into economic history by the historical school in which he had been trained and unaware that the key lines 3379–80 contain a slur upon the hero's birth, the failure of such a prodigious talent to discover and elucidate these two themes must stem in part from a disinclination to see them. While such a depiction of the hero's activities and of the threat to his reputation did not fit the needs of the Generation of 1898, however, it was not only natural but ultimately flattering in the context of economic and social mentalities that prevailed in the period in which the poem was composed. The epic cannot be insulated from ideological currents any more than other genres – far from it – but on that account we should be even more cautious in distinguishing between its functions in modern consciousness and the role it played in the period in which it was first set down in writing.

A heuristic strategy for reconstructing the interpretations of those medieval poets and scribes who produced and first preserved the texts is to pay increased attention precisely to passages that do not fit the models and expectations that prior scholarship has provided. In the history of paradigms it is most often the details that are in some way unassimilable according to the old model that lead to new formulations. In this regard, historically oriented literary studies proceed no differently from, say, physical cosmology or paleontology. Just as the paleontologist, in looking for clues to the evolutionary pathway of the vertebrate under study, focuses on a morphological feature present at the embryonic stage but absent from the skeleton of a mature specimen, or investigates a seemingly useless appendage that turns out to reveal that the creature is related to a previously unsuspected species, so the philologist is led by the elucidation of obscure or apparently useless textual features to posit new ways to understand the text and, occasionally, a new paradigm. This strategy first led me to want to clarify the etiology and function of the apparently anomalous passage in the *rieptos* scene, which in turn led to a hypothesis concerning the historical milieu in which the poet, on the basis of traditional material, shaped the representation of his hero.

Whether the Per Abbat text itself represents the creation of the poet, that is to say in this instance the person who first gave the literary legend of the Cid substantially the contours in which it has come down to us, faithfully enough to justify speculation about his intentions is, in the last analysis, impossible to determine. Per Abbat was the scribe not of the Biblioteca Nacional manuscript but of an older one in the same line of descent. Modifications introduced between the poem as the poet recited it and the text as Per Abbat wrote it down (see chapter 8), and between his text and the surviving folios of the fourteenth-century manuscript, may well mask important aspects of a prior state. But one must attempt to explain the artifact in the form in which it is extant before going on to hypothesize about other possible forms. After that, one is, I believe, not only free to conjecture about what is lost or not directly perceivable, as Menéndez Pidal did so masterfully in his great edition, but even obligated to do so.

The primary object of this book is to reconstruct inferentially the ways in which the poet's earliest audiences understood the text. In fact we have no choice but to infer their interpretations from the text and from the historical milieu to which its analysis leads, since there is no other way of knowing them.

One of my conclusions will be that the poet was himself the receiver of a text that he then transformed into the poem that Per Abbat copied. The poetic legend of Rodrigo Díaz of Vivar came down to the poet in a form that he internalized and re-generated for his own purposes in keeping with the preoccupations of an audience that probably included both nobles and clergy. The poem has an historical kernel, as Menéndez Pidal believed, but it is severely restricted, most of the plot and characterization deriving not from historical events and personalities but rather from the poet's desire to create a poetic fiction that would appeal to his audience. This book thus assumes a double hermeneutic quality: it takes received interpretations of the poem as a given and attempts to correct them in the light of themes that the critical tradition has by and large neglected (or refused) to address, thereby arriving at a new interpretation; and it assumes a model of the poetic process in which the poet received an interpretation of Rodrigo Díaz and transmuted it in the light of his audience's needs. What its conceptions owe to the thinking of María Eugenia Lacarra will be obvious to those who have read her ground-breaking study *El Poema de mio Cid: realidad histórica e ideología* (1980a).

The nature of the evidence available to a person dealing with a society six or seven centuries anterior to his own requires a few remarks, particularly since the history of scholarship on the *Cantar de mio Cid* reflects – inevitably – a series of changes in historical method. What degree of truth is to be assigned to statements about a poem whose text is available in only a single witness, whose author cannot be identified with certainty, and whose date and place of composition are matters of speculation? In the absence of data that might give us a more specific idea of the poem's *état civil*, we are forced to approximate it through a series of inferential maneuvers.

One criterion for judging these inferences is consistency: do the various hypotheses correspond to conditions obtaining in Castilian society in the period to which one assigns the poem?[1]

Does one hypothesis account for the diverse phenomena by simpler means than its competitors (fewer logical steps, fewer premises), all other things being equal? In the absence of specific documentation on the author and his milieu, a series of probabilities converging toward a "best hypothesis" is all that can be hoped for, and what I attempt to present. At times possibilities will have to suffice where probabilities are desired.

One of the conclusions of the present book is that the *Cantar de mio Cid* as found in the extant manuscript[2] represents an orally composed text. That

Historical and theoretical framework

proposition is based partially on an analysis of formulaic density published over a decade ago (Duggan 1974), but also rests upon further analysis of the poem's contents and upon external considerations.

The extended debate over whether the *Cantar de mio Cid* was composed orally or in writing has proceeded with little discussion of a presupposition that deserves analysis. It is often taken for granted that poems elaborated in oral tradition are not as well constructed, as subtle, or as aesthetically appealing as those that were created in writing; or, to state the proposition in another way that amounts to just about the same in this context, that poems written by learned authors (ecclesiastics, for example) are better structured and more sophisticated than the songs of the unlettered.[3] This is an assumption that I do not share and that I consider unprovable. I shall return to this issue in the Conclusion.

The *Cantar de mio Cid* is saturated with the theme of wealth: its acquisition, distribution, and benefits, the conduct it inspires, and the moral flaws that unjustified participation in it reveals. As will become clear in chapters 2 and 3, I believe this is the aspect that most clearly sets the poem apart from its medieval congeners in the Romance languages. It is, in fact, an aspect that is so obvious once it has been pointed out that afterward one is struck by the paucity of comment on economic matters in the abundant critical literature that the poem has occasioned. One searches in vain for allusions to it in the works of Menéndez Pidal, who laid the groundwork not only for literary scholarship on the poem but also for historical treatments of the period in which the Cid lived. The collection of economic data is a long process, and while for Spain it was begun during Menéndez Pidal's early career, the kind of historical study that it represents did not reach maturity until the mid-twentieth century. In addition, Menéndez Pidal considered his primary task, at least early on, to be the rehabilitation of Rodrigo Díaz of Vivar, maligned, according to him, by the treatments of previous historians and especially of Dozy. While the image of the Cid that Menéndez Pidal promoted – that of a just, merciful, consistently victorious captain embodying the ideals of military and political leadership – contributed to the rewriting of history in the mode of the Generation of 1898, it is not at all clear that emphasis on the hero's acquisitive qualities, associated in the modern world with commoners of the mercantile class, would have added to the Cid's stature in the minds of the early twentieth-century Spanish public.

The efficacy of many of the arguments of this book, especially those found in chapters 5, 6 and 7, is contingent on dating the poem's composition to the end of the twelfth century. Justification for a dating to around the year 1200 rather than to the mid-twelfth century will be presented here; I will return to the issue of dating in chapters 6 and 8, in which I suggest an occasion on which the *Cantar de mio Cid* might have been composed and discuss further the significance of certain linguistic features, namely the archaisms that mark the poem as one of the earliest Spanish texts of substantial length.

The work on the dating of the manuscript and the dating and localization of

The *Cantar de mio Cid*

the poem that has exerted the most influence was carried out by Menéndez Pidal. The manuscript is written in a fourteenth-century hand, which Menéndez Pidal situates early in the century. The poem's colophon includes an indication of date according to the Spanish Era, "en era de mill e cc xlv. años" (i.e. AD 1207), but Menéndez Pidal conjectured, following a suggestion of Tomás Antonio Sánchez, that a third "c" had occupied the space before the "x" in which there are signs of an erasure. Menéndez Pidal also believed that the colophon was composed by the fourteenth-century scribe (1954–56, 1: 18).

Despite discrepancies among the three *cantares* in the average number of lines per *tirada* and in the preference for various vowels at the assonance, Menéndez Pidal at first believed that the poem was the work of a single author (1954–56, 1: 72–3, 122–3). In 1961, however, he published a study in which he modified his long-held opinion about the poem's unity: it was now to be attributed to two poets, the first a near-contemporary of Rodrigo Díaz of Vivar from San Esteban de Gormaz, and the second an inhabitant of Medinaceli working sometime between 1123 and 1146 (194) and probably in 1140 (196–7; see below), long enough after the events to have forgotten that, contrary to what the poem represents, Medinaceli was not in Christian hands during the lifetime of Rodrigo Díaz of Vivar. The poet of San Esteban de Gormaz, living at a time when the details of the Cid's career were still well known, would have recounted betrothals between the Infantes and the Cid's daughters, rather than the unhistorical marriages, and would have told how they were broken off when Alfonso became angry with the Cid in 1089 and imprisoned his wife and daughters. To the poet of Medinaceli Menéndez Pidal attributed a greater story-telling freedom, *reformas novelescas* (192), and a diminished knowledge of the hero's life. Among this second poet's many innovations would have been the extensive role played by Álvar Fáñez, the conversion of the betrothals into marriages, transformation of the breaking off of the betrothals into the *afrenta de Corpes*, the introduction of the character Avengalbón and the episodes of the lion and the three judicial duels, and the error of having the Cid's daughter María (the poem's Sol) marry the Infante of Aragon. The poet of Medinaceli would have altered the *Cantar del destierro* little, the *Cantar de las bodas* substantially, and the *Cantar de Corpes* extensively, and Menéndez Pidal went to great lengths detailing exactly which passages he identifies as belonging to each poet.

In the section of his edition devoted to dating the text, Menéndez Pidal based his conclusions on three main points: 1. The poem styles Alfonso VII "el buen emperador" (l. 3003) without naming him, which shows that the king, who died in 1157, must have been present in the memories of both poet and audience (1954–56, 1: 21–2; see also 3: 1167–8). 2. The lines "Oy los reyes d'España sos parientes son,/ A todos alcança ondra por el que en buen ora naçió" (ll. 3724–5 of Menéndez Pidal's critical text) imply that most, if not all, of the reigning families of Spain were related to the hero. Contrary to another of the poet's claims, however, the Cid's daughters were never queens

Historical and theoretical framework

of Navarre and Aragon. Rather than placing too much weight on the accuracy of the two lines, then, one is better advised to identify an event of some resonance that might have impelled the poet to make such a statement, which for Menéndez Pidal was the marriage in 1151 of Blanca of Navarre, the great-granddaughter of Rodrigo Díaz, to Sancho III "el Deseado," or better still their betrothal which took place under dramatic circumstances in 1140. In addition, the poet's error in calling the husband of one of the Cid's daughters the Infante of Aragon whereas she actually married Count Ramon Berenguer III of Barcelona could perhaps best be explained if one supposed that the poet (the second poet, according to the revised theory of 1961) lived in the period in which the count's son, Ramon Berenguer IV, was regent of the kingdom of Aragon, namely 1137 to 1162 (1954–56, 1: 22). 3. The *Poema de Almería*, written after the conquest of Almería in 1147 but before Alfonso VII's death ten years later, includes the lines:

> Nullaque sub celo melior fuit hasta sereno.
> Ipse Rodericus, Meo Cidi sepe uocatus,
> De quo cantatur quod ab hostibus haud superatur,
> Qui domuit Mauros, comites domuit quoque nostros.
> Hunc [i.e. Alvar Fáñez] extollebat, se laude
>   minore ferebat.
> Sed fateor uerum, quod tollet nulla dierum:
> Meo Cidi primus fuit Aluarus atque secundus.
>   (cited here after Juan Gil [ed.] 1974: ll. 232–8)

Menéndez Pidal took this passage, which refers to the hero with the epithet "mio Cid" characteristic of the *Cantar de mio Cid*, as a reference not merely to *a* song about the hero, but – and he insisted on this point – to the text preserved in our manuscript (1954–56, 1: 23–31; see also 3: 1169–70). These arguments led him to date the poem between 1140 and 1157, and the poet's pronunciation of the sound proceeding from Latin short *o* in stressed position as *uo*, an archaism even in the second half of the twelfth century, persuaded him to propose the earlier rather than the later date.

Specifically, then, in the last decade of his life Menéndez Pidal suggested that the poem was composed in 1140 in more or less the form in which we have it, that is in the form given to it by the second of his hypothetical two poets, for the marriage of the Cid's great-granddaughter with Sancho "el Deseado," later to be Sancho III of Castile (see also Menéndez Pidal 1961: 196–7, where he assigns the 1140 date to the second poet, and Catalán 1985: 818–19). But since the poet's representation of the Cid's daughters' marriages is patently unhistorical, Louis Chalon is right in asking (1967: 232) why a poet would have invented for such an occasion a totally fictitious story about the failed marriages of the ancestors of one of the contractants, marriages that supposedly took place only fifty years before the date of composition.

Several of the supplementary observations Menéndez Pidal added to his edition beginning in 1944 concern dating. He remarked that, according to a study of Eduardo de Hinojosa (1899), the legal procedures and institutions reflected in the poem correspond to those of the twelfth century and not the beginning or middle of the thirteenth, a finding that Menéndez Pidal viewed as supporting his dating (1954–56, 3: 1165–6). In addition he noted that various linguistic traits – including the patronymic in -*oz*, syntactic phonetics ("toveldo" for "tuve te lo"), *uó* or *o* as the reflex of Latin short *o*, extensive apocope of the personal pronoun, the post-positive use of *ser* and *aver* as auxiliaries when the main verb begins the hemistich, and the graphy *Oiarra* for *Ocharra* – were archaic features (3: 1166–7); that the poet only uses the names of characters who actually existed in history (3: 1168–9); and that the reference to the king of the Montes Claros in l. 1182 is best explained as stemming from a period in which the Almoravid Empire existed, i.e. before 1146, during which time a struggle between the Almoravid emperor and the king of the Montes Claros in Morocco was still plausible (3: 1170).

The numismatist Felipe Mateu y Llopis devoted a study (1947) to the types of money mentioned in the poem. The Christian monetary system of the time of Alfonso VI was based on the *dinero* (ll. 252, 804, 3734), a coin made of billon, whence the reference in l. 64 to a *dinerada*, the value of one *dinero*. The *dinero malo* (ll. 165, 503, 1042) refers, according to Mateu y Llopis, to a debased billon coinage, one made with an alloy that held a reduced silver content, and since the *dineros* of Alfonso VI were not debased, the poet must be living after the period in which counterfeit coins began to appear, that is to say the beginning of the twelfth century, or, more probably, after the introduction of coin made from poor alloys under Urraca or Alfonso VII.

The only way a person could possess coins of gold and silver in the period in question would be to acquire Arab money, such as the gold *dinares* of Yusuf ibn Texufin, which normally entered the Christian kingdoms in the form of tribute. The *morabetino* or *maravedí*, a gold Almoravid coin, did not make its appearance until after Alfonso VIII conquered Murcia (1172) and in fact although gold and silver Arab coins play a role in the poem, it nowhere mentions them by name – in contrast to the Oxford *Chanson de Roland* which mentions *manguns*. Mateu y Llopis takes this absence of the *maravedí* to indicate that the *Cantar de mio Cid* developed before the coin was introduced into the Christian economy (54), and concludes that, to judge from the money that appears in the text, the earliest layer of the poem dates from the first third of the twelfth century (56).

The chronological results of Mateu y Llopis's investigation are not as sound as they might at first appear, however, since they are based upon an *argumentum ex silentio*: because the poet (that is to say, in this case, the poet responsible for the earliest layer of fabulation) does not mention a certain type of coin, he must not have known that coin, or at least must not have lived when it circulated in the Christian economy. In fact other solutions present themselves; the *maravedí* could have been introduced during the poet's adult lifetime, and he would then have known better than to include it in a narrative about the reign of Alfonso VI; or his omission could simply be a matter of chance and thus not a clue to intentionality or chronology at all. It is preferable to interpret the findings of Mateu y Llopis more conservatively, then, and say simply that the depiction of coinage in the *Cantar de mio Cid* is not incompatible with dating some aspects of the poem to the first third of the twelfth century, but that it does not rule out a later date of composition for the extant state of the text.

Only a few scholars took exception, beginning in the 1950s, to Menéndez Pidal's conclusions on dating, notably Russell (1952) and Ubieto Arteta (1957).

Ubieto's stand against the 1140 date culminated in the publication of his "El *Cantar de mio Cid* y algunos problemas históricos" in 1972, a study that was published in book form in 1973. After reviewing Menéndez Pidal's arguments for dating, Ubieto turns to the study of, successively, geographic-historical anachronisms, geography, historical data, anachronistic historical personages, characteristic institutions, features peculiar to the Aragonese dialect complex, and the historical evolution of the Cid legend.

Basing himself on paleographic data, Ubieto believes that the extant *Cid* manuscript was copied in the mid-fourteenth century rather than early in the century, perhaps in the vicinity of Burgos (15). He also interprets various conflicts in the poem – those between the Cid and the Infantes de Carrión, the Cid and the count of Barcelona, the Cid's men and the Infantes – as reflecting anti-nobiliary sentiments and thus perhaps responsible for arousing the interest of the fourteenth-century scribe (14–15).

Ubieto takes up Menéndez Pidal's arguments one by one. He demonstrates that numerous documents dated as late as 1224 and literary texts up to 1270 simply call Alfonso VII "Imperator" or "Emperador" without naming him (22–3). The line "Oy los reyes d'España sos parientes son" must refer to the kings of Castile, Navarre, Aragon, and Portugal, in which case those kings could not all be said to descend from the Cid until the early years of the thirteenth century, that is to say after Berenguela and Urraca, the daughters of Alfonso VIII of Castile, married respectively Alfonso IX of Leon in 1197 and Alfonso II of Portugal in 1201 (28; for a critique of this idea see Lapesa 1985: 33–5). Derek Lomax later proposed reading the verb of this line as an historical present, in which case it may refer simply to the Cid's daughters' betrothals to the infantes of Navarre and Aragon as depicted in the poem itself (1977: 75).

Eduardo de Hinojosa's studies on legal institutions, notes Ubieto, led Hinojosa indeed to the conclusion that the poem was composed in the twelfth century, but in the second half of the century rather than specifically toward its midpoint. Considering himself unqualified to judge Menéndez Pidal's linguistic arguments, Ubieto passes over them. The abundance of the names of characters who really existed in history he rejects as a criterion of dating. The reference to the king of the Montes Claros is ambiguous, since there are ranges called the Montes Claros in Spain as well as in Morocco and in any case the reference would only be useful in fixing a *terminus a quo* (32–3).

Ubieto agrees with Menéndez Pidal that the Latin *Poema de Almería* refers to songs about the Cid, but not to *this* song. In a related development, Miguel Barceló (1967–68) has found that the epithets "Campeador" and "Cid" are distributed sequentially in the *Linaje navarro del Cid* (dated to before 1194), "Campeador" being found exclusively up to the narration of the siege of Valencia, "Cid" from that point to the end. Since the *Linaje* does not follow the version of the hero's life contained in the *Cantar de mio Cid,* but nevertheless uses the epithet "Cid," Barceló contends – against a claim of Menéndez Pidal – that the use of "Cid" was not confined to popular poetry in the twelfth century and that the *Poema de Almería* does not necessarily refer to the epic. He concludes furthermore that the traditions characterized respectively by the two epithets did not converge until the end of the twelfth or the beginning of the thirteenth century. I concur that the *Poema de Almería* does not necessarily allude to the *Cantar de mio Cid* as we have it, but it does refer to *a* poem or poems in the tradition of the Per Abbat version; the companionship in arms that the *Poema de Almería* posits between Rodrigo Díaz of Vivar and Alvar Fáñez, unattested in history and in fact impossible for the period in which the poem situates it, is sufficient to establish the link with the epic tradition, and the shared use of the designation "mio Cid" does nothing to detract from that conclusion.

Among the geographical anachronisms that Ubieto Arteta discusses, perhaps the most telling is that in the poem Medinaceli is treated as a Christian stronghold whereas it was held by the Bani Hūd dynasty of Saragossa, then by the Almoravids, until it was conquered by Alfonso "el Batallador" in the period 1120–22, with the exception of a four-year interval beginning in 1104, five years after the death of Rodrigo Díaz (Ubieto Arteta 1973: 37–9; see also Menéndez Pidal 1954–56, 1: 74 and 3: 1172). Another apparent anachronism, the mention on two occasions of Mont Real (ll. 863, 1186), that is Monreal del Campo, a town established only in 1124 (1973: 40), is not necessarily problematic since the poet may only be using Mont Real as a point of geographical reference: l. 863 may be understood as "y ffinco en un poyo que es sobre [the present] Mont Real," and a similar construal is possible for l. 1186, "amaneçio a mio Cid en tierras de Mon Real." The same might be said for the poet's mention of Cetina in l. 547, and Derek Lomax has further pointed out (1977: 78) that the formal establishment of a town often followed its settlement and even its naming. The attribution of Montalbán and Huesa to the jurisdiction of the count of Barcelona in ll. 951–9 appears to fit only the historical situation of the period after 1154 (1973: 48).

The denomination "Valençia la mayor" for the city that the hero conquers indicates to Ubieto that the poet must have been composing toward the end of the twelfth century or later, since, as Menéndez Pidal believed (1954–56, 2: 873), he appears to be distinguishing the city on the Mediterranean coast from Valencia de Don Juan or Valencia la Alcántara, towns that only took on the name "Valencia" in that period (1973: 68). Rafael Lapesa has pointed out, however, that the poet occasionally uses *mayor* in a positive rather than a comparative sense (see ll. 2023, 2176), even employing the phrase *Barcelona la*

Historical and theoretical framework

mayor (l. 3195) in the absence of any competing Barcelonas, so that the phrase *Valençia la mayor* is simply the equivalent of *Valençia la grand* (l. 3316) and thus of no use in dating the poem.

In an interesting analysis, Ubieto shows that the tactics used by the poetic Cid in the battles of Alcocer and Cuarte, whereby the army makes a frontal attack on a specified point of the enemy's forces, in no way resemble those of the late eleventh century or most of the twelfth, but are, rather, similar to the tactics employed by the Christian forces at the disastrous Battle of Alarcos in 1195 (1973: 56–63), an insight of major importance for one of the theses of this book.

Citing P. E. Russell's study of diplomatic (1952), Ubieto notes that the use of pendant seals in the poem corresponds to the historical reality of the second half of the twelfth century rather than to the time of Rodrigo Díaz and Alfonso VI (1973: 64–7). Richard Fletcher has subsequently presented evidence, however, that seals were employed on royal mandates as early as the middle of Alfonso VII's reign (1976: 332), so they might well reflect chancery practice from before 1150.

Ubieto concludes that the *Cantar de mio Cid* was composed in the year 1207, the date given in the colophon of the fourteenth-century manuscript. Per Abbat would be the poem's author, although his text, which Ubieto believes to have been couched in the Aragonese dialect, would have been a reworking of previously existing songs. The *Cantar del destierro*, prosified in the *Estoria de España*,[4] had an independent existence, and songs corresponding to the second and third *cantares* may also have had their own separate lives. In the mid-fourteenth century, a *juglar* of Burgos would have copied the text, Castilianizing it in the process.

Ubieto Arteta has returned to the question of dating, attempting to link the poem with Fernando Ruiz de Azagra, lord of Albarracín and governor of Teruel, Calatayud, and Daroca – lands that figure in the *Cantar de mio Cid* – who probably died in 1197 in the expedition which Pedro II of Aragon undertook against Leon on behalf of Alfonso VIII of Castile (1980: 569), and maintaining that it can only have been composed after 1196 since Carrión was a Castilian town except for the years 1196 and 1197 when it was in Leonese hands (573).

In another study, Ubieto points out (1982: 674) that, although the first documentary proof of the existence of the king's *cortes* is from the period of Alfonso VIII, this king convened them in the very places in which the poem has Alfonso VI claim he has held them (see ll. 3129–31), namely Burgos (1169 and 1177) and Carrión (1188, 1192–4). He notes that courts were held in the Middle Ages in many Castilian cities and refuses to write the correspondence off to mere coincidence, concluding that the poem is transferring an activity of Alfonso VIII to Alfonso VI and considering this as evidence that it must have been written after 1188 (677).

An argument similar in kind to Ubieto's has been put forward by José María Lacarra (1975), who notes that the word *hidalgo*, found frequently in the poem under the form *fijo d'algo*, is attested in documentary sources only from the year 1177 in Leon and only from 1201 in Castilian territory. Lacarra doubts, then, that the poem could date from as early as 1140.

D. G. Pattison has examined suffixal derivation in the *Cantar de mio Cid* (1967), in particular that involving the suffix *-ada/ida* in deverbal formations to indicate the place of the verbal action and the suffix *-(d)ura* in deverbals signifying the concrete result of the verbal action rather than the abstract action itself, concluding that the state of both derivations found in the poem was typical of the thirteenth century rather than the early or mid-twelfth. These findings were challenged by Rafael Lapesa in an article entitled "Sobre el *Cantar de mio Cid*: crítica de críticas," published in 1980 and reprinted in Lapesa 1985. Lapesa adduced a large number of examples of the phenomena in question proceeding from documents that are earlier than the year 1200. Pattison has replied to these criticisms (1985–86), claiming that most of Lapesa's examples were taken from documents that are extant only in later copies and thus subject to doubt, and that in any case the conclusion concerning a thirteenth-century dating was based on the comparative frequency of patterns of derivation and not on absolute occurrences.

Several of the arguments of this book are predicated on the assumption that a number of the criticisms addressed at Menéndez Pidal's dating by Ubieto Arteta and others are correct: that is to say that the *Cantar de mio Cid* as we have it was composed toward the end of the twelfth century or the beginning of the thirteenth in a version close to that passed on by Per Abbat.

Particularly telling are Hinojosa's ascribal of the poem's legal climate to the second half of the twelfth century and Ubieto's arguments that Medinaceli was held by the Almoravids until 1122 – an occurrence that would surely not have been outside the ken of a putative poet of Medinaceli composing only eighteen years later – the placing of Huesa and Montalbán in the jurisdiction of the count of Barcelona, the poet's apparent knowledge of military tactics employed by the Christian army at Alarcos in 1195, and the fact that Alfonso VIII, like the poem's Alfonso VI, held courts at Burgos and Carrión. Ubieto's evidence that Alfonso VII was referred to simply as "Emperador" well into the thirteenth century eliminates one of Menéndez Pidal's principal arguments in favor of a mid-twelfth-century dating. I agree with Ubieto that, while the author of the *Poema de Almería* knew a *Cantar de mio Cid*, it was not necessarily the one known to us. Louis Chalon's observation that there would have been no reason for a poet composing for the betrothal of Blanca of Navarre and Sancho "el Deseado" in 1140 to have evoked fictitious marriages for one of Blanca's ancestors is convincing. The line "Oy los reyes d'España sos parientes son" is open to so many interpretations – depending upon one's idea of which kings the poet had in mind – that, while its presence in the poem is highly significant in thematic terms, it is useless for determining chronology. Finally, the linguistic data analyzed by Menéndez Pidal and by D. G. Pattison and Rafael Lapesa are, in my opinion, subject to an interpretation that is compatible with a dating around the year 1200, as is the occurrence of

Historical and theoretical framework

so many historical names in the poem's cast of characters. This conclusion does not exclude the possibility that other versions existed before the one to which Per Abbat had access, as I will argue in chapter 8.

In his *Historia y poesía en torno al Cantar del Cid*, which appeared in 1973, the same year that saw the publication of the book version of Ubieto's analysis, Jules Horrent reviewed the various theories of dating, concluding that "la versión conservada del *Cantar de Mio Cid* comprende cierto número de versos, a lo largo del poema, que justifican mejor los años posteriores a 1150, e incluso 1160, que la primera mitad del siglo, y la segunda mitad del siglo conviene al texto que transcribió Per Abbat más tarde" (262). Derek Lomax also published a survey of the various theories of dating, arriving at a similar judgment, namely that "perhaps it would be safest to conclude merely that the poem was written in the reign, and probably the kingdom, of Alfonso VIII" (81). In chapter 6 I will consider the possibility of a more precise dating.

The text of the poem proper is followed by a colophon of three lines written in the same fourteenth-century hand as the main body of the manuscript, followed by three more lines in another hand of the same period. The colophon reads

> Quien escrivio este libro ¡del Dios paraiso, amen!
> Per Abbat le escrivio   en el mes de mayo
> en era de mill e cc xlv. años.[5]

The additional lines are:

> El el romanz
> ... s leido, dat nos del vino; si non tenedes dineros
> echad ... la unos peños, que bien vos lo dararan sobr'elos.

The two components of this end-matter proceed from different textual situations. The additional lines are not only in a different assonance, but refer to the reading of the text and are thus, as far as textual pragmatics is concerned, a component of the situation(s) in which the manuscript was used for recitation, rather than of the written transmission of the text.

As was noted above, a space follows the second "c" in the date provided by the colophon. Menéndez Pidal, whose opinion prevailed for many years, maintained that a third "c" had been written in that space and then erased, although no trace of ink was visible even when the parchment was treated with reagents. Proceeding on the basis of his hypothesis about what had occupied the blank space, Menéndez Pidal held that the "Per Abbat" mentioned in the second line was the scribe of the extant manuscript who would have written it in May of the Spanish era 1345, that is to say in AD 1307.

Before resorting to complicated theses that involve recourse to hypothetical data, however, one should first exhaust more obvious explanations. While the erasure that is visible in the blank space between the second "c" and the "x" might well have removed a third "c," the act of effacement could just as well have been necessitated by another letter perceived as erroneous or by a slip of the pen. Other erasures that left no trace of the underlying ink are found in the manuscript (see Horrent 1973: 200), and it is best to assume that if a "c" has been erased it was removed for a good reason. The simplest solution is that, as Ubieto Arteta (1973: 10), Horrent (1973: 197–207), and others have maintained, the colophon indicates a date of AD 1207 and was never meant to suggest 1307. I shall proceed in accord with that line of reasoning.

On the basis of lacunae, transposed lines, the incorrect resolution of abbreviations and other errors, Menéndez Pidal has shown that the poetic text as it has been transmitted must represent the copy of at least one previous copy (1954–56: 29).

What role did the Per Abbat of the colophon play in the poem's existence? Colin Smith, Ubieto Arteta, and others have identified him with the poet, but as early as the middle of the eighteenth century other scholars maintained convincingly that he was only the scribe (for a discussion of this question as it was debated up to 1975, see Magnotta 1976). First of all, the verb *escrivir* is used in twelfth- and thirteenth-century Castilian primarily to signify the act of inscribing letters on parchment rather than the process of authorial creation, and that is the only meaning attached to it in other passages of the poem (Horrent 1973: 199; see also the evidence for *escrivir* as "to compose" in Smith 1983: 68–9). *Libro* in this context does not designate the literary work itself, which is referred to at various times in the poem as a *gesta* (l. 1085), or a *cantar* consisting of *coblas* (l. 2276), or as *nuevas* (l. 3729). Rather *libro* refers to the book as an object, the parchment artifact in which letters have been traced.

In his edition in modernized Castilian, Francisco Marcos Marín has noted that "le escrivio" is the only *leísmo* in the text that is applied to an object, with the exception of the *leísmos* used for the swords Colada and Tizón and for Bavieca, all of which are treated for grammatical purposes like persons. On that basis he argues that the colophon was written by someone other than the poet (1985: 174n).

The most obvious conclusion to draw from all this is that Per Abbat was not the poem's author but only a scribe, that he was not the scribe of the fourteenth-century manuscript but of another codex in its line of transmission, and that the scribe or scribes who followed him simply copied his colophon.

Horrent proposes that "Per Abbat" was the name of the fourteenth-century scribe, and that in writing his own name he fell into the error of writing also a date in his own century, which he then corrected by erasing one "c" (1973: 206). This hypothesis is overly complicated: mechanical scribal errors are more frequently independent than related, and furthermore a scribe who corrected to the date found in his model but allowed his own name to subsist would be showing himself to be unscrupulous in one line but scrupulous in the next or, more charitably, to be attentive to the proper correction in one line but negligent in the next, which requires an additional step in the reasoning. I shall consider Per Abbat to be the scribe of a lost manuscript

Historical and theoretical framework

copied in 1207, that is to say probably of the model of the extant fourteenth-century manuscript although other copies could have intervened. The dating of the text to a time in or shortly before 1207 leads me to posit that Per Abbat was the scribe of one of the earliest written states in the poem's textual history.

Since it is improbable that scholars will ever come across a document linking a particular Per Abbat – and their number was legion – with the poem, one must reason by inference in attempting to find a likely possibility. Undoubtedly it would be preferable to rely upon positive documentary evidence, but such evidence is no more available now than it was to Menéndez Pidal when he formulated the hypothesis that the poem was composed for the betrothals of Blanca of Navarre and Sancho "el Deseado." In its absence I will present in chapter 6 two candidates – never before considered, to my knowledge – whose historical and geographical situations accord well with the poem's character, and will describe the milieu in which I believe the poet performed and the one in which Per Abbat worked. This attempt is motivated in part by the conviction that, despite the efforts of Menéndez Pidal, and despite María Eugenia Lacarra's important reformulation of the problem, the implications of the Transierran locale with which the poet was familiar have not been fully exploited.

A manuscript such as that of the *Cantar de mio Cid* is likely to have been of such rarity in 1207 that it must have been copied for someone in high authority who could have afforded the expense it entailed or whose favor could have motivated a monastic scriptorium to absorb that expense. Documents were most frequently created in connection with the activities of kings, high nobles, and monasteries. Since the poem has a secular character one is justified in looking to the monarchy and the nobles of highest rank for the motivations that lie behind its composition.

I will set forth the results of that research after discussing the role and function of economic elements in the poem and relating certain of its themes to the society that surrounded it. The book will then go on to a reconsideration of the poem's thematics, the locus of the battles that it highlights, the milieu in which it may have been performed, what the poet reveals about his social station and compositional habits by his acquaintance – or lack of familiarity – with certain areas of knowledge, and what the poem's language, versification, and style imply. All of these elements are relevant to its mode of creation, which is in turn a function of the poet's position in society. I will conclude with a "best hypothesis" about the poem's creation.

2

The acquisition of wealth

The critic who wishes to trace the complete sequence of motivations in the *Cantar de mio Cid* is at a disadvantage, since the sole surviving poetic manuscript is acephalic, lacking one folio and thus probably about fifty lines of text.[1] To approximate the poet's conception of King Alfonso's intention in proclaiming the exile with which the manuscript opens, one must have recourse to the *Crónica de veinte reyes*, which contains the prosification whose text is closest to the poem (text in Menéndez Pidal 1954–56, 1: 1022–4; Dyer 1975 begins her text with the passage corresponding to the inception of the poetic text).

The chronicle relates that Alfonso had sent Rodrigo Díaz of Vivar to Seville and Cordoba to collect the tribute that the kings of those cities owed him annually. While Rodrigo was in the presence of Mutamid, king of Seville, Mudaffar of Granada attacked Mutamid's territory with the aid of several Christian noblemen – all Alfonso's vassals – including Count García Ordóñez, in spite of Rodrigo's warning that he would not permit one of his lord's tributaries to be threatened without retaliation. Rodrigo gathered an army of Christians and Arabs, overcame the invaders at Cabra, and held Mudaffar's Christian allies captive for three days. It was on this occasion that he pulled out a piece of García Ordóñez's beard, an affront of which Rodrigo strategically reminds the count during the court scene at Toledo in the poetic text (ll. 3283–90). Rodrigo ordered his men to collect the enemy's possessions from the battlefield. The *Estoria de España* adds that of this booty he restored to the Moors of Seville what they claimed as their own, and gave them as much of the remainder as they wished to take. From that time on, says the *Estoria de España*, both Moors and Christians called him "el Cid Campeador."

Returning to Castile with the tribute, the Cid delivered it to Alfonso, but envious courtiers succeeded in arousing the king's animosity toward him. A short time later, while Alfonso was conducting a campaign in Andalusia, the Cid attacked the Moorish kingdom of Toledo on the pretext that Arab bands were operating in the region of San Esteban. He won great renown and rich plunder from this raid, an accomplishment that inspired Alfonso's resentment. The counsellors hostile to the Cid led the king to believe that the Toledo campaign had been inspired by the Cid's desire to put Alfonso and his followers in jeopardy as they passed through the kingdom of Toledo on their return from Andalusia. The poem as we have it bears no trace of this

The acquisition of wealth

accusation concerning the Toledo campaign. In any case, according to the *Crónica de veinte reyes* it was as a result of this counsel that Alfonso decreed that the Cid go into exile within a period of nine days. With the Cid's preparations to leave Vivar the *Crónica de veinte reyes* version reaches the point at which the manuscript begins.

On the basis of the chronicle accounts, the king's decision in the poem to exile his powerful vassal is to be imagined as prompted by a number of considerations. The Cid had acquired renown on one and possibly two occasions at the expense of Alfonso's interests: he had humiliated Count García Ordóñez, later to assume the position of royal *alférez*, and he had perhaps not accorded proper weight to the danger the king might incur on his return trip to Castile from Andalusia. But mixed in with the political motives and intimately connected with them in symbolic and practical ways is the question of accumulated wealth, both the manner in which it was amassed and the uses to which it had been put. The Cid had collected booty from García Ordóñez and the other Christian nobles at Cabra, distributing it to the Arabs in a magnificent gesture that, along with his military prowess, led to his receiving the honorific *el Cid Campeador*. In addition, he had accepted gifts from Mutamid, and had captured 7,000 Moors in his attack on the kingdom of Toledo. Whatever Alfonso's motivation for twice sending Rodrigo Díaz into exile in history – the reliable twelfth-century *Historia Roderici* ascribes it to the attack on the kingdom of Toledo – the poet who composed the text preserved in the fourteenth-century manuscript gives substantial weight to the king's belief – implied in the chronicle account – that the Cid had profited at his expense by retaining part of the tribute. Lacarra's implication (1980a: 22n) that the attack on Toledo was not mentioned in the poem is unverifiable since we do not know the exact content of the missing initial leaves.

Martín Antolínez refers to the supposed theft in a successful effort to establish his lord's creditworthiness during the negotiations with Rachel and Vidas over the loan of 600 marks:

> El Campeador   por las parias fue entrado,
> grandes averes priso   e mucho sobejanos;
> retovo dellos   quanto que fue algo,
> por en vino a aquesto   por que fue acusado.
> Tiene dos arcas   lennas de oro esmerado.   (ll. 109–13)

For the poet the accusation is untrue[2] – otherwise he would have had the chests contain genuine riches instead of sand – but in any case the sole motivation for the *ira regia* in the poem as we now have it is at base an economic one, that the Cid misappropriated wealth belonging by right to his lord. A fine point of irony is made in the Burgos scene: it is only the fact that Rachel and Vidas believe the accusation which the poet considers unjust that enables Rodrigo to finance the military campaign that will in the end result in his restoration to royal favor.

The Cid is at the lowest point in his fortunes while he is camped outside

The *Cantar de mio Cid*

Burgos on the riverbank. He has been constrained to cheat the Jews in order to secure funds for his army, and has only done so reluctantly (*amidos*, ll. 84, 95), whether the reason for his hesitation is personal or, as Lacarra believes (1980a: 191), because the Church disapproved of money-lending. (The *Crónica de veinte reyes* has Martín Antolínez propose the stratagem, a variation that allows the Cid to maintain his nobility of demeanor by simply consenting to a counsellor's advice rather than engendering the plot himself.) Rachel and Vidas believe that the chests contain *aver monedado* (126, 172), so that one might legitimately ask just what the exchange of chests for money is intended to accomplish. Obviously the Cid is represented as wishing to give the impression that he is concerned with the danger of being caught with a large quantity of Arab coins in his possession, such as he might have received from King Mutamid. He thus exchanges the putative gold dinars and silver dirhems of the Arab economy for money of a Christian stamp, silver marks.[3] The Jews are content with this bargain, since money of Arab coinage, unlike the Christian, was fairly reliable in its values. In fact they envision their own prospects in the event that the Cid does not pay them back, which the poet must want his audience to consider a likely possibility: "Gradan se Rachel e Vidas con averes monedados, / ca mientra que visquiessen refechos eran amos" (172–3).

The contract (*pleito*, l. 160) to which both parties consent is of some importance. If Rachel and Vidas break their pledge not to inspect the contents of the chests for a year,[4] the Cid will not have to pay them interest (*ganançia*, 165). Neither the amount nor the rate is specified.[5] Presumably the Jews could then demand to have their 600 marks returned: but why should they, since the contents of the chests are assumed, on the basis of their weight (171), to be worth far more than the principal of the loan? During the second embassy that the Cid sends to Alfonso, Alvar Fáñez encounters the Jews, who fall at his feet asking that their capital (*cabdal*, 1434) be given back to them. If the Cid does not consent, they are ruined. It would seem likely that the poem's audience is to assume that the Jews have in fact looked into the chests, since they are quite willing, even eager, to forgive the interest (*soltariemos la ganançia*, 1434) once the marks are in their hands. This does not mean, however, that they have broken their oath, since the Cid has been away from Burgos for several years by this time (cf. 1169) and they would now be entitled to examine the supposed collateral. In spite of their adherence to the contract's stipulations, however, the Jews are not paid back in the course of the Per Abbat text, although they declare their willingness to settle for the principal. The *Crónica de veinte reyes* version omits the scene in which Rachel and Vidas beg Alvar Fáñez to see to it that the Cid pays them. In the *Estoria de España* they are paid, but only the 600 marks of the original loan (Menéndez Pidal 1955, 1: 594): no mention is made at that point of the interest which had been agreed upon earlier in the *Estoria de España* version. All three texts do devote considerable attention to the loan, which shows that the tradition was in substantial accord on this element.

The acquisition of wealth

That a poem in the genre of the Romance epic should recount in detail how a military campaign was financed at all is extraordinary. In the entire corpus I know of no other poem that elaborates to this extent on economic phenomena.[6] Occasionally one finds references in *chansons de geste* to the need for money to provision armies, but they are rare. In the *Charroi de Nîmes* William of Orange receives poor knights and squires into an army destined to take Nîmes by force from the Saracens, but refuses King Louis's offer of money, stating simply "Ge ai assez quanque il m'est mestier" (McMillan 1972: l. 730). *Girart de Roussillon*, a song characterized by the lavish description of buildings, dress, and precious objects, contains but a few scattered mentions of the expense Girart lays out for mercenary troops, ignoring other potential economic factors in his downfall. The long *Garin le Loherain* (16,600 lines) includes a geographical scenario that rivals the *Cantar de mio Cid*'s in its concern for the appearance of exactness (Parmly 1935), but economic matters enter very little into its motivating elements beyond the initial scene in which Charles Martel persuades the rich clergy to provision his men with arms and horses so that they can repel the invading Hungarians, and a three-line reference toward the end to Fromont's appeal for gold and silver to pay his soldiers (Vallerie 1947). The *Chanson d'Antioche*, recounting, like the *Cantar de mio Cid*, events of the not too distant past, gives no attention whatsoever to the very considerable problems of financing the First Crusade. Thus even in poems where one might expect to find the same preoccupation with economic factors that one encounters in the case of the *Cantar de mio Cid* – because of similarities in theme, in realistic depiction, or in distance between the time of composition and the period of the events being narrated – such factors do not appear to have been among the concerns that French, Occitan, or Franco-Italian poets represent as motivating kings and heroes.

How might this disparity be explained? One might look to differences in social structure for an answer. French feudalism as it is represented in the epic involves above all the exchange of land or office for fealty, requiring the vassal to render certain services to his lord, including military duty – usually for a well-defined period. Land is the classic base for this type of arrangement, but south of the Pyrenees the estate did not play a similarly preponderant role in the relations between men.[7] The conferral of movable goods was much more important in Castile. In addition, whatever benefits might be derived from the territorial base would be denied to the Cid as an exile, and thus the ordinary necessities entailed by his military campaigns would be aggravated by the very pressures that drove him from the traditional sources of revenue. The financial stratagem carried out at the Jews' expense provides the economic power that would normally be drawn from the security of land and castle.

But if these were the only reasons for the extraordinary inclusion of financial dealings in an epic poem, one would expect to find corresponding scenes in other works in which exile figures large as a theme, such as *Girart de Roussillon* from which they are, however, absent. Still other factors must be at work, deriving from the peculiar situation that obtained in late twelfth- and early thirteenth-century Spain, a period in which the Reconquest was taxing the energies of fighting men. Epic is above all an exemplary genre, holding up models for imitation. In an expanding world in which land is available for capture by force, and in which an important political problem is how to incite able-bodied men to leave their familiar surroundings and devote themselves to combatting the Almohads, the *Cantar de mio Cid* furnishes an example of how one noble of relatively low rank rose to the highest level of the social hierarchy without having at his disposal the traditional power base represented by the landed estate. In effect the poem implies a rhetorical question: "If Rodrigo of Vivar could rise to such eminence by fighting the Moors, why can't you?" Viewed in this light, the poem is at one and the same time an inspiring tale of social success and an economic example for ambitious Castilians of narrow means. The depiction of financial dealings may also reflect a particular historical moment, as I will suggest in chapter 6.

Preoccupation with the amassing of wealth is not limited to the scene in which Rachel and Vidas are tricked, although it is perhaps most blatantly presented there. The acquisition of booty, its proper distribution among the Castilian knights and soldiers, the evaluation of precious objects, and the use to which wealth is put join to comprise the major stock of thematic material in the poem. The Cid's reintegration into the social hierarchy is achieved primarily through economic power, and succeeds in direct relation to his personal enrichment. Time and again the types of booty are enumerated: gold and silver (799, 1214, 1737), coined money (1217), shields (795), arms (795, 1800), tents (1783), clothing (481b), slaves (465), camels (2491), horses (1781, 1800, 2489), beasts of burden (2490), and other livestock (466, 481). At times the amounts are said to be beyond reckoning or recounting (799, 1214, 1218, 1738, 2491), although of course this kind of comment on the poet's part is only a rhetorical flourish since he also depicts *quiñoneros* tallying up the loot. The Cid is content that everyone in the army has profited from the plunder: "Sobejanas son las ganançias que todos an ganadas" (2482). Repeatedly, and as early as the capture of Castejón de Henares, the poet terms the fighting men "wealthy":

Del castiello que prisieron odos ricos se parten.	(540)
Refechos son todos esos christianos con aquesta ganançia	(800)
A cavalleros e a peones fechos los ha ricos.	(848)
Tan ricos son los sos que non saben que se an.	(1086)

In contrast, on only one occasion, the taking of Valencia, is there any mention of real estate being distributed to the soldiers:

Los que ixieron de tierra de ritad son abondados,
a todos les dio en Valençia casas y heredades de que son pagados (1245–6)

Movable goods were obviously more highly prized than estates for these knights and other warriors far from their Castilian base, since they could be taken back and converted into money or exchange goods. As the Cid himself

The acquisition of wealth

remarks to Berenguer Ramon of Barcelona, he has been forced to survive through plunder during his exile (1046–8). He leads the life of a robber baron for three years:

> En tierra de moros   prendiendo e ganando
> E durmiendo los dias   e las noches tranochando
> en ganar aquelas villas   mio Çid duro .iii. anos.   (1167–9)

The economic situation presented in the poem with such insistence is clearly one of plunder and immediate gain rather than of long-term exploitation. For a poet composing long after the period in which the events took place, the good sense of this portrayal is obvious, since Valencia was abandoned to the Moors a scant three years after the historical Cid's death.

An example of the importance the poet gives to booty is the battle that takes place in the pine grove of Tévar, which is motivated on Berenguer Ramon's part by the perception that the Cid is succeeding at the expense of lands under the count's protection. The hero, however, sees the *francos* as threatening the safety of his booty ("por toler me laganançia," 999; see also 973, 985). While the Barcelonese is thinking in terms of political and territorial influence, the exile has only the security of his movable wealth to preoccupy him. A certain economic irony results when, as a consequence of parrying this menace, the Cid acquires from the count one of his most valued possessions, the sword Colada (1010).

Another detail that underscores the significance of booty in the poem is the care the hero takes to see that none of his men should slip away from Valencia with plunder:

> Veelo mio Çid   que con los averes que avien tomados
>   que sis pudiessen ir   fer lo ien de grado.
>   Esto mando mio Çid,   Minaya lo ovo conssejado:
>   que ningun omne de los sos   ques le non spidies o nol besas la mano,
>   sil pudiessen prender   o fuesse alcançado
>   tomassen le el aver   e pusiessen le en un palo.   (1249–54)

The Cid is seldom portrayed acting with rigor in the poem: that he should order to the gibbet those of his men who leave with their own gain is a step of unusual severity. To be sure such a penalty would not be anomalous in the period – otherwise it would have been difficult to keep an army together after any major victory. What is extraordinary is that the poet includes it in his portrayal of a hero who is normally fierce only toward the enemy.

The Cid's share of booty is consistently represented as a fifth of the total through each of the four principal battles, Castejón (515), Alcocer (805), and the fights against Yúsuf (1798) and Búcar (2487), as well as in the campaign culminating in the capture of Valencia (1216), and the poet goes out of his way to say that his men were in agreement with this arrangement: "Assi lo fazen todos ca eran acordados" (2488). (See Menéndez Pidal 1954–56, 2: s.v. *quinta* for relevant legal texts.) Lacarra (1980a: 41–3) points out that only the king

The *Cantar de mio Cid*

was entitled to a fifth of the booty, according to the municipal *fueros* – codifications of local privileges granted by the monarchy which are the main sources for our knowledge of laws pertaining to the distribution of the spoils of war in this period – and rightly takes this detail, the fact that the poetic Cid does not turn a fifth over to the king, and his appointment of Jerónimo as bishop of Valencia, normally a royal prerogative, as indications that the poet wished to posit the hero's political independence from Alfonso after his exile.[8] In the absence of any statement to that effect, the economic detail serves as a declaration of autonomy. That there is a hierarchy in the distribution of the rest of the loot, and that horsemen receive twice the amount of footsoldiers (513–14), are matters confirmed by the *fueros*.

The preoccupation with the process of the Cid's enrichment may account in part for the disproportion between events of the historical Rodrigo Díaz of Vivar's life in exile and the poet's depiction of it. After leaving Castile, the poem tells us, the Cid undertook campaigns of plunder in the valleys of the rivers Henares and Jalón. The account of these expeditions centers on the taking of two towns, Castejón de Henares and the mysterious "Alcocer." The surprise attack at dawn on Castejón de Henares is the first engagement in the Cid's three-year-long campaign, and the taking of Alcocer by ruse is the second battle recounted, although several razzias have been mentioned. In spite of the poet's insistence on the capture of these two towns, neither is associated with the Cid's name in historical sources, and I shall present a case for associating the poem with a major monastic center in the valley of the Jalón in chapter 6.

The poet informs us further that while the Castilians held Alcocer, Tamín, king of Valencia, wishing to besiege the town, sent an army of 3,000 men under the leadership of the kings Fáriz and Galve. The entire incident is fictitious, as apparently are Tamín, Fáriz, and Galve who, if they ever existed, certainly did not play the roles assigned to them in the poem. "Tamín" may be a shortened form of the name of al-Mu'tamin, the emir of Saragossa, or possibly a remembrance of "Tamim," governor of Spain after the Cid's death. "Fáriz" may represent "Háriz," a Moor whom the historical Cid apparently killed at Medinaceli according to the *Liber Regum* (Menéndez Pidal 1947: 159), and "Galve" may recall al-Ghalib, son-in-law of Almanzor (Michael 1978: 126n).

The taking of Castejón and the capture and defense of Alcocer are key events in this process not because they correspond to well-known events in the hero's life – they are in fact probably products of the poet's imagination. Thematically their role is to show that the Cid is now on solid financial footing, having put to effective use the investment capital furnished by Rachel and Vidas. The choice of towns in the Transierra and the basin of the Jalón as the scenario for this transformation may well be associated, as Lacarra (1980a: 209) posits, with the poet's desire to depict lands that were of great importance for the crown of Castile in the late twelfth century and under the hegemony of a branch of the Lara family descended from the Cid (1980a: 253). The events

The acquisition of wealth

of the historical Cid's life that are, however distortedly, depicted in the poem, such as the taking of Valencia, are much less interesting for the analysis of the poet's possible motivation than are the patently unhistorical elements, no doubt created under strong imaginative impulse and partly for political motives.

But why did the poet invent the attack by Fáriz and Galve who are, after all, attempting to drive the Cid from a town that he will sell to the Moors shortly after the battle ends – to improve his liquidity – just as he had abandoned Castejón? Until the capture of Valencia, the Cid of the poem is depicted as uninterested in territorial acquisition except to the extent that such conquest leads to the amassing of plunder. Even with the raids carried out in the vicinity of Guadalajara and Alcalá de Henares, the Castejón campaign brought him only 3,000 silver marks (l. 521), although his fifth of the booty would have been worth much more in circumstances in which he would not have been compelled to sell it off immediately. While this amount is five times the principal of the Jews' loan, it is certainly not enough to finance the establishment of a kingdom. Alcocer could be expected to yield less since the poet has the entire army participate in its capture, leaving no one to plunder in the vicinity, and later, in fact, it is sold to the Moors for 3,000 silver marks total (l. 845), of which only a fifth would devolve to the Cid according to the system of division depicted in the poem. But Fáriz and Galve's army represents an abundance of movable goods: horses, weapons, and armor, as well as gold and silver. Rodrigo of Vivar does not have to seek out the wealth of Moorish Spain on this occasion: the poet has it come to him – in the hands, on the backs, and under the saddles of 3,000 Arab fighting men. Five hundred and ten horses are said to have been taken in the battle (l. 796b), as well as incalculable amounts of gold and silver (l. 799). The Cid will no longer have to be concerned about his ability to reimburse the Jews or to pay off his debt (*debdo*, l. 225) of a thousand masses promised to the Virgin Mary: he is now self-financed and has enough surplus to be able to send the first of his offerings to Alfonso, 30 horses saddled and harnessed, each with a sword attached to the saddle-bows.

The modern reader cannot properly evaluate the booty acquired by the Castilians in the *Cantar de mio Cid* without considering the relative values of possessions in the Middle Ages, which is at one and the same time a hermeneutical and a philological question. When the poem mentions the word *caballo*, for example, one thinks of a modern horse, perhaps adjusting the mental image to account for the smaller size of medieval horses. But the notion "horse" also encompasses the value of the horse, not merely in absolute terms but in relation to other values: that of an ox, for example, or a plot of land.

Jaime Vicens Vives remarks that in this period the worth of agricultural property was insignificant when compared to the prices that were placed on precious objects such as chalices, marble coffers, and cloaks of silk brocade. Next in the scale of values came horses, which defined the military profession. On a lower level came fur cloaks and livestock. Lower still was land, and lowest of all the fruits of the land which were theoretically worth nothing since they were not sold on the market (Vicens Vives 1964: 128). The value of land was raised very little when buildings were constructed on it: Reyna Pastor de Togneri (1962: 47n) notes, among other examples of the same type, that in 1090 various manor houses were sold to the monastery of San Millán for 30 solidi each while at the same place and in the same year an ox was worth 20 and a horse between 500 and 1,000 solidi. This system of values corresponds to what we see in the poem, with the addition that finely-crafted articles of a military or paramilitary use are the most precious, namely King Yúsuf's Moroccan tent, whose value is not stated but which the Cid picks out as a gift worthy of King Alfonso (1789–90), and the swords Tizón and Colada, each appraised at a thousand marks or more (ll. 2426 and 1010 respectively). Colada is designated as *la preçiada*, an epithet that no doubt derives from the value of the workmanship that has gone into the manufacture of its hilt as well as from the quality of steel found in its blade. That the poet does indeed consider horses to be valuable is shown by the fact that they are the principal component in all three of the hero's gifts to Alfonso.

Let us consider the amounts of plunder coming into the army's possession in the course of the poem, and the values that it represents. In cases where the Cid's fifth is the figure that the poet supplies to us, it is simply a matter of multiplying by five. The total acquisitions of the Christian forces come to the following amounts for the various campaigns and battles:

1 Castejón: the value of 15,000 silver marks (521);
2 Alcocer: sold to the Moors for 3,000 silver marks (845); 510 horses (796b) acquired from the defeat of Fáriz and Galve's forces;
3 Defeat of the count of Barcelona: "gananças grandes" (1031) plus Colada, worth more than 1,000 silver marks (1010);
4 Capture of Valencia: 150,000 marks in specie alone plus countless additional booty (1216–18);
5 Victory over Yúsuf: 7,500 horses (1780–1) plus tents and tent-posts (1783), including the king of Morocco's tent (1785–6);
6 Victory over Búcar: 3,000 horses (2489) and many other camels and beasts of burden (2490), plus Tizón, worth 1,000 gold marks.

In judging the value of the horses, extremely important animals in the medieval Castilian economy, we are fortunate to have the data provided by Reyna Pastor de Togneri (1962: 47n), who found that in the year 1090, at San Millán de la Cogolla, a single horse was worth between 25 and 50 oxen. A horse's value in monetary terms at that time and place[9] was between 500 and 1,000 solidi; since there were 20 solidi to the pound and the mark of Burgos was a half pound of silver, a mark was the equivalent of 10 solidi. Each horse was thus worth between 50 and 100 silver marks – presumably depending on the quality of the horse. Taking this value into account, one can conclude that the sword Colada, worth "more than 1,000 silver marks," was tantamount in wealth to somewhat more than ten good horses.

Applying these equivalences to the horses acquired in the various

The acquisition of wealth

encounters, and evaluating a horse conservatively on the average (war horses captured from Arab armies were, in fact, probably fine animals) at 75 silver marks, one learns that the 510 horses taken from Fáriz and Galve at Alcocer would have been worth 38,250 silver marks or over twelve times what Alcocer itself brought and twice the revenue from Castejón and Alvar Fáñez's raids combined. Another way of putting it would be to say that, in the system of values operative in the historical world the poet wished to depict, the horses acquired as booty by the army in a single battle were equal to twelve small towns or several large ones. In fact they may have been worth more than that in use value in the Cid's tactical situation since they were movable goods and thus did not have to be defended indefinitely in one geographic location.

The later battles rendered even greater equine wealth, of course. The victory over Yúsuf yielded 7,500 horses, or the equivalent of 562,500 silver marks, and Búcar's defeat 3,000 horses or the equivalent of 225,000 marks. In this light it is likely that for the poet the battles taking place after the occupation of Valencia were of greater significance for the enrichment of both hero and army than the wealth of that city itself, since he only mentions monetary spoils of 150,000 marks from its capture (i.e. five times the Cid's quota of 30,000). Of course houses (*casas y heredades*, 1246) and countless additional objects (*e los otros averes ¿quien los podrie contar?*, 1218) were also acquired in the capture of Valencia; but in the battles against Yúsuf and Búcar weapons and equipment were undoubtedly meant to be understood among the spoils and certainly amounted to a considerable treasure. While few weapons could have equaled Colada and Tizón, each worth a thousand marks or more, the acquisition of thousands of them could hardly have represented a paltry sum. In any event, just taking into account money and horses, the Castilian forces are represented as earning for their pains the equivalent of 993,750 silver marks, of which just over 83 percent was in the form of equine booty.

The Cid's portion of that amount would have come to 198,750 silver marks. It is obvious that the distribution of such colossal sums is an operation on the highest level of priority, to be carried out in writing, according to the municipal *fueros* (Lacarra 1980a: 33). No wonder, then, that Alvar Fáñez, the Cid's own "right hand" in the poem and his personal envoy to Alfonso, is charged with carrying it out and is shown counting up quantities and writing them down after the battle with Yúsuf (1772–3), the most lucrative encounter in the poem.

The appraisal of objects and their relative worth is perhaps of less interest for elucidating the values conveyed by the poetic text than what those objects connote in moral terms. In the *Cantar de mio Cid*, booty and fame are inextricably linked. Where one might expect a call to what are sometimes termed man's higher instincts, that is to say the desire for glory or the appeal to religious ideals, one encounters only the promise of gain. The proclamation that the Cid sends out through Aragon, Navarre, and Castile carries a message obvious in its reliance on the appeal to cupidity:

> Quien quiere perder cueta   e venir a rritad
> viniesse a mio Çid   que a sabor de cavalgar;
> ¡çercar quiere a Valençia   por a christianos la dar!   (1189–91)

The boldness of this proclamation contrasts with the tone of another plea that was uttered only three years after the historical Cid's call for recruits and long before the poem as it has come down to us was composed, namely Urban II's preaching of the First Crusade to the Holy Land at Clermont in 1095. Like the Castilian soldiers of fortune, the Crusaders were placing themselves in a position to profit greatly in worldly ways from their expedition, but among the contemporary sources only Baldric of Dol mentions that Urban's speech included any reference to enrichment through plunder. The Crusade was proclaimed overwhelmingly on the basis of spiritual and moral – rather than materialistic – motives (see Duncalf 1969: 244).

Fame is presented as a significant source of inspiration in the *Cantar*, but wealth is its constant correlative. A token of their relationship is that twenty-five lines are consecrated to the enumeration and distribution of booty after the Castilians repel Yúsuf's attempt to drive them from Valencia, but the engagement itself is recounted in only nineteen lines. The Cid's exhortation to his "nephew" as the two enter Burgos in preparation for his exile, "¡Albriçia, Albar Ffañez, ca echados somos de tierra!" (l. 14), is a rejoicing at the fact that the hero and his followers are now stripped of all resources, with the implication that they are free to acquire through their own skill the trappings of fame. Whatever they come to possess from that moment on will be ascribable only to their merit or good fortune – not to birth or to office or rank. The poet articulates the connection between fame and accumulation of booty after the Castilians have repelled the king of Seville:

> Tornado es mio Çid   con toda esta ganançia.
> Buena fue la de Valençia   quando ganaron la casa,
> mas mucho fue provechosa   sabet, esta aranca[n]da;
> a todos los menores   cayeron .c. marcos de plata.
> Las nuevas del cavallero   ya vedes do legavan.   (1231–5)

Later, in disgust at the Cid's successes, Count García Ordóñez makes an analogous link between honor and booty – here specifically horses that the Cid has sent to Alfonso – and conversely between his enemy's victories and the disgrace of his own party, unable to provide such lavish gifts:

> ¡Maravilla es del Çid   que su ondra creçe tanto!
> En la ondra que el ha   nos seremos abiltados;
> ¡por tan biltada mientre   vençer reyes del campo,
> commo si los falasse muertos   aduzir se los cavallos!
> Por esto que el faze   nos abremos enbargo.   (1861–5)

The hero himself is depicted as viewing display as a desideratum:

> ¡Que lo sepan en Gallizia   y en Castiella y en Leon
> con que riqueza enbio   mios yernos amos a dos!   (2579–80)

The acquisition of wealth

This emphasis on ostentation is in keeping with the poem's lack of internal analysis, as distinct from external psychological depiction, a quality deriving from the state of the society in which it was composed but also a genre characteristic shared by the *chanson de geste*. Just as the characters' thoughts are revealed in dialogue and action, so their true worth is reflected by the accumulation of external signs of wealth, the tokens of reputation and of honor.

Manifestation of wealth takes various forms in the poem, but nowhere is it more intimately associated with a character than with the Cid at the moment of his greatest triumph:

> Nos detiene por nada　el que en buen ora naçio:
> calças de buen paño　en sus camas metio,
> sobr'ellas unos çapatos　que a grant huebra son;
> vistio camisa de rançal　tan blanca commo el sol,
> con oro e con plata　todas las presas son,
> al puño bien estan,　ca el selo mando;
> sobr'ella un brial　primo de çiclaton,
> obrado es con oro,　pareçen por o son;
> sobr'esto una piel vermeja,　las bandas d'oro son,
> siempre la viste　mio Çid el Campeador;
> una cofia sobre los pelos　d'un escarin de pro,
> con oro es obrada,　fecha por razon...
> De suso cubrio un manto　que es de grant valor,
> en el abrien que ver　quantos que i son.　　(3084–95, 3099–100)

At no other point in the poem is the Cid described in this degree of detail, and the poet has chosen to sketch this portrait of his main character not as a fighting man (although the Cid's followers and perhaps the hero himself are in fact wearing mail under their garments at this point) but rather as a richly clad magnate ready to match his knowledge of the law against his slow-witted adversaries. The quality of the garments is persistently stressed: leggings of fine cloth, not just shoes but shoes of embossed leather, a well-fitting shift of fine cloth with gold and silver fastenings, a tunic of fine brocaded silk interwoven with gold threads, a red skin with gold sashes, a fine linen cap also decorated with gold, and, over it all, a cloak of great worth. As in the *chanson de geste*, where the length of a personal description functions as an index of the character's worth (Holland 1966: 397–418), the leading hero is accorded the longest description. The Cid has clad himself as an object of admiration (l. 3100). An aura of wealth surrounds him because he is depicted as carrying on his person not merely rich accoutrements but the magnificent visible symbols of his military and political accomplishments. The contrast with the pegs in his abode, empty of some of these same trappings (*sin pielles e sin mantos/ e sin falcones e sin adtores mudados*) at the beginning of the manuscript (ll. 4–5), is no doubt calculated.

To what extent does the acquisition of wealth as it is depicted in the poem correspond to medieval reality? The spoils of war, in the form of both tribute paid by the Moorish kingdoms and booty won in frontier battles, raids, and major incursions against Muslim territories, played a significant role in the economic life of eleventh-, twelfth-, and thirteenth-century Castile.

While the period of tributes began with Sancho García's return from Cordoba in 1009, their collection only assumed the status of an institution under Fernando I (r. 1037–1065), an institution which Alfonso VI furthered vigorously, especially after the Battle of Zalaca in 1086. Hilda Grassotti has termed the late eleventh century the "classical age of booty" in Castilian history. From the Moorish kingdoms Alfonso received rich jewels, luxurious rugs and cloth, and enormous quantities of gold and silver, which were a major source of wealth for the royal treasury (Grassotti 1964: 55–60). The exact sums that the monarch took in from his tributaries is unknown, but what is recorded is that around the year 1090 the historical Cid collected the following amounts in the Levant: 50,000 dinars from Denia, Játiva, and Tortosa; 10,000 from Santa María; 10,000 from Alpuente; 8,000 from Murviedro; 8,000 from Segorbe; 3,000 from Jérica; 3,000 from Almenar; 2,000 from Liria; and 52,000 from Valencia (Grassotti 1969: 749, based on Sánchez Albornoz). The *Cantar de mio Cid* is not alone in stressing Rodrigo's success in acquiring wealth for distribution to his followers: the *Historia Roderici* mentions the *stipendia largissima* that he gave them at the siege of Liria (see Grassotti 1969: 752n).

A dinar contained, theoretically,[10] 4 grams of gold, and was the equivalent of one solidus. The total of 146,000 dinars that the Cid took in around 1090 would have been worth, then, about 14,600 silver marks, or less than half the value of what the poetic Cid is said to have taken in booty from the army of Fáriz and Galve. That the acquisition of booty in an important battle should have yielded more than the tribute of any town – or perhaps even any region – in a single year is plausible. In any case the poet appears to have been positing amounts that were on an order of magnitude compatible with economic and political reality.

During the last years of Alfonso's life and the reign of his sister Urraca, Almoravid victories resulted in a reversal of the flow of booty and a cessation of tributary payments until after the Battle of Fraga in 1134, when Alfonso VII undertook a policy of aggression that resulted once again in the massive acquisition of booty (Grassotti 1964: 68). The Emperor succeeded in exacting payments of tribute from Ubeda and Baeza, but after his death in 1157 the strife that marked the minority of Alfonso VIII and the advent of the Almohads led to another period of dearth for Castile in which some tribute probably continued to be paid, but not in the quantities won during the reigns of Alfonso VI and, to a lesser extent, Alfonso VII. Despite a short respite around 1182, when Alfonso VIII took booty and prisoners during a devastating expedition into Andalusia, the "balance of predation" was largely unfavorable to the Christian kingdoms. A raid carried out by the archbishop of Toledo provoked a reaction on the part of the Almohads that resulted in the Battle of Alarcos in 1195, disastrous for the Christian rulers. After that defeat, internal conflict among them prevented further gains until the great victory of Las Navas de Tolosa in July 1212, that was financed not with tribute money but through a levy amounting to half the rents recovered by the clergy of Castile (*Crónica latina de los reyes de Castilla*, ed. Cabanes Pecourt 1964: 44).

During Alfonso VIII's reign, then, the late eleventh century must have taken on the appearance of a golden age during which the influx of wealth from the south in the form of booty and tribute improved materially the conditions of life. If there were any period whose economic climate Alfonso VIII might have envied, it would have been the reign of his great-grandfather, and precisely on account of the riches that poured into the kingdom then from the money economy of the Muslim states. Even the impressive booty acquired as a result of the Battle of Las Navas de Tolosa did not suffice to restore the king's economic prosperity, on account of the debts that he had acquired in the victorious campaign (Grassotti 1969: 784).

3
Economy and gift-giving

The terms "vassalage" and "feudalism" as they are normally understood are inadequate to encompass dealings between men, and especially between members of the noble classes, as they are represented in the *Cantar de mio Cid*. Social relationships in the poem are marked by a moral and economic give-and-take that mirrors a particular state of society known as a "gift economy" in which exchanges of money and goods take place continually, but not under conditions that one would normally call "economic" in the modern world. The historian Georges Duby (1973), drawing upon concepts developed by the socio-anthropologist Marcel Mauss (tr. 1954), has interpreted the early economy of medieval Europe as one based on gift-giving. The model he proposes illuminates the meaning of gift-giving and other processes of the eleventh- and twelfth-century Castilian economy as they are found in the poem.

Through conquest and the income from various types of taxes, dues, and rents, nobles of the period were endowed with a quantity of wealth beyond what was needed for their daily sustenance, even granting that they clothed, fed, and equipped themselves on a scale above what was strictly necessary for carrying out the functions of daily life and of warfare. The economic workings of society required that such wealth be passed on to others. Generosity in distributing it was not simply an option open to the powerful: it was an obligation, albeit uncodified and often even unarticulated. Recipients of seignorial largess were by no means all of a station lower than the givers. Naturally almsgiving, the bestowal of gifts upon vassals and other social inferiors, and the conferral of rewards in return for service constituted a major portion of the economic transfers that resulted in the percolation of prosperity down from the higher nobles to the lower and from the nobility to the peasants; but exchanges between equals and gifts from inferior to superior were also immensely important. The king, at the apex of the hierarchy, was forced to have constantly at his disposal sources of wealth that he could distribute to those who would test his liberality. While conquest and plunder provided much of it, so did the offerings of lesser men. The magnificent trappings of royalty were, among other things, a sign that the royal treasure was not empty, and implied that other quantities of gold, silver, and valuable objects would follow what was already being given away in, ideally, a constant stream of abundance. Churchmen also profited from this flow, for

Economy and gift-giving

the powers to be placated were not confined to the temporal. God, controller of mankind's fortunes, had also to be appeased, and the divine kingship guarded its perquisites as zealously as those of any monarch, which directly benefitted monasteries, churches, and individual members of the clergy.

The relationships that depended on these gifts were mutually beneficial. That gift-giving was ever considered disinterested is doubtful. In relationships between fighting men and their retainers, of course, service was commonly rendered for largess; the payment of tribute guaranteed against the attacks of potential plunderers; stipends, legacies to the Church, and donations in atonement for sins or in petition of favors brought a return in the form of heavenly benevolence even when the ecclesiastical intermediaries were not, as they often were, at the same time secular powers capable of bestowing more immediate and tangible benefits. Even the most covert types of almsgiving were thought to be rewarded by good fortune. The economic system fueled by this movement of wealth in many cases had links to mercantile trade, but it nevertheless effected a circulation of goods that sustained the poor, maintained masses of able-bodied monks, gave incentives to the warrior class, and acted in general as a force that held the social edifice together.

While these conditions characterize primarily the early Middle Ages, they still largely obtained in the period 1050–1207, that is, during the Cid's life and the time in which the poem was in all probability composed in the form in which we have it (Duby 1973: 60–9, 287–9). At the same time, one sees in the episode of Rachel and Vidas a sign of the halting emergence of a new kind of economy, represented by the loan granted only after consideration rather than as an obligatory gesture and requiring a fixed interest, yet ultimately, in the Per Abbat text at least, uncollectible. The town-dwelling moneylenders, immersed in the developing mercantile life of prosperous Burgos, participate only marginally in the Cid's ethical and economic universe once the military campaign begins, and the poet in turn apparently viewed his hero as no more compelled to return the money than they were to lend it without deliberation.

The value and frequency of gifts naturally rose with the wealth and social status of the giver. One might then expect King Alfonso to be the principal distributor of largess in the poem. The king, however, is shown infrequently in the posture of giving, and only on official occasions, notably when he bestows a *donadio* or wedding-gift of 300 marks on the Infantes de Carrión after betrothing them to the Cid's daughters, for them to spend on the wedding, and when he returns to the Infantes 200 marks – probably a fine they have paid him for abandoning their wives (Lacarra 1980a: 58–9) – as a contribution toward paying back to the Cid the 3,000 marks in dowry he gave them. In contrast, the Cid makes a show of his wealth by constantly bestowing gifts on those who surround him, thus taking on the aura of a king (see Lacarra 1980a: 115). Several of his gifts are made in expectation of some favor to be sought in return, or in connection with a transaction. Even before he has any substantial possessions to call his own, he gives Rachel a red pelt on the latter's entreaty (l. 178). The Jews, perhaps in imitation of their debtor's generosity, give Martín Antolínez in turn the sum of 30 marks, to compensate for his services as intermediary.

The Cid's gift to the cathedral of Santa María in Burgos functions as a stipend, since he sends it in payment for the thousand masses that he had pledged to have sung there should he succeed. This operation establishes a devotional and financial obligation between the Cid and the Virgin Mary, but the weight of the bargain very definitely falls on the saint's shoulders since the promised masses (and the payment) will be forthcoming only in the event that the Cid receives tangible benefit from the Virgin's protection.

> ¡Vuestra vertud me vala,   Gloriosa, en mi exida,
> e me ayude e(l) me acorra   de noch e de dia!
> Si vos assi lo fizieredes   *e la ventura me fuere complida*
> mando al vuestro altar   buenas donas e ricas;
> esto e yo en debdo   que faga i cantar mill missas.
>
> (ll. 221–5, italics mine)

This passage is noteworthy not only for the materialistic view of religion that it reveals (see Sumption 1975 for this aspect of medieval religiosity), but as an indication of the extent to which the Cid of the Per Abbat text is represented as thinking in economic terms even when he is praying. He takes care later to pay off his debt to the Virgin – in contrast to his behavior toward Rachel and Vidas – but only after he has defeated the Moorish army at Alcocer and taken great booty, telling Alvar Fáñez:

> Evades aqui   oro e plata
> una uesa leña   que nada nol minguava:
> en Santa Maria de Burgos   quitedes mill missas,
> lo que romaneçiere   daldo a mi mugier e a mis fijas,
> que ruegen por mi   las noches e los dias;
> si les yo visquier   seran dueñas ricas.   (ll. 820–5)

The clause of purpose in line 824 may seem a bit strange to the modern reader: why should the hero's wife and daughter need the incentive of a payment to pray for him? Unless one wishes to punctuate the line as an independent sentence, severing it from the thought expressed in 823, it may be taken as an index of the extent to which economic considerations permeate the poem even occasionally in situations in which they seem out of place.

After taking Valencia and repulsing the Moorish king of Seville the hero sends a thousand marks to San Pedro de Cardeña (1285–6), to accomplish the promise he had made previously that the monastery would not suffer losses for taking care of his wife and daughters. Alvar Fáñez only gives 500 to the abbot, however, spending the other 500 on clothing and horses for Jimena, her daughters, and their ladies-in-waiting. Smith (1972) and Menéndez Pidal (1954–56) attribute this inconsistency to the scribe, inserting a compensatory reading in l. 1286. Michael (1978) ascribes it to the poet. In any case, the handsome stipend of 500 marks whets Abbot Sancho's appetite for additional

Economy and gift-giving

gifts (ll. 1443–6) which, he assures the emissary, will only serve to increase the hero's intrinsic worth.

The outstanding examples of interested gift-giving are, of course, the three scenes in which the Cid sends embassies to Alfonso. The poet casts Alvar Fáñez in the role of envoy (accompanied on the final occasion by Pero Vermúdez), having him lead to the king of Castile first 30 horses with saddles, bits, and swords, then 100 horses without mention of their equipment, and finally 200 steeds with saddles, bits, and swords, all acquired by the Cid as part of the fifth of the booty that fell to him.

In terms of the monetary equivalents discussed in the previous chapter, the horses alone given to Alfonso after the campaign in the valley of the Jalón are worth 2,250 silver marks, those given after the capture of Valencia 7,500, and those sent after the victory over Yúsuf 15,000, for a total equivalent of 24,750 silver marks sent in the course of the poem. Since a horse's equipment was often of considerable worth, an extraordinary escalation in value marks the sequence of gifts. If we assume that the equipment mentioned as being sent with each horse in the first and third embassies is together worth about half the value of the animal itself, the first gift comes to 3,375 marks, the second to 7,500, and the third to 22,500 marks. Each gift is thus more than twice the value of the previous one, but each probably represents a lower proportion of the fifth of the wealth that falls to the Cid if we take into account that in the "countless additional booty" (1218) deriving from the conquest of Valencia must have been horses.[1] In any case there can be no doubt that the amount of the gifts far surpasses whatever the hero can have been accused of obtaining from his expedition to collect tribute from Seville and Cordoba, the occasion after which he was exiled.

In addition the Cid declares his intention in ll. 1789–90 to send Alfonso the king of Morocco's tent, the best of all those captured, its posts inlaid with gold, probably the most precious object of booty mentioned in the poem. Although the actual dispatch of this valuable gift is never mentioned, the audience no doubt assumed that it was sent: the versions found in both the *Estoria de España* (Menéndez Pidal 1955: 599a) and the *Crónica de veinte reyes* (Dyer 1975: 77) show Alvar Fáñez and Pero Vermúdez delivering the tent and Alfonso acknowledging its receipt. A line including the tent among the items that comprised the Cid's gift has perhaps been omitted from the Per Abbat version after l. 1810, although it is also possible that the two prosifications are filling in what might have been an obvious omission in their models.

In each embassy the messenger stresses the abundance of booty that the Cid has taken from the Moors:

    Sobejana es, señor,   la su gançia.   (l. 877)
    Grandes son las gançias   quel dio el Criador.   (l. 1334)
    Las gançias que fizo   mucho son sobejanas.   (l. 1852)

This insistence is not merely informational, but rather functions as an announcement – both to the king within the world depicted by the poet and to

The *Cantar de mio Cid*

the audience in the performance situation – that the Cid is rapidly acquiring the economic means by which he can exert powerful influence in the politics of Spain. After each of these declarations, the messenger presents the gifts and relates that the Cid symbolically kisses the king's hands in token of submission.

The presents to Alfonso are neither required by law (see Lacarra 1980: 43) nor accorded on condition of specified benefits: they are gifts made without obligation, in the spirit – and following the uncodified practices – of a gift economy. In accord with those practices Alvar Fáñez on the first two occasions asks for a favor after he delivers the gifts: first for *merced*, that is that the *ira regia* no longer fall upon the Cid, and second that the hero's wife and daughters be permitted to join him in Valencia.

Alfonso is free to reject these requests, as indeed he does when, in gratitude for Alvar Fáñez's service as envoy, he returns to him the honors and lands he has lost by following the Cid into exile (886–8) and even allows others to follow the Cid without incurring the danger that their goods will be confiscated (891–3), but refuses to lift the *ira regia* (889). In doing so he demonstrates that he is less generous than his former vassal Rodrigo Díaz. On the second occasion Alfonso does grant the request made after the bestowal of the gift, and in addition, without being asked, restores all lands and possessions to those who flocked to the Cid's banner (1362–3). By the time the third gift is presented, there is perhaps no need for the messengers to specify what favor they seek: Alfonso promises the pardon (1898b) that Alvar Fáñez had asked for after the first gift, as the poet lays the groundwork for the king's proposal that the Cid's daughters marry the Infantes de Carrión.

Thus the gifts, the pardon, and the marriages are closely associated in the nexus of events that leads up to the complications of the third *cantar*. The pardon is important not because once it has been granted the Cid will be free to take up his former position in Castile – in fact he never does so in the poem – but rather because it prepares the way for the marriages that will ally his house with the family of Carrión. Thus the true effect of the series of gifts is not to return the Cid to the status that he held before incurring the king's wrath, a restoration of which he no longer has need, but to further his dynastic fortunes. The poet associates the marriage with the pardon when he has the Cid say that he is sending the third gift, which will result in lifting the *ira regia*, in gratitude for the king's having allowed his wife and daughters to leave Castile.

The Cid's gifts to Alfonso are not, then, merely an index of his generosity, if by that is meant simply the moral quality of liberality as it is understood in the modern world. They are bestowed not in exchange for benefits either, but definitely in expectation of them and on the third occasion in gratitude for them. And, of course, they are made with the full knowledge that they earn for the giver enormous prestige in the eyes of the populace, the Cid's fellow nobles, and the king himself: "Estos dozientos cavallos iran en presentajas/ que non diga mal el rey Alfonso del que Valençia manda" (1813–14). While

Economy and gift-giving

the poetic Cid apparently no longer considers Alfonso to be his lord in a legal sense (Lacarra 1980a: 46), he is able through the gifts at one and the same time to assert his own integrity, to underscore his faithfulness, to demonstrate that he is worth more as an ally than as an enemy (Lacarra 1980a: 124), to show that the economic grounds for his exile were baseless and have now even been rendered trivial by events, and to spread his reputation through a dramatic gesture. It is not his military exploits that exalt him – they were, after all, on about the same level, in history, as those of Alfonso, the conqueror of Toledo – but rather the use to which he puts his wealth, leading the king to exclaim at the beginning of the court scene, "¡Mejor sodes que nos!" (l. 3116), as he offers to have the Cid sit as his peer on a stool whose symbolic importance the king points up: "quem diestes vos en don" (l. 3115).

Many of the Cid's gifts, however, are granted to strengthen already solid ties to his men, his sons-in-law, his wife and daughters, and the Church. Even his enemy Count Ramon Berenguer of Barcelona is given three palfreys as well as clothing (ll. 1064–5) so that he can make a dignified departure after the scene in which he is persuaded to break his hunger strike.

The Cid offers Minaya Alvar Fáñez a fifth of the booty after Castejón probably because his nephew had led a profitable raiding expedition into the Henares valley as far south as Alcalá while the Cid was occupied with Castejón. The offer to Minaya of the leader's proper share of loot derived exclusively from the razzia would not have been surprising, but the Cid's generosity is shown off to advantage in his stated intention to calculate the fifth on the basis of the combined total from Castejón and the raid. Alvar Fáñez declines this offer, advising his lord instead to send the share in payment to Alfonso. The phrase "pagar se ia della Alfonsso el Castellano" (l. 495) implies not only that the king will be pleased with the gift, but, taking the other sense of *pagar*, that he will consider it as a (partial?) payment for the supposed misappropriation of funds for which he exiled his great vassal.[2] The occurrence of the epithet *el Castellano*, with its emphasis on Alfonso's role as ruler of the land from which the Cid has been excluded, reinforces this reading. The expression *pagarse* has this connotation again a few lines farther on when Minaya explains his gesture:

> Fata que yo me page sobre mio buen cavallo
> lidiando con moros en el campo,
> que enpleye la lança e al espada meta mano
> e por el cobdo ayuso la sangre destelando
> ante Ruy Diaz el lidiador contado,
> non prendre de vos quanto vale un dinero malo.
> Pues que por mi ganaredes ques quier que sea d'algo
> todo lo otro afelo en vuestra mano.   (ll. 498–505)

Perhaps Alvar Fáñez is to be understood as disdaining plunder that has been won in the quick action of raids on unsuspecting towns; more likely his reluctance comes from the fact that his deeds were not accomplished within sight of his lord. In any case the sentiment expressed in this passage is that of a properly humble man, one who is willing to be honored by the bestowal of extraordinary wealth but only if he has earned it to his own satisfaction. As we shall see, this reasoning provides illumination on the specific brand of *menosvaler* that characterizes the Infantes de Carrión in the third *cantar*. After Yúsuf's defeat the Cid makes a gesture toward Alvar Fáñez similar to that following Castejón: "Desta mi quinta – digo vos sin falla/ prended lo que quisieredes, lo otro remanga" (1806–7). That Minaya makes no reply is surely meant to imply his acquiescence this time.

Another recipient of the Cid's largess is bishop Jerónimo, who receives after Valencia's capture one-tenth of the Cid's fifth of the booty, that is to say more than 3,000 silver marks.

But if the Cid is portrayed as transforming his wealth into an instrument of loyalty by giving open-handedly to his vassals and others with whom he comes into contact, he is especially anxious to provide for his family. Before the poet shows him to be aware that the Infantes de Carrión are interested in his daughters, he is depicted as preoccupied with endowing the girls with so much wealth that they will be attractive matches for whatever suitors come along. Thus when Jimena sees the tents of Yúsuf's army and naively asks her husband what they are, he replies ironically that the Moors are bringing her a dowry for her daughters:

> Riqueza es que nos acreçe maravillosa e grand;
> ¡a poco que viniestes presend vos quieren dar;
> por casar vuestras fijas: aduzen vos axuvar! (ll. 1648–50)

The same solicitude applies to Jimena's ladies, to whom their lord ostentatiously gives 200 marks each as he declares his intention of marrying them to his vassals, a deed of largess that he hopes will spread the news of his munificence in Castile (l. 1767; cp. 2579–80). The goods taken from Yúsuf convince the ladies that they are as good as married (ll. 1799–1802). For the women wealth is a correlative of marriageability, as it is of honor and reputation for the men. The Cid's generosity increases as the poem progresses, perhaps not surprisingly since at the start of his exile he had little to give away. From a person constantly in other people's debt – the Jews of Burgos, Martín Antolínez, the Virgin Mary – he is transformed into a bestower of riches on others.

This metamorphosis affects the portrayal of the Infantes de Carrión, who are presented as laboring under a misconception about the worth of worldly goods that marks them through the whole poem. For them birth is by itself a value superior to anything that can be added by merit as reflected in acquired possessions, which is decidedly not the poet's or the hero's point of view. But they do share with the Cid the premise that wealth and marriage go hand in hand. Their first thought is for the financial profit they can derive from association with him: "Bien casariemos con sus fijas pora huebos de pro" (l. 1374), although at first they decide not to make overtures because their lineage is greater than his. They show a certain degree of inconsistency in their

Economy and gift-giving

articulation of the exchange of values constituted by the marriage, depending on whether their utterances are presented as public or private.

Within the space of six lines (ll. 1883, 1888) the poet has them use *ondra* in the two acceptations that it conveys within the contexts of the Cid's moral universe and their own. In both statements their own profit is mentioned ("e iremos adelant"; "a nuestra pro"). First, in secret, they state that marriage with the Cid's daughters will bring them honor (1883; see also 2530), but in their public approach to the king they speak of the prospective marriages as bringing honor rather to the daughters, a thought that is much more in keeping with the ethos of the class that they represent: "Casar queremos con ellas a su ondra" (l. 1888). The king shares this conception of *ondra* as a quality deriving from high birth, advising the Cid accordingly that the marriage will bring him increased honor (ll. 1905, 1929).

But whatever the Infantes' presumed idea of the advantages that will accrue to them, the poet makes it obvious that solvency is chief among them since he has them act as if they were already enriched at the *vistas* on the river Tagus, having them contract new debts and pay off old ones as if they are already in possession of the wealth that will be at their disposal as sons-in-law of the lord of Valencia (ll. 1975–8). Both at the *vistas* and at the wedding itself the Cid gives impressive gifts to those in attendance, sixty horses at the *vistas* and a hundred horses and mules at the wedding – distributions on the same order of magnitude as the first two presentations to the king, as the audience no doubt appreciated. In addition he gives Alfonso a fourth gift at the end of the *vistas*, twenty palfreys and thirty battle horses. His invitation to the wedding appeals frankly to the most materialistic expectations of the prospective guests: "Qui quiere ir comigo a las bodas o reçebir me don/ d'aquend vaya comigo; cuedo quel avra pro" (ll. 2129–30). In contrast, while naturally the Infantes give their wives the obligatory *arras*, in this case estates the visitation of which will be the pretext for taking them from Valencia, on no occasion does one actually see the Infantes distributing gifts to subordinates, contrary to what might be expected from nobles of such an exalted rank. For nobles of such high station, they comport themselves quite shabbily.

Still, it is not their cupidity that sets the Infantes apart from the Cid and his men, surely the most acquisitive heroes in any epic poem composed in a Romance language – and perhaps in any Indo-European language. The difference between the Cid's followers and the Infantes is that the former have worked to convert their valor into wealth, while the latter, lacking courage, are incapable of doing so. Beginning with the lion episode, a second sequence of motivations is introduced into the poem. The first, it will be recalled, was initiated by the accusation that the Cid had kept for himself part of the wealth he collected on an expedition to the Moorish kingdoms of Seville and Cordoba, and comprises a series of actions inspired by the hero's desire to finance his exile which will lead to the capture of Valencia and the striking victories over Yúsuf and Búcar. While the Infantes benefit from those actions and share the eagerness to amass riches that characterizes the Cid and his followers, their cowardice makes them ill suited to emulate the conquerors of Valencia. Once they have been shown up as cowards, Fernando hiding under the bench where the Cid lies sleeping and Diego taking refuge behind a wine press, the course of their actions leads them to sever themselves from their new-found source of wealth as their sense of having been shamed motivates them to channel their desire for revenge toward the weakest creatures in the poet's cast of characters, the Cid's daughters.

After viewing with trepidation the tents of King Búcar of Morocco, against whose troops they will have to do battle, Diego and Fernando sum up their consternation in a metaphor drawn from the semantic field of finance: "Catamos la ganançia e la perdida no" (l. 2320), "we considered the profit but not the loss." Still, they have at this point not yet acted counter to the code of the Castilian knights. It is only when they accept booty from the victory over Búcar in spite of having behaved in a cowardly manner on the battlefield that their true nature is rendered manifest. Each of the Cid's men took his just share, *so derecho contado* (l. 2486), but the poet and his audience know that the equivalent of 5,000 marks that fell to the Infantes as their portion (2509) – a sum with which they are more than content (see ll. 2470, 2510, 2529, 2542) – was not earned by the sword. Presumably Pero Vermúdez, who had rescued Fernando from public shame when the latter fled the battlefield, received only the 600-mark part that went to all the other knights (l. 2467), less than an eighth of each of the cowards' shares. Fernando had the ideal opportunity on which to give a gift when Pero presented him with the horse of the Moor he killed on Fernando's behalf,[3] but did not do so, contenting himself with promising to do twice as well the next time (or perhaps to give him a double gift: see the notes to this line in Smith 1972 and Michael 1978): "¡Aun vea el ora que vos meresca dos tanto!" (2338). On this occasion Fernando proves the truth of Pero Vermúdez's later characterization of him as "lengua sin manos" (3328). In fact neither brother gives a gift, unless one counts the *arras*.

The Infantes' grasping behavior contrasts sharply with Minaya Alvar Fáñez's conduct after the taking of Castejón: like him they should properly have refused the offer of wealth that they had not earned, and the poet moves Alvar Fáñez skilfully into the foreground in the aftermath of this victory, having him greet the Infantes as they enter the court (l. 2516) and characterizing his actions on the battlefield in the very terms that he had used after Castejón to set forth his own goals of knightly achievement: "Por el cobdo ayuso la sangre destellando,/ de .xx. arriba ha moros matado" (ll. 2453–4; cp. ll. 498–503).

Diego and Fernando have actually set their sights low, expressing repeatedly their contentment with the portion of 5,000 marks, which is only a small fraction of the amount that has accrued to the Cid during his various campaigns. Although they remark to each other that the wealth they have earned from Búcar's defeat is so extensive that they will never be able to spend it (l. 2542), the audience is already aware that 5,000 marks is not all that much to support Elvira or Sol on the scale to which their father's successes have accustomed them. After all, Minaya is said to have spent 500 marks in Burgos just providing the Cid's wife and daughters and their ladies-in-waiting with horses, mules, and finery in preparation for the journey to Valencia (ll. 1423–8). One has the impression that the poet is holding the Infantes up to ridicule by endowing them with a false sense of material values to match their moral bankruptcy. Perhaps we are meant to imagine that they have not been given the opportunities to acquire financial acumen on the Cid's scale.

This inability to reckon with wealth allows Diego and Fernando to plot the outrage of Corpes, since they imagine that they are now rich enough to aspire to marriage with the daughters of kings and emperors, a notion the audience is obviously encouraged to take as mistaken. The manner in which they express this idea reflects a subtle sense of irony on the poet's part. He once again juxtaposes in their speech utterances that suggest a confusion in their minds about the relationship between inner worth and reputation:

> D'aquestos averes   sienpre seremos ricos omnes,
> podremos casar con fijas   de reyes o de enperadores
> ¡ca de natura somos   de condes de Carrion!
> Assi las escarniremos   a las fijas del Campeador
> antes que nos retrayan   lo que fue del leon.   (ll. 2552–6)

Four ideas are compressed into these lines: that the newly acquired riches are sufficient to make the Infantes wealthy for the rest of their lives, that they can rise in the noble ranks through marriage, that they are from a high-born lineage, and that they will anticipate any ridicule that might be heaped upon them for their conduct in the lion episode. The *ca* best reveals their distorted sense of values, creating as it does a causal relationship between the innate qualities of their heredity and their ability to marry above their station. If they did have this capacity, it would be because of the 10,000 marks in booty (but the last two lines reveal their unworthiness even to partake in that share of the plunder). The poet has them express contradictory values: if the relationship between the first two lines of their assessment is a causal one, that is to say if they can aspire to higher marriage because of their wealth, then the supposed causality between the second and third lines is vitiated. Thus both their perception of the financial situation and their reasoning about its role are muddled.

The Cid's reaction to the Infantes' proposal to take his daughters off to Carrión – a project justified by the husbands' feigned desire to show their brides the *arras* that they have given them, in this case estates – is to bestow on the sons-in-law a dowry of 3,000 marks in addition to mules, palfreys, battle-horses, silk brocades, and other clothing. The crowning gifts, precious but, in the light of what both the audience and the Cid's vassals know (cp. ll. 2532–6), inappropriate in what they connote, are the swords Colada and Tizón, conferred with words of a heavily ironic ring: "Bien lo sabedes vos que las gane a guisa de varon" (l. 2576). The scale of these wedding gifts, exceeding the 10,000 marks worth of booty that Diego and Fernando have already been granted, has two justifications: the lord of Valencia wishes to spread word of his munificence in Galicia, Castile, and Leon (ll. 2579–80), and he offers the gifts as an incentive for the Infantes to treat his daughters well: "Si bien las servides yo vos rendre buen galardon" (l. 2582). With the greater financial skill the poet has conferred on him, the Cid is thus depicted as realizing that the Infantes' wealth, even with the addition of the wedding gifts, is not enough, as indeed turns out to be the case.

The Avengalbón episode only serves to sharpen the portrayal of the Infantes as nobles who covet goods that they did not earn by their own valor: "Ellos veyen la riqueza que el moro saco,/ entramos hermanos conssejaron traçion" (ll. 2659–60). They are shown to have become aware that in terminating their marriages to the Cid's daughters they are cutting off their source of wealth, and they wish to steal the Moor's as a supplement (ll. 2661–3).

Indeed, although one usually supposes that the Cid is to be considered full of anxiety for his daughters' physical well-being when he hears of the outrage inflicted on them at Corpes, his utterances represent him as occupied to a greater extent with how the affair reflects upon him: "¡Grado a Christus que del mundo es señor/ quando tal ondra me an dada los infantes de Carrion!" (ll. 2830–1), a sentiment similar to his reaction to the exile (l. 8) and to the king's espousal of the marriage proposal (ll. 1933–7).

The Cid is immediately determined to find a new marriage alliance for his daughters (ll. 2834, 2867, 2893), but he does not mention the physical abuse done to them by their husbands until his third appeal for justice at the *cortes* (l. 3265), after he has dispensed with the two civil demands. His one conversation with them is taken up by statements about revenge upon the Infantes, a possible new marriage, and why the old one was consented to in the first place. The physical abuse is mentioned to the king by the Asturian Muño Gustioz (ll. 2944–6) who in history was the Cid's brother-in-law. Indeed loss of the wealth that the Cid so freely gave to Diego and Fernando weighs upon him more heavily, according to the poet's depiction, than any other consideration except the fact that the marriages have been terminated: "Mios averes se me an levado que sobejanos son,/ esso me puede pesar con la otra desonor" (ll. 2912–13). Just as considerations of profit and honor dominated the sequence of events leading up to the marriages, to the exclusion of sentimental factors, so the feelings and physical well-being of Elvira and Sol are little exploited by the poet after the Corpes scene itself and are not seen to touch the hero.

The preoccupation with goods as signs of worldly grandeur continues during the *cortes* at Toledo. The Cid adopts a stance of refusing to admit that he has been dishonored by the Infantes' rejection of his daughters because only Alfonso, as their sponsor, can be affected in his dignity by the outrage. As a result, the Cid's first demand is that the swords Colada and Tizón be returned to him, gifts that were only occasioned by a kinship relation now dissolved. The symbolism of these valuable weapons, one captured from a Christian prince (who, incidentally, included Moors among his forces: ll. 968, 988), the other from a Muslim, no doubt leads the poet to make them the object of the first suit. No sooner are they in the Cid's hands than he gives

Economy and gift-giving

them away to two vassals to whom he is morally indebted, Pero Vermúdez the standard-bearer, and Martín Antolínez. The Cid's generosity to the latter fulfills his previously expressed desire to reward him for arranging the loan: "¡Aun vea el dia que de mi ayades algo!" (l. 205). Martín Antolínez, alone among the Cid's followers, is thus a key figure in both the first and the last episode of his climb from penury to glory.

That in having the Cid demand the return of the swords the poet intended to stress economic and moral concerns rather than simply the legal requirements of the situation is suggested by Lacarra's finding (1980: 61) that the request for return of gifts has no basis of legitimacy in twelfth- or early thirteenth-century legal sources.

The second legal demand is also for the return of material wealth, the 3,000 marks in dowries that the Cid here identifies as one of the Infantes' goals in contracting the marriages: "En oro y en plata tres mill marcos (de plata) les di (y)o./ Hyo faziendo esto, ellos acabaron lo so" (ll. 3204–5). According to the *Fuero Juzgo*, he had a perfect right to demand that these *ajuares* be given to his daughters now that the marriages have been dissolved (Lacarra 1980a: 61). No mention is made at this point of the other presents that accompanied the 3,000 marks and the swords: Louis Chalon rightly considers them to be outright gifts, the dowry consisting solely of the 3,000 marks (Chalon 1976: 151n).

When Alfonso, to whom the judges defer, grants the Cid's petition, the Infantes encounter a liquidity problem, having already spent the dowry and possessing no money of their own. Their previously demonstrated lack of judgment concerning quantities of wealth finds confirmation in this new imprudence, and they are forced to pay in kind (*en apreçiadura*, l. 3240) from their familial goods (*heredades*, l. 3223). The debt is finally made good from a combination of valuable possessions (horses, mules, swords), loans from third parties, and the 200 marks returned to the penniless heirs by Alfonso.

This last detail is surely meant to be the most humiliating: while the Cid is shown manifesting generosity on every occasion, the Infantes must accept back the only amount they are depicted as having given. Hinojosa (1899: 578–9) hypothesized that the 200 marks were the obligatory gift which, according to Germanic law, the husband was to present to the person who transmitted to him power over the bride, but Lacarra's conjecture (1980a: 58–9) that they represent fines of 100 marks each that were to be paid by men who abandoned their wives is probably correct. If so, the Infantes give no gifts at all in the course of the poem.

One should not conceive of the *Cantar de mio Cid* merely as a poem dominated by indiscriminate economic concerns: some economic matters, such as the amount of revenue the Cid derived from the Moors in Valencia, the damages due to knights who have been wounded in battle or whose horses have been killed (on which the *fueros* are quite specific), and the much-debated question of whether the hero ever did pay back the Jews' loan, are simply passed over in silence. Of the economic matters that are presented, however, gift-giving stands out as a dominant theme.

The *Cantar de mio Cid*

In a poem about a society whose economic mechanisms are based on the circulation of wealth through gift-giving, one can measure the exemplary value of characters by examining the extent to which they exhibit largess and the circumstances under which they give and take. Just as the Cid is the major accumulator of wealth, he is the person who is most frequently shown distributing it. While Alfonso is the chief recipient of his largess,[4] the king's gestures of giving up the 200 marks of the Infantes' fine, apparently without being obligated to do so, and of refusing to accept the Cid's horse Bavieca as a gift (ll. 3515-21), reveal him as a figure of generous spirit. Rachel and Vidas, unlike the other characters, request a specific gift from the Cid but also give one to Martín Antolínez. The hero's relatives, vassals, and footsoldiers, and the clergy associated with him, also profit richly from his distributions, as was to be expected, but they never confer gifts in turn. The Infantes de Carrión, finally, display a meanness of character that is echoed in their grasping conduct in economic matters.

4

Social status, legitimacy, and inherited worth

The relationship between the Cid and the Infantes de Carrión in the poem, totally fictitious from the vantage point of history (Spitzer 1948, Horrent 1973, Chalon 1976, Smith 1980, Lacarra 1980a), may have been conceived in part, as Lacarra has argued cogently (1980a: 137–56), to depict as reprehensible the Beni-Gómez, García Ordóñez, and Alvar Díaz – ancestors of the Castro family, one of the most powerful in the political life of late twelfth- and early thirteenth-century Castile and Leon. Lacarra believes that the force behind this portrayal is the clan that was the Castros' most intense rival, the Laras, one of whose members, the royal tutor Manrique de Lara, was killed by Fernando de Castro in 1164 at the battle of Huete. But the clash between the family of Carrión and the Cid also serves another function in the poem: to provide a context within which a question can be raised and answered concerning the nature of the Cid's descent from Diego Laínez and, concomitantly, his progeny's worthiness to contract marriages with partners of the very highest social rank. This last development may well be motivated by the fact that, as Lacarra has stressed, both the Laras of Molina and Alfonso VIII himself were related to Rodrigo Díaz of Vivar.

The Cid's third judicial demand opens the criminal part of the legal proceedings, occasioning a full-scale controversy about personal status, a subject that the Infantes had raised before. For the lord of Valencia, whose gifts until now have only implied a personal dignity corresponding to their high value, the time has come to settle directly the question of intrinsic worth, involving primarily in this period the values conferred by lineage. His gifts regained from the Infantes, the Cid announces that he will not let them off without proceeding to *riepto*, the formal challenge leading to judicial combat that will resolve the issues once and for all. Attacking the Infantes for taking his daughters from Valencia under false pretenses and for striking them with cinches and spurs, he declares in succinct juridical language: "¡Por lo que les fiziestes menos valedes vos!" (l. 3268). The sense of such an indictment is that the accused parties should not enjoy the privileges of the status they have held, in this case because of conduct inappropriate to persons of that rank.

In the municipal *fueros* that often reflect other legal aspects of the *Cantar de mio Cid* more faithfully than do the Castilian national lawcodes, specific legislation concerning noble status is difficult to come by, probably because an individual's nobility was only challenged infrequently in local jurisdictions.

Even the *Fuero viejo*, extant solely in its revised, "systematic," fourteenth-century form but deriving from elements going back as far as 1055 and probably reflecting in this instance the lost *Ordenamiento de Nájera* of 1128, only takes up the challenge to noble status in language that implies an inquiry into matters of birth (Jordan de Asso 1771: xix; I, v, xviii).

The *Siete partidas* of Alfonso X "el Sabio," on the other hand, begun in 1256 and completed in its first redaction nine years later (Craddock 1974: 370, 378n), deals with loss of status through conduct in VII.v, "De las cosas que fazen los omes, por que valen menos," with supplementary treatment in vi, "De los enfamados." The *Partidas* state that the ancient sages – "sabios antiguos," by which is undoubtedly meant the formulators of orally transmitted law (see Pérez-Prendes 1978: 404) – made *menosvaler* an issue subject to *riepto*. It results in rendering the convicted party disabled at court and before the law, namely in judicial combat, in bringing accusations, in giving testimony, and in filling offices, since he becomes *enfamado* and must suffer rejection from the company of men (VII.v.1).

In the following title, "De los enfamados," Alfonso specifies that the infamous are not as seriously disabled before the law as those guilty of treason or *aleve*, but that they cannot be chosen for any dignity or office and that they should be dismissed from any that they held before. Neither can they act as judges or royal counsellors, take part in political administration, act as spokesmen, live at court, or in fact participate in courts of any kind.

Menosvaler is, then, very high on the list of disabling legal statuses, just below treason. In the case of the Infantes de Carrión, who insist repeatedly that they are *de natura de condes de Carrión* (2549, 2554, 3296), proof that they are "worth less" would be tantamount to preventing them from ever performing comtal functions, such as taking part in courts or advising the king. In fact we know that the historical Diego and Fernando González of Carrión were members of the court of Alfonso VI between 1090 and 1105 (Fernando until 1109), which means that they could not possibly have been convicted of *menosvaler* and that the trial scene and its outcome must thus be fictitious (see Menéndez Pidal 1961: 154–5; Chalon 1967). Nevertheless the Infantes of the poem, who have neither courage nor military abilities, do engage in outrageous conduct justified only by the supposed privileges of their birth, which the Cid's charge has now challenged.

A person incurs *menosvaler* for stating falsely that he will bring suit or render homage, for taking back something that was said in a trial or at court, and for many other causes (VII.v.2). In "De los enfamados" these additional causes are divided into two types, arising respectively from fact and from law. The infamous on the basis of fact include those who are born of illegitimate unions, who are defamed in their fathers' wills, who are chastised for their manner of living by king or judge, or who have been ordered to restore stolen goods (VII.vi.2). On the basis of law a man is infamous if he marries off his daughter within a year of her husband's death, if he marries a woman widowed within the year, if he employs a woman for immoral purposes, if he

Social status, legitimacy, and inherited worth

is a public entertainer (*juglares* and others are specified) – unless he only entertains his friends, kings, or other lords – if, being a knight, he is expelled from an army for misconduct or deprived of his knighthood, or if he is a usurer or breaker of promises. Also infamous are those convicted of treason, falsehood, adultery, and other serious crimes, and those bribing persons who might bring testimony against them (VI.vi.3–4).

According to the *Partidas*, the Infantes would indeed be subject to the challenge of *menosvaler* since they have broken the promises constituted by their acceptance of betrothal to the Cid's daughters, an arrangement that the king himself effected at the *vistas*, as well as by their participation in the marriage ceremonies. By beating their wives and treating them as concubines (*barraganas*) rather than as legitimate spouses, they have thus gone back on an agreement made at court. If the Infantes were to be convicted of the charge of *menosvaler*, they would be on the same social level as *juglares*, pimps, bastards, and usurers, not only dishonored in public but subject to legal disablements; it is even possible that such a lowering of status would impose encumbrances of shame on their descendants in the genealogically-minded world of a poet composing in the late twelfth or early thirteenth century.

Concubinage (*barraganía*) was a legal form of union in medieval Castile, although it carried with it certain stigmas, with the result that children issuing from such arrangements had the status of natural offspring, could not succeed their fathers, and could not inherit if their fathers died intestate unless special provision were made (Gacto Fernández 1969: 25, 49, 96n). A man could terminate a relationship of *barraganía* without ceremony, at his whim, which would lessen the gravity of the Infantes' cruelty if their relation to the Cid's daughters was indeed concubinage.

The Cid's charge of *menosvaler* provokes an intervention from the Infantes' ally García Ordóñez to the effect that they are of such high birth (*natura*) that they should not have sought out the Cid's daughters as concubines (*varraganas*), much less as legitimate wives (3276), echoing the Infantes' own statement to that effect at the end of the Corpes scene, "Non las deviemos tomar por varraganas" (2759). The critical tradition has always taken these statements of García Ordóñez, Diego, and Fernando as bravado, exaggerations meant to emphasize by purely rhetorical means the supposed gap between the Infantes' level of noble status and the hero's. In previous interpretations of the poem these references to *barraganía* are puzzling, a debilitating link in an otherwise cogent motivational sequence, since both the betrothals and the marriage ceremonies were carried out in public, before witnesses who could testify to their legitimacy, and the unions received the Church's blessings (*bendictiones*) at mass in the sacrament of marriage (l. 2240). As we shall see, however, there is a hidden reason, brought forward by Ansur González, why Elvira and Sol might not qualify as spouses *de bendición*, a potential impediment which, if validated, would be so debilitating socially as to block the Cid's daughters' ascent in social dignity. The claims of the *vando* of Carrión are meaningless unless the Cid is himself "worth less" than he purports to be – a good deal less: less, in fact, than a noble. Then his daughters, born of a marriage between noble (Jimena Gómez) and non-noble (Rodrigo Díaz), would in turn be encumbered under law and might well not be worthy to serve even as concubines to men *de natura de condes*. Count García Ordóñez's intervention comes to nothing, nullified when the Cid undercuts the status that would allow him to pursue the charge in court by covering him with ridicule, referring to the incident at Cabra in which he pulled out some of the count's beard with impunity (Zahareas 1964: 166). Because the count never pursued a legal action against the Cid for that affront, he is permanently *enfamado* (Lacarra 1980: 97n), and thus, as Partida VI.V.1 tells us, unable to make accusations in court. Diego and Fernando then take up the nearly aborted line of defense proffered by their legally disabled ally, maintaining that, far from having lost status through their conduct, they are of too high a station to remain content with marrying the daughters of an *infanzón*.

Fernando claims that the Cid should cease his charges since he has already received restitution for his goods (l. 3294), and reasserts the Infantes' privileged hereditary comtal status:

> ¡De natura somos   de condes de Carrion!
> Deviemos casar con fijas   de reyes o de enperadores
> ca non perteneçien   fijas de ifançones.
> Por que las dexamos   derecho fiziemos nos.   (ll. 3296–9)

His reply to the charge of *menosvaler* is couched in the same valuational diction as the accusation, echoing its terminology as was specified by medieval law codes: "Mas nos preçiamos sabet, que menos no" (l. 3300). Notably he does not repeat García Ordóñez's allegation that the Cid's daughters would have been unworthy to serve as concubines for him and his brother, but rather only points up the gap between the statuses of counts and *infanzones*.

In countering this defense, Elvira's and Sol's first cousin Pero Vermúdez calls Fernando a liar (3313), an act tantamount to the challenge to judicial combat, and repeats the charge of *menosvaler* (3314). He narrates Fernando's craven demeanor in the battle against King Búcar and in the lion episode, which deflates Fernando's justification, based solely on the privileges of hereditary eminence, and exposes his infamy and worthlessness, this time not for his conduct toward his wife, but for cowardliness in hiding under the Cid's bench in order to escape the lion: "¡Por o menos vales oy!" (l. 3334). Lacarra points out (1980a: 87) that the revelation of cowardly conduct in the battle against Búcar is the equivalent of a legal accusation, since fleeing was specifically forbidden by law codes of the period. Fernando's conduct in the lion episode was probably likewise illegal: what Pero is accusing him of is not cowardice, which however undesirable was only a legal offense under certain well defined conditions, but rather that he did not protect the sleeping and thus helpless Cid as did the latter's vassals who were present on that occasion: "Nos çercamos el escaño por curiar nuestro señor/ fasta do desperto mio Çid

Social status, legitimacy, and inherited worth

..." (3335–6).[1] Pero draws an analogy between Fernando's conduct in those two instances and the abandonment of the wives, repeating the Cid's accusation: "¡Por quanto las dexastes menos valedes vos!" (l. 3346). Both he and Martín Antolínez, the latter in accusing Diego and recalling once again the lion episode, assert that Elvira and Sol (Pero: "although they are women," 3347–8) are worth more than the Infantes (ll. 3348, 3369).

According to Lacarra (1980a: 86), the formal accusation made before the king that gives rise to the judicial duels is not that the Infantes acted wrongly at Corpes, but rather that they were guilty of cowardly conduct, Fernando in the battle against Búcar and both he and Diego in the lion episode. I would nuance that conclusion: the accusation is *menosvaler*, and the evidence for it is Fernando's conduct against Búcar and both brothers' abandonment of their father-in-law in a moment of peril.

In replying in his turn to Pero Vermúdez, Diego does not refer directly to the accusation that Fernando conducted himself in a cowardly fashion in the lion incident; rather he takes the same line of defense as Fernando in asserting that he and his brother belong to an untarnished lineage:

> ¡De natura somos   de los condes mas limpios!
> Estos casamientos   non fuessen apareçidos
> por consagrar   con mio Çid don Rodrigo.   (ll. 3354–6)

The import of these lines is that the Infantes were ill-advised to have established a kinship relation with the Cid. The distinction between full marriage and concubinage or *barraganía* underlies *consagrar*, properly "to enter into a relationship of son-in-law to father-in-law," which derives from *CONSOCRARE but is influenced by CONSACRARE, "to consecrate," on account of the sacramental nature of the marriage ceremony (Menéndez Pidal 1954–56, 2: 589–90). The assertion with which Diego ends his rebuttal, "¡por que las dexamos ondrados somos nos!" (3360), is probably meant to reflect that now that the Infantes are free of the union of *barraganía*, they are able to contract what according to their claim would be their first legitimate marriages. Diego's renewed insistence on comtal descent is an appropriate consideration under the circumstances, since the Infantes must stress a quality that would weigh against cowardly and treacherous behavior that, if proven, would certainly constitute a blot on their reputation.

The Infantes' reliance on the defense of high birth (*natura*) and purity of line (*limpios*) might seem strange. They have, after all, embarked on their outrageous course of action in retaliation for the scorn they received subsequent to the lion episode (see l. 2719). But unless the poet had conceived of them as figures whose actions were based upon some calculation that might counterbalance the potentially disastrous animosity they would inspire in the king for having broken marriage ties that he arranged personally, their characterization would have been extremely weak. There is a hidden consideration, however, that only comes to light in the third controversy of the *rieptos* scene, occasioned by Ansur González's obscure taunt, the gist of which is precisely that the Cid – and thus his offspring as well – is not of legitimate lineage and is consequently *enfamado*.

At the height of the *cortes* scene, Ansur González, elder brother of the Infantes, enters the palace flushed from having eaten and launches an insult in the Cid's direction:

> ¡Hya varones!   ¿Quien vio nunca tal mal?
> ¡Quien nos darie nuevas   de mio Çid el de Bivar!
> ¡Fuesse a Rio d'Ovirna   los molinos picar
> e prender maquilas   commo lo suele far!
> ¿Quil darie   con los de Carrion a casar?   (ll. 3377–81)

This curiously phrased intervention appears on the surface to be only an attack on the hero's standing at the low end of the noble hierarchy, since *infanzones* were entitled to collect dues on the use of mills that came under their jurisdiction. As Menéndez Pidal (1947: 119) points out, however, mills were prized possessions of the seignorial class; it is thus difficult to conceive that their mention would naturally lend itself to scornful effect.

Menéndez Pidal conjectured that Ansur was mocking the hero "como si administrase demasiado directamente la molienda, a modo de pequeño propietario" (1929: 129), phrasing which he later revised to: "como si picase con sus manos las ruedas molares y cobrase directamente la molienda, a modo de pequeño propietario" (1947: 119–20). In his article proposing that two poets were responsible for the text as we have it, he speculated that ll. 3378–81 were the reminiscence of a *cantiga de escarnio* making fun of the Cid as a poor miller subsequent to the breaking off of what Menéndez Pidal hypothesized were historical betrothals rather than marriages between the Infantes de Carrión and the Cid's daughters (1961: 173–4). That Ansur González is simply assimilating the Cid's possession of the mill to the actual operations performed by the miller or claiming that he is administering it too directly is, however, improbable; for as rude as such a quip might be, it is lacking in point and would not justify a challenge to mortal combat such as Muño Gustioz subsequently proffers.

Above all, Ansur's statement would be out of proportion with the outrage at Corpes that was the ultimate motivation for the accusations of cowardice that were to be avenged by the other two duels if it merely referred to an excessively close association with mills. Muño Gustioz's challenge uttered in reply to Ansur is of the utmost gravity: he addresses Ansur as "alevoso, malo e traidor," terms endowed with a legal status that raises the issue to the highest level of jeopardy and makes it subject to *riepto*. The correctness of at least the first of these terms, *alevoso*, is confirmed by the *Fuero real* when it states: "Sy algun fidalgo dixiere mal a otro en tal manera que si nol emendare lo quel fizo que es por ende alevoso" (IV, xxv, 4; quoted in Serra Ruiz 1969: 221). Although the *Fuero real* is from 1255 and thus later than the *Cantar de mio Cid*, it is little affected by the revival of Roman law in its provisions concerning *iniuria* (Serra Ruiz 1969: 222) and probably reflects earlier practice.

Social status, legitimacy, and inherited worth

The seriousness of Ansur González's intervention is underscored by the fact that King Alfonso, who had the power of decision in cases such as this (Otero 1959: 167), accepts the validity of Muño's challenge and allows the third duel to take place. In contrast, immediately afterward he rejects the attempt of Minaya Alvar Fáñez, who, in addition to being Elvira's and Sol's cousin, gave them away in marriage and thus is very directly touched by the outrage at Corpes, to set up a fourth judicial combat with the Infantes' party (3463–6). Their champion in this instance would be Gómez Peláyet, a person with no other function in the poem (3457).

The basis for the king's decision is no doubt that the claim that underlies Minaya's intervention, namely that the Cid's daughters were legitimate wives ("parejas pora en braços ... tener," l. 3449) and not the *barraganas* of the Infantes, who took them "a ondra e a bendiçion" (l. 3439), will logically be settled by the outcome of the duel between Muño Gustioz and Ansur González, rendering the additional duel otiose. But this consideration only increases the probability that Ansur has raised a distinct matter that is not redundant with what is to be settled by the first two duels. It also suggests that the poet introduced Minaya's challenge specifically to stress the significance of Ansur's obscurely phrased insult.

The *maquila* was a portion of wheat given to the miller in return for his services and the Cid as an *infanzón* would hardly be entitled to receive recompense under that rubric, although he might well receive other types of payment from a miller working under his jurisdiction. Line 3379, scornfully exhorting the Cid to go to his mill on the river Ubierna (on which Vivar is situated) and roughen the millstones, can, on the other hand, mean that Ansur González is taunting the Cid for being a miller. There is no question but that the daughters of a person of such low rank would be ill-suited to aspire to a marriage alliance with the powerful comtal family of the Beni-Gómez.

Even a statement to the effect that the Cid is a miller, however, that is to say not a member of the noble classes, makes no literal sense unless it is meant to imply that one of the hero's parents is of an identity or status other than might normally be supposed. Ansur González's words convey a much greater affront than has been recognized in the critical tradition (with the exception of Michael 1978: 292n), an innuendo about the Cid's birth, suggesting that he is descended from a miller and thus entitled to a miller's pay. In fact, Ansur González is accusing the Cid of being a bastard.

A legend preserved in the *romance* "Ese buen Diego Laínez" also has it that Rodrigo Díaz, the youngest of four sons of Diego Laínez according to the ballad, was a bastard (Michaelis 1871: 6–8; Wolf and Hofmann 1856: 94–6; cited according to Menéndez y Pelayo, 1903: 55–6):

> Ese buen Diego Laínez – despues que hubo yantado,
> hablando esta sobre mesa – con sus hijos todos cuatro.
> Los tres son de su mujer, – pero el otro era bastardo,
> y aquel que bastardo era, – era el buen Cid castellano.

In that text Diego submits his sons to a test to see which of them will avenge him against Count Lozano: the father bites a finger of each in turn. Only Rodrigo is brave enough to survive the selection process, threatening to slap his father if the latter does not release his finger. Joyfully Diego then confers on the young man his arms and the duty of taking vengeance on the Count. It is probably no accident that Rodrigo's bastardy is mentioned not only at the beginning of the ballad, but also just before the boy undergoes his painful ordeal ("Al Cid metiera el postrero,/ que era el menor y bastardo," ll. 35–6), since in popular literature bastardy is often a trait that renders characters hardier.

In the *Crónica particular del Cid*, printed in 1512 (facsimile edition: Huntington 1903), the story is told that Diego Laínez, riding home one day in July, encountered a peasant woman (*vilana*), whom he raped and impregnated. Lying with her husband later that day, she became pregnant again, and eventually gave birth to two sons. The first-born, being the offspring of Diego, was baptized Fernando Díaz. The chronicler sets the record straight at this point: "Los que non saben la historia, dizen que este fué mio Cid Ruy Diez, mas en esto yerran." He goes on to explain that Fernando Díaz later became the father of five sons, the Cid's cousins, among whom were Martín Antolínez, Pero Vermúdez, and Alvar Salvadórez, while Diego Laínez went on to marry Teresa Núñez, daughter of Count Nuño Alvarez de Amaya[2] (Huber 1844: 9).

In fact suspicions about the Cid's illegitimacy were much older, since the *Crónica particular* is here only echoing earlier chronicles. The *Cronica geral de Espanha de 1344* begins its version of the tale, based on the *Crónica de Castilla*, with the allegation that "alguus dizem que o Cide era de barrègaa" only to deny it immediately: "Esto no he verdade." A denial corresponding to that of the *Crónica particular* follows the tale. The 1344 text also lists Martín Antolínez and Pero Vermúdez among the Cid's cousins, but not Alvar Salvadórez (Lindley Cintra, 1951–61, 2: 480.9–19). The *Tercera crónica general* takes pains to deny the allegation in similar wording: "Los que leen la estoria dicen que este fue Mio Cid, mas en esto yerran." The author of a genealogical treatise found at the end of the *Crónica particular* rejects a second alternate version of the Cid's descendance that is pertinent here:

E por que algunos que no han leydo la cronica del Cid: piensan que este don Diego laynez ovo al Cid ruydiaz en vna molinera. sepan que no es assi: antes es como en este capitulo se ha dicho. y la declaracion desto mas cumplida hallar la han en el .j. capitulo desta cronica del Cid.   (Huntingdon 1903, fol. 104v, col. a)

Thus in the early sixteenth century a variant was extant to the effect that the Cid's mother was a miller's wife.

This particular form of the legend surfaces again in Francisco Santos's *La verdad en el potro y el Cid resucitado* (1671), in which a character inquires:

¿Si seria cierto que huuo Cid? Si (respondiò) yo tengo un libro manuescrito, que dize que hubo y que fue bastardo, avida en vna molinera; y en verdad que he leido infinitos libros, pero jamas he oido dezir quien fuesse su madre: Calla mala lengua (dixo el Cid)

Social status, legitimacy, and inherited worth

que no ay huesos libres de tu rabiante filo. Si fuera hijo bastardo, no heredera de mi padre el hazienda que di en arras a mi muger Ximena Diaz, nieta del Rey Don Alonso el Quinto que dio fueros á Leon. Y la infanta Dona Vrraca su prima, no pretendiera casar conmigo, á no ser yo tan bien nacido como ella.
(Santos 1671: 109–10; ed. Rodríguez Puértolas 1973: 146–7; see p. 85 of the 1686 edn.)

In having the hero refute the slur of bastardy, Santos places in his mouth words that might well have expressed some appropriate consequences of the bastardy in the context of the *Cantar de mio Cid*, namely that Rodrigo would have been unworthy to inherit from his father or to marry into a royal lineage.

That this legend accords with Ansur González's insult cannot be coincidental. Those who would maintain that it is must be prepared to explain how the wish that the Cid should be filing down mill-stones and taking payments in kind could constitute an insult so grave that it should be avenged on the same level, and in the same circumstances, as accusations motivated by the assault upon the hero's daughters, an assault that has occasioned nothing less than the convoking of a royal court. That the insult should concern bastardy provides an indication as to why the poet invented the duel between Muño Gustioz and Ansur González in the first place, since after all the latter would otherwise only be involved in the dispute peripherally, through his kinship with the Infantes, and plays no role in the poem other than in these scenes. The insult he offers to the Cid would be purely gratuitous and superfluous within the context of the plot unless his taunt has some relevance to their legal stance, which in turn is based on a claimed difference between the dignity of their lineage and that of the hero.

Furthermore, one naturally expects not three duels but two, corresponding not only to the two Infantes but to the swords Colada and Tizón, that Pero Vermúdez and Martín Antolínez will use to fight on their lord's behalf. But in view of the poet's organizational habits, if there are indeed to be three duels the third should not be over a trivial matter, for when the poet sets up triadic scenes he arranges them in crescendo: the Cid's three gifts to Alfonso, his three judicial demands. Considering the duels, then, one would anticipate that if there is for any reason to be a third, it should be in some way climactic, surpassing the first two in importance, as indeed it does since it concerns the hero's legitimacy, the very foundation of any pretense he might have to rank and status in this type of society and an issue at the heart of the defense that the Infantes de Carrión put forward. Thus it is perfectly apt that Ansur should end his intervention with a question to which he does not expect a satisfactory answer and which concerns status by right of birth: "¿Quil darie con los de Carrion a casar?" Unlike most of the heroes of medieval epic, the poetic Cid does not come equipped with the honor of an unchallenged birthright. On the contrary, his noble status must be established on the field of combat.

Ansur González's innuendo is naturally a grave affront. In the municipal *fueros* one finds laws concerning two types of insults, those involving actions and those deriving from verbal aggression. Generally the latter are limited to a specified number of words, typically referring to betrayal ("traydor"), heresy

The *Cantar de mio Cid*

("tornadizo," "herege"), leprosy ("gafo," "malauto"), cuckoldry ("cornudo"), sodomy ("fodido," "sodomitico," "fodidinculo," "fijo de fodido"), or prostitution ("puta"). Some *fueros*, however, leave the possibility open to recognize other, similar, words as insults. Thus the *Fuero de Salamanca* (from 1081) speaks generally of "rancura ... de desondra" (Américo Castro and Federico de Onís 1916: par. 18), and the *Fuero de Soria*, in its extensive redaction (possibly anterior to 1255), forbids calling a person "gaffo o ffududincul o cornudo o traydor o herege o a mugier de su marido puta o otros denuestos feos que ssean a desonrra o a menosprez" (Sánchez 1919: par. 481; see also Serra Ruiz 1969: 247). In the territorial *Pseudo-ordenamiento I de Nájera*, possibly formulated by Alfonso VII in 1138, and the *Fuero viejo*, compiled in the second half of the thirteenth century but perhaps going back to an original composition of the first half of that century, *fornesino* figures in the *numerus clausus* of grave insults (García Gallo 1936–41: 367; Jordán de Asso and de Manuel y Rodríguez 1771: III, v, viii). While the poet has Ansur González so formulate his innuendo as to avoid words that might be forbidden in law, the very gravity of what he is circumventing lends impact to his taunt.

But even if an insult specifically proscribed by the law codes is not employed, what Ansur implies, if taken at face value, was, as Francisco Santos was to have his Cid character specify, a serious and legally debilitating charge. Two types of illegitimacy, sometimes with subcategories, were recognized in twelfth- and thirteenth-century law codes: if a child was born of the union of a man and woman each of whom had no other marital ties but who were not married to each other (*barraganía*), the child was a "natural offspring" (*hijo de soltero y soltera*); if, on the other hand, either party was encumbered by another marital tie, or if any other impediment existed (in cases of incest, for example), the child was illegitimate (*hijo malfecho* or *fornezino*, the latter classed as an insulting term, as we have just seen, by the *Pseudo-ordenamiento I de Nájera* and the *Fuero viejo*). While natural children could inherit under certain circumstances, illegitimates could not: the *Fuero de Molina de Aragón*, compiled in 1152 in the Transierran region that dominates the poem's geography, is uncompromising in its brevity: "Fornecino non herede" (Gacto Fernández 1969: 65n). *Hidalguía* could be passed on to natural children, sometimes after they were legitimized, but not to illegitimates (see for example *Partidas*, VII.xi.1).

Full appreciation of the legal implications of bastardy may be impossible to achieve through perusal of the municipal *fueros*, which, after all, were only recording in writing for royal confirmation the oral customal law of their localities. If particular cases required interpretation, men skilled at law (*foreros*) indicated the proper course of action, that closest to custom (Pérez-Prendes 1978: 401). When the *Fuero viejo* specifies that if an *hidalgo* is defied by a *labrador* he can challenge the veracity of the latter's proofs by insulting him as an excommunicate, a perjurer, or an *hijo de matrimonio no velado* – charges that cannot be used with impunity by the *labrador* against the *hidalgo*

Social status, legitimacy, and inherited worth

(Serra Ruiz 1969: 121–2) – it takes for granted that bastards are as unworthy of belief as those who are proven to have taken false oaths, allowing us to catch a glimpse of the disabling quality of bastardy in medieval legal actions.

The Cid's father in history, and presumably in the poet's imagination, had a legitimate wife, although her name has not been passed down to us in trustworthy historical sources. She was the daughter of Rodrigo Alvarez, who held *honores* from King Fernando I of Leon and Castile, and the niece of Nuño Alvarez, an important figure at the royal court (Menéndez Pidal 1947: 124). Normally there would thus have been no question about the noble status of her offspring. If Ansur González's insult were to reflect reality, the Cid would be not an *hijo de soltero y soltera* – his father not having been a bachelor – but rather an *hijo fornezino* and thereby illegitimate. As such he would not have inherited nobility. If one is to take the *Partidas* into account, he would be *enfamado* and subject to all the legal restrictions specified for the infamous, including the prohibitions against holding offices, giving testimony or bringing accusations in court, and taking part in judicial combats.

The Cid's daughters would in that case indeed not be fitting legitimate wives for the Infantes de Carrión: as daughters of an infamous non-noble they might not even have been appropriate concubines. The *Partidas* (IV.xiv.3) explain that in the case of counts and other high nobles, not every woman would make a fitting *barragana*:

Illustres personas son llamadas en latin las personas honrradas e de grand guisa, e que son puestos [sic] en dignidades assi como los Reyes e los que descienden dellos e los condes ... E estos atales, como quier que segund las leyes, pueden rescebir las barraganas: tales mugeres y a que non deuen recebir, assi como la sierua, o fija de sierua. Nin otrosi la que fuesse aforrada nin su fija, nin juglaressa nin sus fijas nin tauernera, nin regatera, nin alcahueta, nin sus fijas, nin otra persona ninguna de aquellas que son llamadas viles, por razon de si mismas, o por razon de aquellos do descendieron. Ca non seria guisada cosa que la sangre de los nobles fuesse embargada, nin ayuntada a tan viles mugeres.

As we have seen in the discussion of *enfamados*, *juglares* are on the same level as illegitimate offspring, whose descendants would be just as inappropriate to serve as concubines to counts. Any issue of such a mismatch would also be of low status:

E si algunos delos sobre dichos fiziesse contra esto, si ouiesse de tal muger fijo, segund las leyes, non seria llamado fijo natural, ante seria llamado spurio: que quier tanto dezir como fornezino. E de mas tal fijo como este non deue partir en los bienes del padre, nin es el padre tenudo de criarle, si no quisiere.

This concatenation of legal reasoning explains García Ordóñez's outburst after the Cid opens the criminal section of the trial:

> Los de Carrion   son de natura tal
> non gelas devien querer   sus fijas por varraganas
> ¡o quien gelas diera   por parejas o por veladas!
> Derecho fizieron   por que las han dexadas.
>   (ll. 3275–8)

The *Cantar de mio Cid*

The Infantes approach this level of hyperbole, stating that they would not have taken the Cid's daughters as *barraganas* unless they were asked to do so.

> Non las deviemos tomar por varraganas
> si non fuessemos rogados,
> pues nuestras parejas non eran pora en braços. (ll. 2759–61)

One of the reasons why *barraganía* was so common in Spain in the Middle Ages was precisely that it allowed the union of persons of unequal social standing. Noble status is much more important in the poem than the issue of the inheritance of property, of course, since by the time the third *cantar* opens the Cid has already acquired by conquest much more wealth than he could have inherited from his parents.

The complex of legal charge and countercharge that one encounters in the trial scenes poses challenges to the modern reader's competence to understand it. Phrases that the characters appear to be uttering haphazardly or in passing take on weighty meanings when placed in the context of medieval Castilian law. Obviously the poet took for granted that his contemporaries would understand their import, but as moderns we have to overcome the mental distance between the poet's audience and ourselves by puzzling over seeming inconsistencies, searching out relevant *fueros* and legal codes, and scrutinizing the characters' arguments. That process is not without its aesthetic rewards in this case, however, since it also reveals a calculation on the poet's part. By having the Cid proffer the charge of *menosvaler*, he has set up a situation in which the potential social consequences for the hero's family and the Beni-Gómez are symmetrical. Following Lacarra's argument that one of the poem's purposes was to further in the late twelfth or early thirteenth century the interests of the Lara clan at the expense of the Castros, it becomes apparent that what is at issue is a double placing in question of the dignity derived from lineage: in the Infantes' case their own dignity (descendants of the counts of Carrión) and that of their progeny (the Castros), in the Cid's that of his daughters (possible descendants of a *fornezino*) and of their progeny (the Laras). The trial scenes thus take on a hitherto unsuspected conceptual symmetry.

One might well ask why the poet has chosen Muño Gustioz as the Cid's champion in the third duel. The answer lies perhaps in the nature of the insult. Muño, who is identified in the poem only as the Cid's *vassallo de criazón* (737, 2901–2), performs other functions linked to Jimena, Elvira, Sol, and the Infantes de Carrión. He goes with Pero Vermúdez and Martín Antolínez to Molina to meet Alvar Fáñez and the Cid's daughters and accompany them to Valencia (1458–1609); during that trip he takes the initiative in conveying the Cid's message to Avengalbón (1481), which would imply that his standing in the Cid's *mesnada* was higher than that of the other two knights. His lord charges him, along with Pero Vermúdez, with keeping an eye on Diego and Fernando when they come to Valencia (2168–71, 2177–9), and while carrying out that assignment he overhears the Infantes' timorous conversation before

Social status, legitimacy, and inherited worth

the battle against Búcar and advises the Cid to have them sit out the battle in Valencia (2324–30). He is one of those who are enumerated as accompanying the Cid to the *vistas* (1995). In history, the Asturian noble Muño Gustioz was married to one of Jimena's sisters, Aurovita (Menéndez Pidal 1947: 723). In 1113, fourteen years after the Cid's death, he witnessed the sale of lands that had come to his sister-in-law from the Cid as *arras* (Menéndez Pidal 1954–56, 2: 767). Although the poet does not mention Muño's kinship by marriage with Jimena, it is possible that he knew of it from the tradition of poems concerning the Cid and decided to associate Muño with Jimena in the poem. If so, Muño would be a logical choice to defend the Cid against the charge that he is a bastard, since if that accusation were true his sister-in-law would have been dishonored by marrying a person below her status. Acceptance of the Cid's daughters as queens of Navarre and Aragon (3399) implies that the slur on the hero's birth was false, but the defeat of Ansur in single combat proves it definitively, since Muño Gustioz's *riepto* specified Ansur's mendacity as the basis for his challenge:

> Non dizes verdad [a] amigo ni ha senor,
> falsso a todos e mas al Criador.   (ll. 3386–7)

Ansur would not have been subject to punishment or disgrace if he were to have won his combat with Muño, as naturally that would have been considered proof that the insult was true and would have indemnified him from what would otherwise be serious consequences. The Navarrese *Fuero de Viguera y Val de Funes*, granted by Alfonso "el Batallador," specifies in its language: "Todo home que dixiere a otro: cornudo o gafo, o traidor o fornecino *et no lo fuere*, dar l'a, si con quereylla non fuere, meio homjzidio de calonja..." (Ramos Loscertales 1956: no. 447; italics mine), as do the *Partidas* (VII, ix, preamble):

Pero si aquel que deshonrrasse a otro por tales palabras, o por otras semeiantes dellas, las otorgasse, e quisiesse demostrar que es verdad aquel mal que le dixo del, no cae en pena ninguna si las prouasse.

In losing the combat, on the other hand, Ansur has placed himself in a dangerous situation since by making his charge before the king and in public, he has aggravated the circumstances of the insult. The *Partidas* again specify (VII, ix, 19):

La segunda manera porque puede ser conocida la desonrra por graue es, por razon del lugar del cuerpo ... o por razon del lugar do es fecha la desonrra: como quando desonrran a alguno de palabra, o de fecho delante del Rey ... o en otro lugar publicamente ante muchos.

Since in fact Ansur is defeated and the trial's outcome is by definition in keeping with divine justice, God has pronounced in favor of the purity of the hero's lineage.

Ansur González's insult also poses a subsidiary threat to the Cid's economic image. The *maquila* is after all a payment in kind for services rendered. In the poem the Cid is depicted as seizing the goods of Arab kings, town-dwellers, and armies, as well as those of the Count of Barcelona when the latter attempts to despoil him of his plunder. Towns formerly under Arab dominion pay him tribute. Through judicial means he takes back gifts that were received under false pretenses. He distributes gifts freely to those who deserve them, including the two trial judges Counts Anrrich and Remond, and uses presents to secure influence with Alfonso. But never is he seen receiving gifts or dues, although both unquestionably came to the historical Rodrigo Díaz of Vivar. Indeed rents are only mentioned once in the poem (the *enfurción* that the inhabitants of San Esteban want to give Minaya Alvar Fáñez, l. 2849), and even then it is not clear whether the term in question is to be taken literally or metaphorically. Only in Ansur González's taunt is one presented with the image of the Cid receiving payment, and there it is a question not of coins, precious metal, or livestock, but of the practically valueless wheat. The portrait of an archetypal gift-giver is in danger of being marred only by this one enemy, who is eventually defeated so decisively in the final *tirada* that in order to spare his life his father is obliged to intervene with the legal declaration that his cause is lost.[3] In the end the figures whom the poet has chosen as a foil for this portrait are at the lowest point on the moral scale, having completely lost face, as well as on the scale of economic liquidity ("Grant est la biltança de infantes de Carrion" [l. 3705]), but the Cid's lineage is exalted.

The Cid thus rises in status not merely from the level of an *infanzón* without further qualification, but from that of an *infanzón* who was rumored to be illegitimate, with all the social impediments implied thereby, the most serious of which was that bastards were prevented from inheriting nobility. His social ascent is portrayed in the poem as resulting from his military capabilities, the practice of which during his exile is first made possible, financially, by the tricking of Rachel and Vidas. His tactical prowess and courage bring their reward in the form of immense wealth the distribution of which, to his men, to the clergy, to Alfonso, and to the Infantes de Carrión, makes possible his family's meteoric rise in the social hierarchy, an ascent that is still incomplete when the poem's action comes to a close but has reached its culmination by the period in which the poet is speaking: "Oy los reyes d'España sos parientes son."[4]

The legend that the Cid's illegitimate mother was a miller's wife must have been known not only to the poet but to his audience; otherwise an innuendo of the degree of allusiveness that characterizes lines 3379–80 would have served no purpose. At least one medieval reader recognized that lines 3378–80 were of particular importance: on folio 74 verso of the manuscript, on whose recto the poem ends, a fourteenth-century hand has written some lines from an unknown Castilian version of the *Altercatio Hadriani Augusti et Epicteti philosophi*, and then:

Social status, legitimacy, and inherited worth

> E ...
> Deçir vos quiero nuevas de Mio Cid de Bivar
> que fuese ... rio ... rna los molinos a ...
> ... prender maquilas ... suele (?) far.

These are obviously a slightly modified version of the lines spoken by Ansur González which someone living in the fourteenth century has picked out from the poem. The deviations from the readings found in the text proper are minor with the exception of the second line: l. 3378 reads "Quien nos darie nuevas" rather than "Deçir vos quiero nuevas," as if to say that the person who wrote the lines is insisting on their meaning for those who will read them later. The *nuevas* referred to are probably not the hero's exploits, as Ian Michael appears to interpret the word in his edition (1978: 55n), but the news that the Cid was suspected of being a bastard.

Another hand has added below the lines in Spanish on f. 74v: "Pater noster qui es noster" and "Dixit dominus domino meo sede adestris meis." The latter line is the incipit of Psalm 110, and Menéndez Pidal believed that someone might have written it thinking of the Cid's triumph over his enemies: more likely is that the writer was thinking specifically of his triumph over the impediments that would have accrued to him if his champion had lost the third judicial duel, or even of the relationship between God the Father and God the Son, who, according to the Nicene Creed, "sedet ad dexteram Patris." "Pater noster qui es noster" draws a similar analogy, after all, with its pun on the first line of the Lord's Prayer, and the substitution of the second "noster" for the prayer's "in coelis" points up the very issue that Ansur González's challenge raises: paternity.

In fact there is a slim possibility that the *Altercatio* in this particular version also had something to do with the theme of paternity. No complete text of a version corresponding in its opening to this one is known in Castilian, but Menéndez Pidal noted (1954–56, 1: 3n) the fifteenth-century *Tratado del ynfante Phiteus* begins in an analogous way (see now Severin 1985), and a printed version found in *El libro del infante Epitus* (Burgos: Juan de Junta, 1540) relates how the child Epitus was born clandestinely.

In any event, one of the earliest readers of the extant manuscript of the *Cantar de mio Cid* of whom we have tangible evidence apparently had no trouble recognizing the importance of Ansur González's words, selecting them for reiteration and perhaps evoking another work related to their theme. A second reader of the same period added allusions that might be taken as referring to the same theme. The first documented receptions of the poem are thus in accord with the interpretation presented here.

5

The poet's milieu

In having the clan of Carrión cast doubt on the noble pedigree of Rodrigo of Vivar, the poet has chosen to give a particular emphasis to the final part of his tale, the section that a listening public or a reader of the manuscript would experience last and go away remembering. Since, as most commentators would now agree, the relationship between the Infantes de Carrión and the Cid's daughters is largely and perhaps entirely fictitious, the *afrenta de Corpes*, the court scene at Toledo, and the three trials by combat – that is to say almost the entire second half of the poem – must also be fictitious. The confection of those episodes is a key to the poet's purposes. He does what other epic poets composing in the Romance traditions did before him, appropriating the name and some historical details from the life of a figure who has caught the imagination of his compatriots and employing them in his narrative for his own purposes (see Duggan 1985). Those purposes are revealed by the selections that the poet makes in telling his tale.

The primary choice is, of course, that of the principal topic, the rise to power of Rodrigo Díaz of Vivar and his relationship with Alfonso VI.

A second area of choice is found in discrepancies between the poem and what is known about the Cid and his contemporaries from the historical record. Each deviation from what is known about the life and circumstances of Rodrigo Díaz offers a potential clue to the poet's intentions, since it raises the possibility that he distorted the historical account for his own purposes and the deviations might allow us to identify those purposes. Of course it is also possible that variances from history represent the story as he received it, and are not imputable to his intentions.

Among the discrepancies are the compression of Rodrigo Díaz of Vivar's two exiles of 1081 and 1088 into one, the representation of three battles after the capture of Valencia whereas there was in history only one (Ubieto Arteta 1973: 113–15), the names assigned to his daughters (Elvira and Sol for the historical Cristina and María), their marriages to the Infantes de Carrión, their identification at the end of the poem as the queens (*señoras*) of Navarre and Aragon (whereas they actually married respectively Ramiro Sánchez, lord of Monzón and Infante of Navarre, and Count Ramon Berenguer III of Barcelona),[1] and the names of the count of Barcelona (don Remont Verenguel in the poem, but Berenguer Ramon in history) and the abbot of Cardeña (Don Sancho, but in history Sisebuto), as well as the latter's role in sheltering Jimena.

The poet's milieu

A major deviation from history is the portrayal of the Cid's relationship with the Muslims. His status as a mercenary captain for King Mutamin of Saragossa in the period 1081–85 is never referred to. In fact the choice of the name "Tamín" for one of the Cid's Muslim enemies suggests that the poet knew nothing about this aspect of his hero's life or even perhaps that he wished to conceal Rodrigo's service under a Moorish king. Also passed over in silence is the fact that the Cid was aided in the siege of Valencia by the Muslim holders of the castles surrounding that city (Horrent 1973: 70).

In fact the poetic narrative of the siege itself is quite misleading: during the historical Rodrigo of Vivar's first exile he played the role of military protector of Alcadir of Valencia; and during his second exile Alfonso VI attacked the city while Rodrigo was absent from it, in retaliation for which the Cid led a punitive expedition against the Rioja. Valencia was only captured by the Cid's forces after an uprising by supporters of the Almoravids led to Alcadir's murder. Although the poet repeatedly describes the wealth that the Cid and his men acquired in their struggles against the Moors, he never mentions that Valencia was the Cid's client city, paying him extensive tribute, which perhaps means that the poet did not know about it (see Hook 1973: 121–3). The poem has the Valencians attack the Cid and his men first (ll. 1098–1156), while he is in Murviedro, an action with no basis in history.

Some characters play roles in the poem that they did not play in history, or assume unhistorical characteristics. Alvar Fáñez is portrayed as the Cid's steadfast companion and right-hand man during his exile. In fact, however, the historical Alvar Fáñez, an impressive and powerful figure in his own right, married to Mayor, the daughter of the influential Count Pedro Ansúrez (Rodríguez Fernández 1966: 50, 55) who was the uncle of the Infantes de Carrión, could not have played the role that the poet assigns to him and may not have accompanied the Cid into exile at all (Horrent 1973: 277). "El Conde don Beltrán," a minor character, does not appear to have had an historical existence, unless he is the Beltrán who became count of Carrión in 1117, in which case the designation *conde* given to him by the poet is premature; neither does Ansur González, who plays a small but key role in the poem as the older brother of the Infantes de Carrión and challenges the Cid's legitimacy, fighting the third judicial duel. Félez Muñoz is called the Cid's nephew (741) and the cousin of his daughters, but there is no historical record of anyone of this name who could have been Rodrigo Díaz's nephew. While there are historical traces of the characters Ojarra and Yéñego Semenones (Iñigo Jiménez), they are not datable as contemporaries of Rodrigo Díaz of Vivar but rather are attested only from the 1120s on (Ubieto Arteta 1973: 131–2). The historical Jerónimo, bishop of Valencia, is not known to have taken part in battles, as he is said to have done in the poem, although such warrior-bishops did exist in medieval Spain; in any case he did not arrive in Valencia until 1097, three years after the battle of Cuarte in which the poet claims he fought.

Turning to the Muslim characters in the poem, Yúsuf, king of Morocco, an important historical figure, probably did not attack Valencia in person, contrary to what the poet represents, but rather sent an army under the command of his nephew. Although the supposed king of Morocco, Búcar, is thought to represent the historical Almoravid general Abu Bakr, Ubieto Arteta (1973: 133–4) has expressed doubts about this identification and has pointed out that one of the neighborhoods of the town of Albarracín is called "Búcar." Tamín, a Muslim king who is alarmed at the taking of Alcocer, was not the king of Valencia as he is said to be in l. 636. But an historical king of similar name whom an ill-informed poet might have considered likely to have been roused to action by the military activities of a Christian general in the valley of the Jalón was Mutamín, emir of Saragossa, for whom Rodrigo Díaz was, as I have mentioned, not an enemy but a friend. Neither Fáriz nor Galve, the kings who attack the Cid's army in the poem after he captures Alcocer, played those roles in history. According to the *Historia Roderici*, Háriz (= Fáriz) was also the name of a Muslim that Rodrigo Díaz of Vivar killed in single combat in Medinaceli.

A third area of choice is the absence from the poem of elements that one might naturally expect to be in it. Chief among these is the lack of any mention that Jimena was the granddaughter of Alfonso V of Leon and was thus the cousin of Alfonso VI and herself of royal lineage. Jimena's brother in history, Count Froila Díaz of Leon, is mentioned (l. 3004), but his relationship to Rodrigo's wife is not. Both of these lacunae may be related to the anti-Leonese sentiment that permeates the poem. Rodrigo of Vivar and Jimena had a son, Diego, who was born around 1075 and died at the Battle of Consuegra in August 1097; one would at the very least expect the poet to include him in the scene in which the Cid takes leave of his family before going into exile (see Chalon 1967: 217–19). In addition, Alvar Alvarez was Rodrigo Díaz's nephew in history, but the poet fails to allude to that relationship; nor does he recall that Muño Gustioz was married to Jimena's sister, Aurovita, another case in which a character with Leonese ties is de-emphasized. He also omits any specific indication of the type of kinship that linked the Infantes de Carrión with their uncle Pedro Ansúrez and their presumed brother Ansur González, and García Ordóñez with his brother-in-law Alvar Díaz. The silence in the last-mentioned case may be only incidental, however, and it is not certain that Pedro Ansúrez, absent from the extant folios, appeared in the poem in its intact state. The Abbey of Santo Domingo de Silos, which is located along the route that the Cid takes on his journey into exile and to which the historical Rodrigo Díaz made a donation in 1076 (Menéndez Pidal 1947: 220) figures nowhere in the poem.

Fourthly, the poet has also chosen to give a pejorative cast to the depiction of certain characters. Presumably the systematic portrayal of García Ordóñez and the family of Carrión as cowardly, excessively proud, and cruel does not correspond to the conduct of those characters in history. It appears too that the poet does not sympathize with the moneylenders, and he is obviously not favorably disposed toward the count of Barcelona.

The poet's milieu

A fifth area of choice is geographical. While I do not subscribe to Menéndez Pidal's theory of two poets, one from San Esteban de Gormaz and the other from Medinaceli, the poet was obviously familiar with the region between San Esteban and Calatayud, and he could have been a native of San Esteban, whose inhabitants he praises,[2] or of Medinaceli, Calatayud, or Molina, or another locality in the area encompassed by those towns. He seems also to have been familiar with Burgos and may have been acquainted with its environs.

Finally, the poet has highlighted certain themes. The inclusion of a challenge to the Cid's legitimacy as the final issue to be decided in the judicial duels of the third *cantar* is noteworthy. No historical reference to the Cid's being challenged by anyone in this regard is extant. If such a challenge had occurred and had been resolved by judicial combat, an event of such magnitude certainly would have left a trace of some kind in the historical record. The rise in status that could not have occurred if the challenge had been upheld is also emphasized at the end in the passage that recalls the Cid's kinship with the kings of Spain. The poet has, in addition, chosen to stress throughout his work the economic aspects of military and political life, specifically the acquisition of wealth through booty and its distribution among the warriors, and gift-giving as the cement of social relationships.

Taking this knowledge of history and these deviations from it, these silences, and these emphases into account, one might then, in considering the identity of the poet and the milieu in which he composed, think of a person who had some access to historical knowledge but not to historical documents (the misnamings would be inexplicable otherwise).

The poet would have been favorably inclined toward the Abbey of San Pedro de Cardeña and the monastery of San Servando in Toledo but was not a partisan of the former and did not have access to its records (or the misnaming of the abbot as "Sancho," a reading assured twice by the rhyme, instead of "Sisebuto" would be unthinkable: see Menéndez Pidal 1954–56, 1: 40 and 3: 1171). The Cid's body was reburied at Cardeña after Jimena was forced to leave Valencia in 1102; although he died in the month of July 1099 (according to the *Historia Roderici*, published in Menéndez Pidal 1947: 968) the poem situates his decease on Pentecost Sunday, in accord with the legend of the Cid as propagated by Cardeña, which places it in the month of May (for this and other details of the cult of the Cid at Cardeña, see Russell 1958). The monks are portrayed in the poem not only as sympathetic to the hero, but as willing to defy Alfonso by provisioning him and caring for his wife and daughters.

The poet would probably *not* have been particularly well disposed toward the Abbey of Santo Domingo de Silos, would have been hostile to García Ordóñez, the family of Carrión, the count of Barcelona, the Leonese, and perhaps the moneylenders (either those of Burgos or moneylenders in general), would have wished to link Alvar Fáñez, who was the more or less autonomous prince of Toledo from 1111 to 1114 (Reilly 1982: 90), with his more illustrious contemporary Rodrigo Díaz, and would have wanted to exaggerate the extent to which Rodrigo's deeds (rather than his lineage and marital ties) were responsible for his rise in power, would perhaps have wanted to portray a bishop as engaging in cavalry warfare, and would have been familiar with the region bounded by San Esteban, Molina de Aragón, Calatayud, and Medinaceli. The poet would have had motives for emphasizing the economic aspects of warfare and of society in general, and for placing in question and then confirming the legitimacy of his hero's birth. He could have had a direct interest in representing the history of Rodrigo Díaz and of his society in this way, or could have been intent on appealing to the interests of his patrons.

The poet's purposes are conditioned by his place in and knowledge of the society of his own time, an observation whose consequences depend in part on the period in which he was working and on the nature of its prevailing political climate. As was made clear in chapter 1, I hold with those who date the composition of *this version* of the poem shortly before the time at which the colophon was composed, that is to say in the years just prior to 1207.

Some critics (Russell, Smith, Lacarra) have concluded, rightly, that the poet is familiar with various points of law, specifically in regard to marriage, the distribution of booty, court procedures, and the *riepto*, and also with the physical aspects of documents.

In an influential article published in 1952, P. E. Russell called attention to the poet's references to documents, and in particular to royal pendant seals. The *carta* that Alfonso sends to Burgos in l. 24 is described as "fuerte mientre sellada," but Russell maintained that royal seals were probably not used in Castile until after 1150, and not on *mandatos reales* such as the one in question until late in the reign of Alfonso VIII. This type of argument *ex nihilo* is subject to the discovery of new evidence, however, and Richard Fletcher (1976: 332) has since shown that royal *mandatos* which may well have had pendant seals were being sent to urban communities probably from the middle years of the reign of Alfonso VII.

Russell was impressed by the fact that the poet noticed seals at all, which would "imply that the circumstances of the poet's life had been such as to make him at least acquainted with the appearance of a type of document unlikely to be much seen outside public offices or ecclesiastical or seigneurial chanceries" (1952: 341). But the fact that a poet describes certain objects or processes cannot in itself be taken as evidence of technical expertise. Critics of Homer debated this question in the eighteenth century, eventually coming to the conclusion that Homer was not necessarily a priest (although he describes sacrifices in great detail) or a sailor (although he evokes the winds and the weather and depicts voyages) or skilled at any trade in particular beyond that of composing epic poetry, but rather was merely incorporating observations of life as it went on around him. So with the Cid poet. A royal seal was no doubt an impressive object to a medieval observer, and the lower the social status of that observer, the more striking the sight. Alan Deyermond quotes Pero López de Ayala's *Rimado de palacio* to the effect that a well-written and well-sealed document was one of the nine attributes through which a king's majesty was known (Deyermond 1969: 78). The royal seal would have had the same visual effect attached to a document as a scepter or a crown would have had when carried or worn, but to be impressed by it one does not have to have knowledge of diplomatic. Peter N. Dunn has remarked that the threat contained in the *mandato*, according to the poet, namely that anyone giving the Cid shelter "perderie los averes e mas los ojos de la cara/ e aun demas los cuerpos e las almas" (ll. 27–8), a version of the Latin formula sometimes used in royal documents and in contracts but not in *mandatos*, shows that the poet was not acquainted with contents of true *mandatos* (Dunn 1975: 264; I will have more to say about this threat below). The kind of non-technical and wholly external acquaintance betrayed by the phrase "fuerte mientre sellada" has no bearing on the question of the poet's background.

Various legal questions surface in the *Cantar de mio Cid*, leading some to ask what the knowledge of law reveals about the poet's station in life. In the eleventh and twelfth centuries, and including the period in which the *terminus ante quem* of the Per Abbat version of the *Cantar de mio Cid* is situated, the "legal profession" was not composed primarily of what we would call today "lawyers," that is to say experts skilled in the complexities of written law or whose principal occupation and means of sustenance were derived from legal activities. The sources of our knowledge of medieval Castilian law are fragmentary, but a number of its features are clear: in the period between the Cid's death and 1207 the law was not widely available in a systematized form in writing; it was essentially a customal law that was only committed to parchment occasionally, most frequently for localities whose ordinances were confirmed by a king or magnate in acknowledgment of local customs and privileges (*forum, fuero*).

The *fuero* has, in fact, been defined as "la versión escrita del Derecho consuetudinario de una localidad que se somete a la aprobación del rey o del señor para poderse juzgar con arreglo a él" (Lalinde Abadía 1981: 69). Only in the later thirteenth century was the attempt made to impose the principle embodied in the famous declaration of the *Libro de los fueros de Castilla*:

> Esto es por fuero: que los alcaldes de Burgos jusgan por fuero los privilegios que tienen escriptos de los reyes e lo al lo que semeja derecho a ellos e a los otros omnes buenos de la villa, e lo que es escripto de los reyes, eso es fuero; e lo al que non es escripto de los reyes e non es otorgado o jusgado en casa del rey, non es fuero, fasta que sea jusgado e otorgado en casa del rey por fuero. (Cited from García González 1963: 619n)

Whether they were written or not, however, in the twelfth and early thirteenth centuries the legal customs of a locality constituted the principal collection of laws according to which the local society regulated relations among its members. The writing down of the laws was not necessary to give them force: in most instances the law was passed down from generation to generation memorially in the absence of written texts (Pérez-Prendes 1978: 389). As José Manuel Pérez-Prendes expresses it, "la fuerza viva del grupo fue dando forma de padres a hijos, plasmando en sus memorias el criterio jurídico de la masa popular" (1978: 396).

Obviously, written lawcodes were available to some: the *Liber Judiciorum* (also known as the *Forum Judicum*, *Fuero juzgo*, or *Lex Wisigothorum*, *Ley de los Visigodos*) was used in the Christian kingdoms from the seventh century and formed the basis for some municipal *fueros*, although its persistence varied from region to region; in Catalonia it survived while in Aragon it was largely forgotten by the tenth century and only surfaced in the twelfth in communities of exiled Mozarabs such as that of Huesca (Lalinde Abadía 1976: 19–20). The early eleventh-century *Fuero de León* dealt with the urban community as a whole and not merely with a few social groups, but was an isolated case. Towns undergoing rapid evolutionary transformations such as Nájera, Logroño, Sepúlveda, Toledo, or Cuenca, whether these changes were brought about when a town developed out of a rural center or when it was repopulated or reconquered, were granted rights that appear to have been in place in older cities (Gautier Dalché 1979: 177), even though written codes are lacking. In some established centers, privileges were embodied in oral codes. The *usos* of Monzón referred to in 1169 in the *carta de población* of Selgua were probably never written down (Lalinde Abadía 1976: 20). When Alfonso VI granted a *fuero* to Sepúlveda in 1076, he specified that he was confirming "hoc quod *audivimus* de isto foro sicut fuit ante me" (quoted in Gautier Dalché 1979: 199; my emphasis). The influential *Fuero de Cuenca*, influenced by the *Fuero de Teruel*, granted in 1190 by Alfonso VIII, and in turn the basis for the *fueros* of many other towns, codifies a series of customs and practices that were already in effect (Gautier Dalché 1979: 248).

The *Fuero viejo de Castilla*, written in the second half of the thirteenth century by a private jurist, collected Castilian territorial law that had not been written down before that time. Its prologue describes the king's motivation in having customs and legal precedents recorded on parchment:

Et estonces mando el rey a los ricos homes e a los fijosdalgos de Castiella, que catasen las istorias e los buenos fueros, e las buenas costumbres e las buenas façañas que avien, e que las escriviesen e que se las levasen escritas, e que el las verie, e aquellas que fuesen de enmendar, el ge las enmendarie, e lo que fuese bueno a pro del pueblo que gelo confirmarie.[3]   (Quoted from Pérez-Prendes 1978: 399)

That this text was written in the second half of the thirteenth century is pertinent to the question at issue here since it shows that the oral transmission of legal knowledge persisted alongside written lawcodes into a period well after the time in which Per Abbat copied the poem. Even in the mid-thirteenth century, after many municipal *fueros* had been consigned to parchment, the law was largely an orally transmitted body of customs, precepts, and precedents. Intimate knowledge of the law, the customs, and the procedures of a specific region would by no means imply that the person possessing such knowledge was *culto* in the sense of being learned, or even literate. The law was preserved primarily, as one text puts it, "in ore hominum veteranorum" (Pérez-Prendes 1978: 401).

The poet's milieu

Certain men, termed *foreros*, were particularly knowledgeable about the law. A number of *foreros* are mentioned in medieval texts, particularly in collections of *fazañas* (exemplary legal decisions, often used as precedents: see García González 1963). In the group of *fazañas* found in Madrid, Biblioteca Nacional 431, are mentioned "Gil Ordonnez de Balegora, que era buen caballero et forero," "Ferrant Ladron de Roias ... que era cauallero ançianno et forero," and "Roy Peres de Soto que era el mas forero que auya entonçe en Castiella" (Suárez 1942–44: 584, 586, 589). Note that two of these men proficient in the law are not clerics but rather *caballeros*, and the social station of the third is unspecified. Pérez-Prendes notes that "forero" does not designate an office; some *foreros* occupied high judicial positions, others minor offices, and others no post at all. The term only refers to their knowledge of customal law. Pérez-Prendes sums up (1978: 401) the way in which legal knowledge functioned in the period:

Lo importante, en fin de cuentas, es que la presencia de estos individuos [i.e. *foreros*], generalmente alrededor del monarca y de los funcionarios judiciales, supone la existencia de un ordenamiento jurídico no formulado por escrito, salvo en muy pequeña parte, mantenido vivo en la memoria y la equidad de los más expertos, quienes indagan ante cada situación concreta cuál es la conducta más aproximada a la costumbre.

In some areas the *fuero* was never recorded on parchment but was simply preserved in the memory of the inhabitants. Pérez-Prendes is of the opinion that the *fuero* of Burgos that was in effect until 1256 and was restored after 1272, although constantly alluded to, was in fact never written down (1978: 404).

Foreros are present in the *Cantar de mio Cid*, although not under that designation. When Alfonso assembles the court he has proclaimed in Toledo in order to hear the charges leveled against the Infantes de Carrión, "Fueron i de su reino otros muchos sabidores/ de toda Castiella todos los mejores" (ll. 3005–6). Among those whom the Cid designates to accompany him is "Malanda, que es bien sabidor" (l. 3070). The term *sabidor* is equivalent to *forero*, "one who is knowledgeable about the law" (see the examples given in Menéndez Pidal 1954–56, 2: 833 and the phrase "sabidores de fuero e de derecho" in Torres Fontes, cited in Pérez-Prendes 1978: 406). Menéndez Pidal (1954–56, 2: 740) glosses *sabidores* as "letrados," but there is no reason to make the connection specifically with *written* law; Lacarra (1980a: 99–102) follows him in this regard, calling the *sabidores* "letrados profesionales" and "nuevos letrados," and goes further in assigning partially to their initiative the growing influence of Roman law. According to her analysis, the poet is attacking the notion of private vengeance that is incorporated in the customal law, in favor of the public law that the king wishes to foster. The author may, then, according to Lacarra, have been a "letrado defensor del nuevo concepto del derecho." As more and more local customals came to be written down, the *sabidor* was no doubt more and more frequently a lettered expert, but he did not necessarily have to be. The influence of Roman law in the poem is minor, if it surfaces at all.

The *Cantar de mio Cid*

Menéndez Pidal cites the mention of a "terra de illo molino de Mal Anda," occurring in a charter in which a "terra de Per Uermudez" is also mentioned, from 1144. If the charter is authentic, it may show that Malanda was an historical character whose memory may well have been preserved in legend or poetry in the late twelfth century – perhaps even in earlier versions of the Cid's exploits – as one who had exemplary knowledge of the law. Michael conjectures (1978: 276n) that Malanda may be the corruption of an Arabic or Hebrew name.[4]

In any case the world of the *Cantar de mio Cid* is one in which primarily customal law, not written law, is at issue, which makes it natural that, although documents such as *mandatos* play a role in the work and although the *cortes* and the judgments of God constitute dramatic high points, no scene shows a character consulting a written lawcode. Certainly the designation "lawyer" that Smith attempts to attach to the poet carries with it connotations that are more a hindrance than a help, since it implies that he was primarily concerned with law, or made his living in legal matters, or was available to be hired out for his legal knowledge, connotations that are probably anachronistic in the context of eleventh-, twelfth-, and early thirteenth-century Castilian society. "Lawyer" is to be rejected as a descriptive term in the present instance.

Lacarra concludes that the author must have known the legal profession intimately and may even have been attached to some chancery (1980a: 255); she goes so far as to call him an "hombre culto, perito en la práctica jurídica" (1980a: 262). On the basis of the phrase "el Poyo de myo Cid asil diran por carta" (l. 902), she reasons that he knew the *Fuero de Molina de Aragón*, in which the "Poyo de Mio Cit" is given as one of the points marking the boundary of Molina (1980a: 258). The place-name passed out of usage before the modern period, and today the place in question is simply known as *El Poyo*. The *Fuero de Molina* was first set down in writing in 1154, and the earliest version that is preserved today is from the period between 1272 and 1283 (Sancho Izquierdo 1916), long after the Per Abbat colophon was written. Even if one could show that the pertinent passage of the *Fuero de Molina* was in the earliest version, all that the presence of the place-name in the *fuero* shows is that the hill was still associated with the hero in the twelfth and thirteenth centuries and that the poet knew this fact was recorded in some written document. To maintain that he must have read the *Fuero de Molina* in order to have been able to state that the hill would be known as "el Poyo de myo Cid" in written documents is an abuse of the evidence.

Lacarra maintains not only that the poet was skilled at legal practice, but that he was knowledgeable in Roman law. She connects this – unjustifiably in my opinion – with the rise of experts in law, *sabidores*, who have already been discussed. Just when did Roman law begin to have a strong influence in Castile? The reception of Roman law is associated with the rise of the universities, the first of which in Castile was Palencia, founded by Bishop Tello Téllez de Meneses (1212–40); in Italy, Bologna attracted students from all over Europe for the study of Roman law. Alfonso X "el Sabio" was among the foremost proponents of a unified law for the whole kingdom of Castile, and constructed the *Fuero real* for this purpose. The first town to receive it as law may have been Sahagún in 1255 (Pérez-Prendes 1978: 544). In his *Curso de historia del derecho español*, Pérez-Prendes does not even include Alfonso VIII among the monarchs during whose reigns the work of receiving Roman law was carried out (Pérez-Prendes 1978: 567). The *Fuero de Zorita de los Canes* was granted by Alfonso VIII and the Master of the Order of Calatrava in 1180 (Pérez-Prendes 1978: 434), but it was based on customal, not Roman, law. The most widely distributed of the municipal codes granted by Alfonso VIII was the *Fuero de Cuenca*, established in 1189–90 (although the extensive text is dated to around the end of the thirteenth century), in which certain features reflected the influence of Roman law; it was later adopted, with modifications, in Béjar, Zorita de los Canes, Plasencia, Sepúlveda, Soria, Salamanca, and many other towns. While Roman law was, then, in the process of being received in the period prior to 1207, it had only begun to have influence.

That the poet did possess expert knowledge of the law is unlikely, since the references to law are such as might have been made by any intelligent and well-informed person in the period. Furthermore, the legal elements in the poem correspond now to one code, now to another, and thus do not show knowledge of the law of one area, as might be expected if the poet was a *peritus* in the law of a particular town or region, but rather the same type of imaginative reconstruction of the legal aspects of the Cid's life as one finds for the poem's historical aspects. Finally, if the use of law in a literary work were to be taken as sufficient proof that its author was "in the legal profession" – whatever that would mean in the period – one would have to assume that many, if not most, of the major narrative works of twelfth- and thirteenth-century French literature are the product of "legal minds" – *Lanval*, for example, in which Marie de France (a *perita* then?) narrates a trial in great detail and with all the essential procedural steps intact (Francis 1939), and the Oxford *Chanson de Roland* in which Ganelon is tried both by jury and by combat, and the *Prose Lancelot* in which the trial of Queen Guinevere plays a central role, and the Tristan romances in which Queen Yseult is tried for adultery (see the comprehensive treatment of the subject in Bloch 1977). That French literature of the twelfth and thirteenth centuries is dominated by "legal minds" is, however, manifestly untrue. And even if it were, the expertise involved would be in oral customal law. This would also have been the situation for the *Cantar de mio Cid* if one could indeed show that highly technical and obscure aspects of the law were involved, which as a matter of fact is not the case.[5]

But if there is no evidence that the poet was connected with legal matters in a professional way, his steady attention to the economic aspects of warfare shows that he was actively interested in promoting military values and attracting fighting men to the Reconquest.

The *Cantar de mio Cid*

José Fradejas Lebrero has interpreted the *Cantar de mio Cid* as "todo un programa de incitación heroica y guerrera" (1962: 63), the product of a Mozarabic poet who wished to inspire knights to take part in the Reconquest and stressed the wealth they could gain in doing so. The poem's structure reflects its thematics, the three *cantares* being devoted respectively to *riqueza*, *hombría*, and *honra* (Fradejas Lebrero 1962: 49), appealing to nobles but also to peasants and implying that their deeds too might be told in song. Fradejas Lebrero points out that what he calls the "colophon" of the first *cantar* (i.e. l. 1084) is not a sentence of thanksgiving or praise but rather the statement that the hero's followers are rich. The poet distorts the conditions of warfare, only recounting vaguely the death of "more than fifteen" Christians in the course of several campaigns while passing over in silence the normal difficulties of military life such as thirst, fatigue, heat, and illnesses. He portrays the Moors, however, as dying in quantities that strain the imagination, thus emphasizing, along with cupidity, the supposed ease with which one could engage in war against the infidel (41). The *Cantar de mio Cid* is even more exaggerated in this respect than the *Chanson de Roland* since the Cid's 3,970 men not only do battle against Búcar's fifty thousand, but come out of the battle intact.

In searching for a time at which this propagandistic aspect of the poem would have been most fitting, Fradejas Lebrero observes that, in all of the twelfth century, only in the period after the defeat that Alfonso VIII suffered at Alarcos in 1195 was there a need to assemble a huge army to give strong impetus to the Reconquest (52). According to him, the *Cid* poet must have written his work, on the basis of earlier poems, under that king's patronage sometime between 1195 and the Battle of Las Navas de Tolosa in 1212, attempting to be historical but at the same time inventing much of his material. I believe that Fradejas Lebrero is correct about the poem's propagandistic function and its relation to the darkest period of the later Reconquest.

As I have attempted to demonstrate in chapters 2 and 3, the poet places enormous stress on the process by which wealth is obtained in warfare. The principal means is the acquisition of booty, which is distributed according to set customs to the leader, the knights, and the footsoldiers. Another important mechanism for the distribution of wealth – probably *the* most important both in the time of Alfonso VI and in the period in which the poet was composing – is gift-giving, which, as we have seen, is amply (almost obsessively) represented in the thematics of the *Cantar de mio Cid*. Economic considerations were of course always a matter for concern to the king of Castile, but, as Fradejas Lebrero holds, never more than in the period between the Battle of Alarcos (19 July 1195), a crushing defeat in which the Christians lost enormous quantities of men and goods (González 1960, 1: 964–7), and the victory of Las Navas de Tolosa (16 August 1212), perhaps the most decisive battle of the Reconquest (see Lomax 1978: 129).

Alfonso VIII was profoundly affected by the disaster of Alarcos: he had fought in the thick of the combat and was only saved from capture by his men, who took him off against his will, according to the reliable *Crónica latina de los reyes de Castilla*. The same chronicle tells how the king was obsessed during the seventeen years between the two battles by the memory of the great defeat, and prayed often to be allowed to avenge it (ed. Cabanes Pecourt 1964: 39). He labored to rebuild both the physical resources and the morale of Castile.

Rodrigo Jiménez de Rada, archbishop of Toledo and primate of Spain, devotes an entire chapter of his *De rebus Hispaniae* (book VIII, ch. 4) to the king's generosity, between his accounts of the coming together of the Christian forces in May and June 1212, and the attack on Malagón of 24 June. The prelate is no doubt concerned to parry the charge that the foreign contingents returned home just before the great battle because they were not sufficiently rewarded, as well he should be since the *Crónica latina* relates that the king sent him north of the Pyrenees to try to persuade the king of France and other princes to add their reinforcements to the Spanish army. But what he says in that chapter reflects the supreme importance of the distribution of wealth in medieval warfare. Alfonso's personal physician, Arnaldo, was sent to Poitou and Gascony for the same purpose, "multa promittens ex parte regis" (ed. Cabanes Pecourt 1964: 44).

The normally laconic *Crónica latina* stresses the king's expenses both in sustaining the trans-Pyrenean contingents and in subsidizing his ally Pedro II of Aragon:

Dum convenirent nobiles et populi regis Castelle et regis Aragonum, cunctis qui venerant de Pittavia et de Uasconia et de Provincia et de aliis partibus et ipsi regi Aragonum expensas omnes nobilis rex Castelle sufficienter ministrabat. Ubi tanta copia auri effundebatur cotidie, quam vix et nummeratores et ponderatores multitudinem denarriorum qui neccessarii erant ad expensas poterant numerare. Universus clerus regni Castelle, ad petitionem regni, medietatem omnium redituum suorum in eodem anno concesserant domino regi. Preter stipendia cotidiana regi Aragonum, multam sumam pecunie misit antequam ipse de regno suo exiret: pauper enim erat, et multis debitis obligatus; nec sine adiutorio regis Castelle potuisset militibus suis, qui eum sequi debebant, stipendia necesaria largiri. (ed. Cabanes Pecourt 1964: 44)

This is an account of the preparations for a battle that took place five years after the date that Per Abbat's colophon assigns to the copying of the *Poema de mio Cid*: nevertheless it points up the economic problems with which Alfonso VIII and Pedro II of Aragon had to cope in placing their kingdoms on a footing sufficiently secure that they could undertake to inflict a decisive defeat on the Almohad Empire. The poetic Cid, also short of money at the beginning of his exile, but with neither the facilities nor the power to coin it or to constrain the ecclesiastical authorities to place their economic resources at his disposal, has to undertake to finance his campaigns in a more devious fashion, but his needs and concerns mirror those of Alfonso VIII in the period 1195–1212 and the Cid's appeal to the knights of Aragon and Navarre as well as those of Castile for their assistance in attacking Valencia – "Quien quiere perder cueta e venir a rritad ..." l. 1189 – is no more venal than that of his great-great-grandson Alfonso VIII. The Aragonese and Navarrese were likewise the allies of Alfonso, who had to do battle at Las Navas without the support of the Leonese.

Do the historical circumstances of the period between the battles of Alarcos and Las Navas de Tolosa correspond to that other major and hitherto neglected theme of the *Cantar de mio Cid* – legitimacy of birth? To answer this question, it will be necessary to consider in greater detail the state of Castilian politics in the late twelfth and early thirteenth centuries.

Aside from the difficulties of the Reconquest, hostile relations between Castile and Leon constituted the major political problem with which Alfonso VIII had to contend. As soon as the young Alfonso IX took the throne of Leon upon the death of his father Fernando II in 1188, the Castilian king launched an attack, taking possession of ten castles (González 1960, 1: 703) – despite the accord of Fresno-Lavandera at which Alfonso VIII and Fernando II had made peace and pledged to join their forces in the struggle against the Moors. Alfonso IX found it expedient to placate his uncle the king of Castile, and at the *cortes* held at Carrión that same year, he was armed a knight by the older king and kissed his hand – a gesture of questionable prudence since it corresponded to the symbolic act of vassalage.

A marriage alliance was perhaps the surest way to establish peace between Castile and Leon, and accordingly an agreement was made to the effect that – *contra Deum et canonicas sentiones* [sic], as the *Crónica latina de los reyes de Castilla* puts it (Cabanes Pecourt 1964: 27) – Alfonso IX would marry one of the daughters of Alfonso VIII, her identity left unspecified. Two months later, also at Carrión, Alfonso VIII's eldest daughter, Berenguela, was betrothed to Conrad, son of the Holy Roman Emperor Friedrich Barbarossa, but that engagement was broken the following year (González 1960, 1: 709).[6] Apparently Alfonso IX, who felt that he had been humiliated at Carrión, thought twice about marrying his rival's daughter, because in February of 1191 he wedded Teresa, daughter of Sancho I of Portugal, a union that yielded the desirable politically important male offspring even though in the same year it was declared incestuous by the new Pope, Celestine III, on the grounds that the parties were first cousins (González 1960, 1: 711). Peace among the various Christian kingdoms of Spain was obviously subject to such variables as the stability of marital relations, royal fertility, and the availability of dispensations from canons regulating consanguinity.

In 1191, Alfonso II of Aragon, Alfonso IX of Leon, and Sancho I of Portugal concluded a treaty of mutual aid against Castile. Three years later the Papal Legate Cardinal Gregorio de Sant Angelo intervened to re-establish between Castile and Leon the good relations that were a necessary prerequisite to warfare against the Moors, dictating the treaty of Tordehumos, among whose terms were that most of the castles under dispute were restored to Leon, that a number of castles on both sides would be designated as security in the custody of the Orders of the Temple and of Calatrava, and that the kingdom of Leon would devolve upon the king of Castile if Alfonso IX died without male issue. Before the last-mentioned clause could take effect, how-

The poet's milieu

ever, the king of Leon would have to abrogate the homage he swore to Sancho I of Portugal at the time of his marriage to Sancho's daughter Teresa. The rights of the offspring of the now dissolved union of Alfonso IX and Teresa to the throne of Leon were set aside. Castles that had been given to Teresa by the Leonese king as dowry were restored to Leon, and if Alfonso VIII were to aid Sancho I in resisting this restoration, he would be considered to have broken the peace and would lose the castles of fidelity specified in the treaty (González 1960, 1: 713–14; text in Rodríguez López 1907, 2: 325–7). The pact of Tordehumos was a major step toward the reunification of Castile and Leon under a single king, a goal toward which Alfonso VIII aspired constantly throughout his reign. Pedro Fernández de Castro, grandson of Alfonso VII and bitter enemy of both the Laras and Alfonso VIII, whose interests were not favored by any *rapprochement* between the two Christian kingdoms, left Castile to go over to the Almohads a few weeks before the treaty of Tordehumos was concluded and became the principal advisor to the caliph Ya'qub al-Mansur ibn Yusuf (González 1960, 1: 333, 716).

With peace – however precarious – established among the Christian kingdoms, Alfonso VIII, who had previously been conducting raids against the infidel, was able to turn his full attention toward the Muslim south. In either May or July of 1194, the same year in which the treaty of Tordehumos was concluded, he sent the archbishop of Toledo, Martín López de Pisuerga, and the Master of the Order of Calatrava at the head of an army of nobles, knights, and footsoldiers across the Guadalquivir, where the Christians ravaged Muslim territory as far as Seville, returning with large quantities of booty (*Crónica latina*, ed. Cabanes Pecourt 1964: 28; González 1960, 1: 951–2; Serrano 1935, 2: 140). This raid had an unfortunate result in that it provoked Ya'qub into crossing the Strait of Gibraltar with a large army in 1195. Alarmed at this threat, Alfonso VIII made arrangements to collaborate with the Leonese king and set out for Toledo, where he assembled his forces. It is perhaps worthy of note that in the Castilian army were numerous Jewish merchants, who had brought an abundance of money with which to buy prospective prisoners and booty for resale (Huici Miranda 1956: 159n). The Castilian king, without waiting for the arrival of either Alfonso IX of Leon or Sancho VII of Navarre, led his army into the field and on 19 July 1195 suffered a monumental defeat at the hands of the Almohad caliph. His men ssaved his life, and he reached Toledo with only twenty knights in his company. Pedro Fernández de Castro had fought on the side of the Almohads and acted as intermediary between Muslims and Christians when Diego López de Haro, the renowned *alférez* of Castile, surrendered the castle of Alarcos to Ya'qub's forces shortly after the battle. The Almohads then conducted deep punitive raids into Castile.

As a result of the Castilian defeat, hostilities broke out once again with the kingdom of Leon, to which Pedro Fernández de Castro returned, assuming the office of *mayordomo* in December of 1195. This opponent of Alfonso VIII arranged an alliance between the Almohads and the Leonese in which Sancho VII of Navarre also took part, subsequent to Alfonso VIII's refusal to cede the castles of Alba, Luna, and Portilla to Leon, as had been agreed upon in the treaty of Tordehumos (Huici Miranda 1956: 170). A Leonese army including Muslim contingents raided the Tierra de Campos in 1196, while Almohad forces under Ya'qub attacked the southern frontier of Castile and captured Plasencia.

At this point fortune came to the aid of Alfonso VIII with the death of one of his old adversaries, Alfonso II, king of Aragon and count of Barcelona. The heir to his throne, Pedro II, was the son of Sancha, daughter of Alfonso VII "el Emperador" of Castile and aunt of Alfonso VIII of Castile. Using funds that he received from the latter, Pedro brought forces to the aid of the Castilian king, under attack now from Leon, Navarre, and the Almohads. A combined army of Castilians and Aragonese counterattacked successfully, conducting raids in Leon.

Pope Celestine III, naturally disturbed at this revival of warfare among the Christian kingdoms – and all the more so since now the Leonese and Navarrese were actively cooperating with the Muslims – excommunicated Alfonso IX of Leon and his counsellor Pedro Fernández de Castro, offered indulgences to those fighting against them, and declared the Leonese troops to be free of their obligations toward the king if he used Muslim forces to attack Christians (Huici Miranda 1956: 180).

The two kingdoms came to terms under this pressure from the Papacy, although hardly in a way that the pontiff would have recommended. Alfonso IX of Leon agreed to marry the seventeen-year-old daughter of the Castilian monarch, his cousin Berenguela (Alfonso IX and Alfonso VIII had the same grandfather, Alfonso VII "el Emperador") despite the fact that recent history had shown that the marriage was unlikely to receive the necessary Papal dispensation. Rodrigo Jiménez de Rada reports that Alfonso VIII was reluctant to enter into the agreement because of the issue of consanguinity, but that Queen Leonor persuaded him to relent (ed. Cabanes Pecourt 1968: 172). The couple were married in Valladolid in the autumn of 1197 (Serrano 1935, 2: 148). Pedro Fernández de Castro, no doubt seeing that this new *rapprochement* between Castile and Leon militated against his interests, left his post as Leonese *mayordomo* and returned to Andalusia.

The marriage agreement between Alfonso IX and Berenguela is dated 8 December 1199, over two years after their wedding, probably because it took that much time to arrange the transfer of authority over the more than thirty castles that Berenguela received as dowry (González 1944, 1: 92–3; see also Serrano 1935, 2: 148n). The Leonese monarch kept several castles that he had already occupied, but gave into the keeping of Alfonso VIII's vassals ten castles as security against the rejection of Berenguela. The dowry guaranteed both the peace between Castile and Leon and the stability of the marriage, since the castles were to come under the authority of Alfonso VIII or his son Fernando or whoever was then king of Castile if Alfonso IX separated from Berenguela or if he mistreated her, held her in captivity, killed her, or had her killed:

The poet's milieu

Et si rex Legionis dimisserit uxorem suam reginam domnam Berengariam, perdat castella fidelitatis, et milites qui arras tenuerit [sic] dent illas ei, posite in potestate patris uel fratris sui regis domni Ferrandi aut fratris sui qui tunc regnauerit, bona fide et sine malo ingenio. Similiter, si rex Legionis eam occiderit uel occidi fecerit, amittat arras et castella fidelitatis. Et si illam captam tenuerit aut ei tam malam continentiam habuerit que sit preter rationem, et hoc emendare noluerit sicut mandauerit rex Castelle aut eius uxor, regina domna Alienor, aut filius eorum rex domnus Ferrandus uel frater eius qui regnauerit, amittat arras et castella fidelitatis et dentur regi Castelle, aut filio eius regi domno Ferrando uel fratri eius qui regnauerit. (González 1960, 3: 206)

According to the *Estoria de España*, the Castilian king gave whatever he had taken from Leon into Berenguela's hands (ed. Menéndez Pidal 1955: 683, col. b). If she were to bear an heir and die before her husband, the *carta de arras* specified that the castles of the dowry would belong to the heir; if she were to die without an heir in that circumstance, they would belong to Leon; if Alfonso IX were to die before her, they would be her possession for life (González 1960, 1: 729–30). The frankness of this contract, envisioning as it did the possibility of murder and mayhem on the part of the Leonese monarch, is extraordinary.

Although none of the bishops of Alfonso VIII's kingdom witnessed the dowry agreement, no doubt for fear of the consequences from Rome, a delegation of Castilian and Leonese bishops did present the case for an exception to the canons against consanguinous marriage to Celestine III, the Spanish Pope, who died on 8 January 1198. His successor, Innocent III, was intransigent. In a bull dated 24 May 1198, the Pope, while affirming his support for efforts toward reconciling the two kingdoms, authorized his legate Rainerio to impose the penalty of excommunication on Alfonso IX and the bishops of Leon, Astorga, Zamora, and Salamanca (González 1944, 1: 100n). Faced with the recalcitrance of the parties in question, Innocent proceeded with his policy despite the efforts of a delegation consisting of the archbishop of Toledo and the bishops of Palencia and Zamora (González 1944, 1: 102 and 103n39). In a bull of 16 June 1199 (Migne 1890–91, 1: col. 610–15), he mentions having excommunicated Alfonso IX, Berenguela, and all those who had advised in favor of the marriage, having placed the kingdom of Leon under interdiction, and having forbidden the celebrating of divine offices in any location in which the royal couple was present. He orders returned to Leon the castles that Alfonso IX had given to Berenguela as dowry, declares potential offspring of the marriage to be illegitimate, and threatens the king and queen of Castile with excommunication if the matter is not resolved to his satisfaction, observing that he had refrained from imposing the interdiction upon Castile only because Alfonso VIII expressed a willingness to take his daughter back (col. 612). Innocent pointedly reproaches the Spanish hierarchy for not opposing the marriage: "Sed in detestabili copula in Occidente contracta, licet non absque quorumdam ecclesiasticorum virorum assensu fuerit forsitan attentata, auctoritas tamen ecclesiastica nullatenus intervenit" (Migne 1890–91, 1: col. 611). The interdiction also eventually took effect in Castile, and was still remembered a generation later (González 1944, 1: 100n).

Papal intransigence threatened not only the fragile peace that had been established between the two kingdoms but also Castilian ambitions to reunite them as had been the case under Alfonso VI and Alfonso VII "el Emperador," and the monarchs took steps to palliate its effects. Alfonso IX offered to donate 20,000 silver marks to the Church and to maintain 200 knights on a war footing to defend Christendom if the Pope would allow him to live with Berenguela until she could bear him an heir, or for at least three years (González 1944, 1: 101). On the Spanish front, in the marriage agreement written at Palencia on 8 December 1199 it was specified that the dowry should remain intact even if the Pope were to persist in refusing to recognize the legitimacy of the couple's offspring.

Alfonso continued to live with Berenguela, who bore first two daughters (Leonor, probably born in the second half of 1198, and Costanza), then a son (July 1201); the latter was called Fernando, perhaps a somewhat confusing name since it was borne also by his half-brother, the son of Teresa of Portugal. Two other children followed: Alfonso and Berenguela (González 1980–86, 1: 162). In a bull dated 5 June 1203, Innocent III reiterated his declaration that the offspring of Berenguela's marriage were illegitimate, specified that they were therefore incapable of inheriting ("cum prolem ex hujusmodi copula incestuosa susceptam denuntiaverimus spuriam, et secundum constitutiones legitimas in bona paterna nullo unquam tempore successuram," Migne 1890–91, 2: col. 83), and castigated Alfonso VIII for impeding the separation of the spouses by refusing to relinquish control of the castles in Leon. Nevertheless, the young Fernando's father recognized him as heir to the throne of Leon. The king of Castile objected to Innocent that the castles belonged not to him but to his daughter, but in a bull of 20 June 1204 the Pope refused to pay heed to such a distinction. He directed the bishops of Compostela, Toledo, Tarazona, and Coimbra to force Berenguela to give back to Alfonso IX the castles she had received from him in connection with the marriage, under pain of excommunication. Furthermore, until they complied with the Papal command, any place in which Berenguela or her parents lodged continued under interdiction (Migne 1890–91, 2: col. 374–5).

Ceding to the inevitable, Berenguela and Alfonso IX separated at Valladolid in 1204, toward the end of spring, after seven years of marriage during which she had borne five children. Fernando stayed with his father (González 1960: 734). Berenguela was absolved on 22 May 1204, Alfonso IX by October of the same year (González 1944, 1: 116–17).

Alfonso VIII's politically motivated reluctance to accept dissolution of the marriage proved justified, as shortly after Berenguela left the Leonese court several enemies of Castile were restored to it, including Diego López de Haro, the former *alférez* of Castile now living in exile, and Pedro Fernández de Castro, who became once again *mayordomo* of Leon (González 1944, 1: 118–19). Few had a greater interest than he in undoing the results of Alfonso IX's

The poet's milieu

union with Berenguela (González 1980–86, 1: 64). Between Castile and Leon hostilities soon recommenced, a development which the *Crónica latina de los reyes de Castilla* ascribes directly to the break-up of the marriage:

> Causa vero discordie inter gloriosum regem Castelle et regem Legionis fuerat idem: rex Legionis dimiserat filiam regis Castelle reginam scilicet dominam Berengariam. De qua idem rex Legionis iam susceperat duos filios et duas filias.
> (ed. Cabanes Pecourt 1964: 37)

As Julio González remarks, however, the war was caused rather by the affair of the castles (1960, 1: 735).

In his will dated 8 December 1204, Alfonso VIII left the castles of Valderas, Bolaños, Villafrechós, Melgar, Siero de Riaño, Siero de Asturias, Almanza, Castrotierra, Carpio, Castroponce, and Monreal to his grandson Fernando, unless the bishops of Toledo and Segovia, the prior of the Order of the Hospital, and Fernando Díaz of the Order of Santiago should decide that they be returned to the king of Leon (González 1960, 1: 736–7 and doc. 769). As had previously been the case when the interests of the kings of Leon and Castile coincided, Pedro Fernández de Castro once again abandoned the offices he held under Alfonso IX, but this time for good (González 1960: 737).

The following year Alfonso VIII's attentions turned toward Gascony, which he claimed for his wife upon the death of her mother, Eleanor of Aquitaine, but he soon made an attempt to settle again with Leon in the treaty of Cabreros (26 March 1206). The four-year-old Fernando was the focal point of this agreement, receiving from his grandfather the towns mentioned in the will, from Alfonso IX of Leon the castles of the dowry, that is to say Monreal, Carpio, Almanza, Castrotierra, Valderas, Bolaños, Villafrechós, Siero de Riaño and Siero de Asturias, plus Luna, Argüello, Gordón, Ferrera, Tiedra, and Alba de Aliste, and from his mother the town of Cabreros and the castles of the dowry. All of the young Fernando's acquisitions would belong to Leon rather than Castile. Flouting once again the Papal attack upon the legitimacy of the children he had had with Berenguela, Alfonso of Leon affirmed Fernando as his heir and specified that if the boy should die before him, the younger son, Alfonso, should assume the throne of Leon. Berenguela was provided with an income of 8,000 *maravedíes* for life, in guarantee of which eight castles were placed under the control of Castilians who were vassals of Fernando. To obviate any future Leonese recourse to the Pope to recover Berenguela's income under the threat of excommunicating her, Alfonso of Leon undertook to certify that the money was hers alone (González 1960, doc. 782).

Julio González, the authority on the reign of Alfonso VIII, sums up the balance sheet:

> El tratado de Cabreros era favorable a Castilla. Mediando la bula de 1204, en que se anulaba la donación y se ordenaba la devolución de los castillos que tenía doña Berenguela al rey de León, Alfonso VIII no podía obtener mejores ventajas. Por si fuera poco, se restablecía el derecho sucesorio de don Fernando en el reino leonés. Aun

prescindiendo de la voluntad pontificia, parece lógico que el reino se reservase al primogénito del monarca de León, el don Fernando habido de doña Teresa, el cual quedaba relegado. Y para mayor eficacia en el tratado se imponía silencio al rey leonés.
(1960, 1: 739)

The fortunes of Castile and Leon had come to depend upon the fate of children about whose legitimacy there was a marked difference of opinion.

Several uncertainties hovered about the figure of Fernando, the son of Alfonso IX of Leon and Berenguela. Although Alfonso IX had no male offspring that was indisputably legitimate and would thereby have enjoyed an unchallenged right to the throne of Leon, Fernando was not Alfonso's only living son, nor his oldest. As we have seen, he had a half-brother, also named Fernando, the issue of Alfonso IX's marriage to Teresa, daughter of the king of Portugal, Sancho I, which had also been declared null and void for reasons of consanguinity. In addition, since the marriage between Berenguela and Alfonso IX had been declared illegitimate by the Pope, any claim that its firstborn, Fernando, could become his father's heir would come up against the principle enunciated in the *fueros* and discussed in chapter 3 that *fornezino non herede*, Fernando being in the eyes of the Pope the product of an incestuous union. Strictly speaking, even the right to noble status of Berenguela's children might be questioned.

That Fernando should be recognized as legal heir to Leon was decidedly in the interests of Castile. The mortality rate for children – even the offspring of kings – was high, and provision for several future heirs was not misplaced, as was to be confirmed by events. Fernando's half-brother of the same name was to die in 1214 before his father. Alfonso VIII and Leonor had ten children, but none of their three sons survived to mature adulthood: Sancho died in 1181 at two months of age; Fernando, declared heir in Alfonso's will of 8 December 1204, died at the age of 21 in 1211, three years before his father; and Enrique, to be crowned king under the tutelage of his sister Berenguela at the age of 11, only occupied the throne thirty-three months before he was killed by accident while playing with other boys. During his short reign, Enrique I was first betrothed to Mafalda, daughter of the king of Portugal, and then, through the intermediary of Alvar Núñez who had supplanted Berenguela as regent and was inimical to her interests, to Sancha, daughter of Alfonso IX of Leon, in an arrangement that would have made him king of Leon (González 1960, 1: 231) and would have excluded from the kingship Fernando the son of Alfonso IX and Berenguela.

Hostilities broke out between Alvar Núñez and the partisans of Berenguela, who asked for help from her ex-husband the Leonese king. Amid the secrecy that followed upon Enrique's death, Berenguela, now heir to the throne of Castile as the oldest surviving daughter of Alfonso VIII, managed to extract Fernando from Alfonso IX's entourage. When the Leonese king discovered that he had been tricked, he invaded Castile. Berenguela and her partisans declared Fernando king of Castile on 2 July 1217. The potential impediment constituted by Fernando III's illegitimacy was overcome by the

The poet's milieu

fact that his mother designated him as her successor in a moment of acute crisis for Castile, and was backed by the loyalist nobles, particularly those of the Transierra and Extremadura (González 1980–86, 1: 238–9). In his *Memorias para la vida del santo rey don Fernando III*, the eighteenth-century Jesuit Andrés Marcos Burriel reports that Alfonso IX and Berenguela had succeeded in having Pope Innocent III recognize Fernando as the legitimate heir to the throne of Leon (1800: 12), a decision later confirmed by Honorius III in his bull of 10 July 1218 (Mansilla 1965: 141–2).

A truce that recognized Fernando as king soon put an end to these last hostilities between Castile and Leon (González 1944, 2: doc. 352) and specified that the two kings would request Papal ratification of the agreement. Honorius III did in fact confirm it in the bull of 10 July 1218 and intervened again the following month, forbidding any rebellion against Fernando during his minority. After Alfonso IX's death in 1230 Fernando was to rule in Leon, uniting the two kingdoms, and he reigned until 1252.

The *Cantar de mio Cid* was copied by Per Abbat, whose identity will be taken up in the next chapter, in May of 1207, and I will argue that it may have been composed in 1199 or 1200. The legitimacy of its hero Rodrigo Díaz of Vivar, is, like that of the future offspring of Berenguela and Alfonso IX, subject to doubt on the grounds that, like Berenguela's progeny, the Cid is a *fornezino*. That the character who articulates that doubt, Ansur González of the house of Carrión, is defeated in judicial combat by Muño Gustioz (in history Jimena's brother-in-law), indicates the poet's notion that in the divine view of things the hero is in fact to be considered legitimate. King Alfonso VIII and the partisans of Castile, including the house of Lara which governed at this time San Esteban de Gormaz and Molina, could not have wished for a more favorable judgment for the young Fernando.

I am not maintaining that the *Cantar de mio Cid* is an *épopée à clef* with the Cid standing directly for Fernando, who was in fact not yet born in 1200, but rather that, in receiving, transforming, and giving a new slant to his material, its poet used themes and invented outcomes that he knew would please his audience. One of those themes was an unsuccessful challenge to the legitimacy of an important political figure who happened also to be the ancestor, five generations back, of the Infanta Berenguela. The poet emphasizes the issue of legitimacy by making it the subject of the third judicial duel, the final act of heroic achievement, which is followed immediately by the new marriages of the Cid's daughters, by the ringing declaration "Oy los reyes d'España sos parientes son;/ a todos alcança ondra por el que en buen ora naçio" (3724–5), and by the hero's death.

While the consequences of this integration of the Cid's progeny into the royal lines of Spain and its implications for the poem's date have occasioned much controversy, little attention has been paid to the fact that the poet went to great lengths inventing episodes to explain the steps by which the Cid's rise in status was effected when he had no need to: the offspring of Rodrigo of Vivar and his wife Jimena were already of royal blood since Jimena was the

The *Cantar de mio Cid*

great-granddaughter of Alfonso V of Leon on her mother's side and second cousin to Alfonso VI of Leon and Castile. The poet has thus created a set of problems where none existed in history. His purpose, I believe, was to set the Cid up as the model of one who not only enriched himself through warfare against the Muslims, but who managed to transmute the wealth he thus acquired into the highest status of the nobility.

The questions about the Cid's worthiness to mix his lineage with that of a comtal family in legitimate marriage are decided in his favor by the judgments of God, but the worldly judgment comes first in the guise of the proposals of marriage "a ondra e a bendiçion" (l. 3400) from the Infantes of Navarre and Aragon so that the issue has been overtaken by events and the three combats are from *that* point of view superfluous. They still serve a purpose, however, in the poet's world of the turn of the twelfth century, in which the king of Castile was anxious about the possibility that his daughter would be rejected by another monarch. Elvira and Sol will both become queens, according to the poet. The daughters of the historical Cid, Cristina and María, married respectively Ramiro, lord of Monzón in Navarre, and Ramon Berenguer III, count of Barcelona. Thus neither of the daughters became a queen, nor did they marry the infantes of Navarre or Aragon, although confusion on these points might be comprehensible in a poet composing in the late twelfth or early thirteenth century since the son of Cristina and Ramiro, García Ramírez, became king of Navarre in 1134 and Barcelona was united to Aragon in 1137. Questions of title are not normally obscure to contemporaries, which confirms that the poem was composed in the version in which we have it long enough after 1137 for the chronology to have become clouded in people's memories.

Surely not irrelevant to the poet's mention of the infantes of Navarre and Aragon is the state of relations among the three kingdoms in 1199. Alfonso VIII was the ally of Pedro II of Aragon, by the treaty of Calatayud (20 May 1198). Together the two kings had attacked Sancho VII of Navarre in 1198, with the result that, in order to prevent his kingdom from being parceled between Castile and Aragon, Sancho sued for peace, offering the hand of his sister to Pedro. After Innocent III forbade this marriage (yet another incestuous union, in the eyes of the church) from taking place, by a bull of 11 February 1199 – Alfonso VII was the common grandfather of bride and groom – Alfonso VIII probably met with Pedro. In the late winter and early spring of 1199, for a brief time, Alfonso of Castile was at peace with the kings of both Aragon and Navarre, but in the summer of 1199 he launched an attack on Navarre, and during the first days of 1200, while Sancho VII was absent from his kingdom in search of Muslim allies, he captured Vitoria (González 1960, 1: 847–52).

Is there any indication in the text of the *Cantar de mio Cid* that, while mentioning threats directed at the Cid, the poet had one eye on the threats to the royal succession posed by the Papacy? The *mandato real* that arrives at Burgos early in the text specifies that those who give shelter to the hero are in danger of losing their eyes, "e aun demas los cuerpos e las almas" (l. 28).

The poet's milieu

Threats of blinding and death are not unusual in such a context, but how could the king plausibly claim to have authority over the loss of his subjects' souls? This phrase has puzzled previous commentators (see Russell 1952: 345n; Dunn 1970: 262), as indeed it should if one only has the powers of the king of Castile and Leon in mind; but if the poet was composing at a time and in circumstances in which the Pope had imposed an interdiction on communities in which Alfonso VIII, Queen Leonor, or Berenguela resided, placing the souls of the royal couple and their daughter in jeopardy (Migne 1890–91, 2: col. 83), the phrase would be understandable.

The poet's primary choice, that of the hero about whom he was to sing, was motivated by the fact that both the king of Castile and the Laras – in whose Transierran lands the poet must have lived as indicated by the fact that he situates most of the military activity in that region – were related by kinship to Rodrigo of Vivar. This Castilian hero flourished in the time of Alfonso VI, one of the kings under whose reign the unity of Castile and Leon, a major goal of Alfonso VIII, had been achieved. The time of Alfonso VI was also regarded as the "classic age of booty," a period of enviable economic prosperity derived from plunder. The conflation of the historical Cid's two exiles into one was inspired by poetic considerations, as a stratagem for unifying the action, although it is not clear whether it was first carried out by the poet who is responsible for this text or by one of the predecessors in a line of transmission that also conveyed to him the names of the minor historical characters. That he did not get the latter from documentary sources is indicated by his errors concerning the names of the abbot of Cardeña, the count of Barcelona, the Muslim king of Valencia, the Cid's daughters, and the daughters' second husbands. Although Horrent doubts that Rodrigo's son Diego ever visited Valencia (1973: 79n), the poet's failure to mention him among the Cid's children is to be ascribed not to his absence from his father's *mesnada* in history but rather to considerations of lineage. Cristina and María bore progeny, but Diego did not and thus had no value in the genealogical coin of the poet's world.

The poem's narrative of the unhistorically systematic and straightforward conquest of Valencia is no doubt motivated by a desire to present the Cid's achievement as a logical progression, that is to say by literary considerations (Hook 1973), and the emphasis on the military achievements of the campaign rather than on the imposition of a tributary relationship reveals just how little the poet knew of the historical Cid's political shrewdness.

The portrayal of Bishop Jerónimo as a fighting prelate may owe something to the example of Martín de Pisuerga, bishop of Toledo, who led the expedition into Muslim territory in 1194, or to the bishops who took part in the Battle of Alarcos, although other models are not lacking (see Grassotti 1969: 384–6 and chapter 6 below). That Yúsuf attacks Valencia himself is probably a poetically motivated detail, although the representation of an Almoravid emperor's attack may have been designed to attract the attention of Alfonso VIII, whose most pressing ambition was to meet and defeat the Almohad emperor in battle. As María Eugenia Lacarra has stated, the poet's depiction of the Infantes de Carrión as villains is aimed at the Castro family, enemies of both Alfonso VIII and the Laras, the most visibly villainous of whom, in 1207, was Pedro Fernández de Castro, who fought in the Battle of Alarcos on the Moorish side. The Leonese king whom he served was suspected of being capable of treating his spouse, Alfonso VIII's daughter Berenguela, as the Infantes de Carrión treat their wives in the poem. In fact, the poet's seemingly otiose generalized condemnation of those who mistreat their wives, uttered just after the end of the third duel, "Que buena dueña escarneçe e la dexa despues/ ¡atal le contesca o si quier peor!" (3706–7), might well have been aimed in the direction of Alfonso IX of Leon.

Ansur González of Carrión, unattested in history, whom the poet has issue the challenge to the Cid's legitimacy, is probably a fictional character created for an *ad hoc* purpose, as is Félez Muñoz, whose only significant function is to rescue the Cid's daughters in the aftermath of the fictional *afrenta de Corpes* (but see chapter 6).

The theme of potential illegitimacy corresponds to Alfonso VIII's desire that one of his grandchildren be recognized as capable of inheriting, and the emphasis on economic considerations to the monarch's strategic preoccupations after the Battle of Alarcos. It is possible that the depiction of the moneylenders of Burgos derives from the difficulties Alfonso must have experienced in raising funds for his wars against the Almohads, although specific evidence for this is lacking. That the poetic Cid is intent on recovering the dowry he has given to the Infantes de Carrión corresponds to Alfonso VIII's concerns over the castles of Berenguela's dowry.

A very important social message that the poem projected when it was composed in the form in which we have it was that the Cid, according to the poet not just an exiled *infanzón* making his way in the world without the advantages of an influential marriage alliance but an *infanzón* whose nobility of birth was subject to challenge, was nevertheless able to raise himself up to the level of his own king. He did so by acquiring wealth from the Moors and from a Christian prince whose army, like Alfonso IX's, included Moors. The implication is that any knight, however obscure his origins, could aspire to accomplish similar feats.[7] Most knights, obviously, would have been content with lesser achievements. What better way to enlist the cooperation of able-bodied fighting men than to hold up for their contemplation the example of the Cid, properly exaggerated and set in circumstances that, while they deviated from history, served admirably the needs of the interested parties? Jerry R. Craddock (1986) analyzes the ways in which medieval historiographers in the Alphonsine tradition rewrote history to suit dynastic needs in the dispute between Sancho IV and the Infantes de la Cerda. While the *Poema de mio Cid* became rewritten history when it was recorded in the Per Abbat manuscript, it was first, as I shall argue in chapter 8, "resung" history.

The *Cantar de mio Cid* as we have it in the poetic text differs thematically from all other epics in the Romance languages because it was designed to fit

The poet's milieu

the needs of the Reconquest at a specific moment, with an example detailed in its portrayal of economic and social advancement, needs which were not topical for poets composing in French, Occitan, or Franco-Italian.

The implications of the poet's knowledge of the area bounded by San Esteban, Calatayud, Guadalajara, and Medinaceli, the motivation for his hostility toward Count Berenguer Ramon II of Barcelona, and the possible identity of Per Abbat will be taken up in the next chapter.

6

Geography and history

Rodrigo Díaz of Vivar is known to history above all as the man who conquered Valencia. The *Cantar de mio Cid* includes that feat in its narrative, but recounts the actual conquest in only eleven lines while devoting several hundred to military campaigns that are undocumented in history, or have been displaced from their rightful chronological place in the life of Rodrigo of Vivar, or did not take place at all. None of the historical sources on the Cid's life details the itinerary of his journey into exile, but the *Historia Roderici* reports that his first destination was Barcelona (Menéndez Pidal 1947, 2: 923), which would have required him to follow a route leading directly east rather than the south-southeastern trajectory that he takes in the poem (Chalon 1976: 83). See map 1. His activities in the valley of the Henares may reflect a raid he carried out in 1081, that is to say shortly before his first exile, but Jules Horrent has pointed out (1973: 273–4) that according to Rodrigo Jiménez de Rada the valley of the Henares was occupied at the time of the Cid's first exile by troops that Alfonso VI had led into the Moorish kingdom of Toledo. The Cid's stay at El Poyo recalls the period in 1089 when, reconciled with Alfonso VI, he imposed a tribute on the region around Calamocha (see Chalon 1976: 89n, 91, 97). The exploits in the region north of Valencia that the poem recounts at the beginning of the second *cantar*, just before the conquest of the Levantine city, are fictitious (Chalon 1976: 102–5).

Although Menéndez Pidal defended the poem's essential historicity, the disproportion between Rodrigo of Vivar's military activities and their representation in the poem led him to posit that the poet or poets must have been motivated to associate with the Cid's campaigns towns of which they were natives. He settled on two in particular, San Esteban de Gormaz and Medinaceli. If one is to assent to this type of reasoning – as I in fact do, although without espousing the Pidalian theory of the two poets or the association with Medinaceli – it makes sense to look also to a geographical area to the east of Medinaceli that is highlighted in the poem to a greater extent than either that town itself or San Esteban.

Upon leaving Castile, the poetic Cid conducts a military campaign along the Henares, attacking the town of Castejón (l. 435), which he captures, and sending Minaya Alvar Fáñez as far as Alcalá on a raiding expedition. Subsequently, abandoning Castejón, he leads his men up the Henares, crosses over into the valley of the river Jalón, and camps between Ariza (the Fariza of l. 547) and Cetina. The capture of Alcocer follows.

Geography and history

No place-name corresponding to "Alcocer" is found in the immediate region in which the Alcocer of the poem appears to be situated (between Ateca, the "Teca" of l. 571, and Terrer, to the west of Calatayud).

Reasoning that Alcocer derives from the Arabic *al-qasr*, "castle," corresponding to Castilian Castejón, "large castle," Criado de Val, followed by Ian Michael, has conjectured that the town in question may be Castejón de las Armas, one kilometer south of the Jalón (Criado de Val 1970; 95–7; Michael 1978: note to l. 553). One difficulty with this interpretation is, however, that the Cid's men are not said to cross the Jalón to reach Alcocer. Another is that when the poet maintains that "açerca corre Salon, agua nol pueden(t) vedar" (l. 555), he probably does not mean simply that the Jalón is a kilometer to the north of the town, but that the river runs beside it. There is a stream by Castejón de las Armas, but it is the Piedra, not mentioned in the text.

Ubieto Arteta, following up on a suggestion of Russell, has proposed that "Alcocer" is Peñalcázar, called "Alcázar" by the local inhabitants (1973: 87–8), but this solution is even less convincing than Castejón de las Armas since Peñalcázar is over 30 kilometers to the north of the road that links Ateca and Terrer, between which towns it is said in the poem to be located. As one can see from ll. 550–4, Alcocer is represented as being situated close to Ateca. It is also near a river, and since the Jalón is the only river named in this section one must assume that that is the river in question. When the Cid and his men ride in the valley of the Jalón, they are seen by the inhabitants of Alcocer, a feat that would hardly have been possible if the latter were looking out from a point thirty kilometers from the Jalón. Furthermore the inhabitants of Alcocer pursue the Cid down the valley of the Jalón, upon which he looks back and "vio que entr'ellos y el castiello mucho avie grand plaça" (l. 595). *Grand plaça* surely does not signify a distance of thirty kilometers. I agree with Ubieto (1973: 92) that "el autor del *Cantar* conoce perfectamente la geografía de la región comprendida entre Ariza y Calatayud," but his statement is true only if his identification of Alcocer with Peñalcázar is rejected.

The poet represents Alcocer as a town of some importance: its capture is the most extensively narrated of the Cid's conquests and provokes the emir of Valencia to send an army under the leadership of kings Fáriz and Galve to liberate it. The Castilians defeat this force, killing 1,300 Moors; Fáriz flees to Terrer, Galve to Calatayud. Afterward the Cid sells Alcocer back to the Moors for 3,000 silver marks (l. 845) and is able to send gifts to Alfonso as a result of his conquest.

Alcocer is probably a fictitious place (see Russell 1956: 102; Pattison 1983b), created by a poet who wanted to have the Cid achieve an important victory in the valley of the Jalón even though no towns in that valley possessed local legends to the effect that he had occupied them. In fact, there is no record that the historical Rodrigo Díaz carried out military activities of any kind in the valley of the Jalón during his first exile. The poet simply made up Alcocer, allowing his audience to assume that the town had disappeared between the period in which the Cid lived and his own time. He also reveals an imperfect

The *Cantar de mio Cid*

knowledge of the geography of Arab hegemony, assigning Alcocer to the sphere of influence of the kingdom of Valencia whereas it actually belonged to the kingdom of Saragossa in this period (Menéndez Pidal 1954–56, 2: 874). I conjecture below (p. 100) about a geographical collocation that may have suggested the name "Alcocer" to the poet.

The other toponyms mentioned in this section of the poem are "las Alcarias" (the Alcarria), "Anquita" (the town of Anguita on the river Tajuña), "campo de Torançio" (Campo Taranz), "Alfama" (Alhama), "la Foz" (more correctly "la foz," a curve in the Jalón), "Bovierca" (Bubierca), "Teca" (Ateca), "Terrer" (the town of Terrer), and "Calataut" (Calatayud), all readily identifiable. The topography about which the poet demonstrates the most intimate knowledge in the entire *Cantar de mio Cid* is that of the valley of the Jalón, between Medinaceli and Calatayud and including Ariza, Cetina, Alhama de Aragón, Bubierca, Ateca, "Alcocer," and Terrer. See map 2.

The dating of the poem to the late twelfth or early thirteenth century and the presence of thematic parallels with the social and economic situation of Alfonso VIII of Castile and his family in the period between the battle of Alarcos and Las Navas de Tolosa has led me to link the *Cantar de mio Cid* with the interests of the Castilian court. When the poet's geographical knowledge is taken into account, the same line of reasoning leads to a great center of religious influence situated in the valley of the Jalón and patronized by Alfonso VIII, the monastery of Santa María de Huerta.

Huerta is located fourteen kilometers west-southwest of Ariza, close to the path that the poetic Cid takes after abandoning Castejón de Henares. It was within the precinct of the diocese of Sigüenza. The monastery was founded in 1169 when the Cistercian community of Cántavos (García Luján 1981, charter 13), which had been established in 1144 (Alvarez Palenzuela 1978: 105) on a site donated by Alfonso VII "el Emperador" (García Luján 1981: charter 1), moved to a new and healthier emplacement (Cocheril 1964: 252) on the confines of Castile and Aragon.

Unlike most Cistercian monasteries, which were purposely built in locations that were difficult to reach, Huerta was located a few hundred meters from a major road, the one linking Saragossa with Medinaceli, Guadalajara, and Toledo (Maur Cocheril 1964: 258). The poetic Cid follows a section of that road on his way from Ariza to "Alcocer," whence he sends his first gift to Alfonso and where he orders Alvar Fáñez to have a thousand masses said at the altar of the Virgin Mary in the cathedral of Burgos. Precisely because of its convenient location, Huerta was an ideal meeting place for prelates and princes (see Zamora 1962a and 1962b).

Alfonso VIII placed the first stone of the buildings of Huerta on 20 March 1179 in the presence of Count Pedro de Molina, referring to its church shortly afterward as "quam ego propriis manibus meis aedificavi" (García Luján 1981: charter 38). Alfonso visited Huerta again on 15 March 1184 to define the limits of its properties (González 1960, 2: no. 420). In August of 1197 he was present in Calatayud when his young ally Pedro II of Aragon extended protection to Huerta (González 1960, 3: 857). Alfonso's donations to the monastery include the estate of Estenilla near Medinaceli (García Luján 1981: charters 14, 35), first a quarter (charter 24) then the whole of a well in the *salinas* of Landet in Medinaceli (charter 26), an estate near the castle of Valera within the jurisdiction of Cuenca (charter 52), and an annual gift of 100 *maravedíes* from the royal *salinas* of Atienza (charter 58). He confirmed Huerta's possession of Cántavos and other properties in 1176 (charter 36), of Albalate (charter 59) and the hermitage of Santiago in 1195 (González 1960, 3: 855), of all of Huerta's holdings in 1199 (García Luján 1981: charter 62), of Albaladejo near Cuenca in 1200 (charter 67), and of Bliecos in 1210 (González 1960, 3: 879). His devotion was apparently reciprocated by the monks: Angel Manrique mentions that the anniversary of Alfonso's great victory at Las Navas de Tolosa was celebrated annually at three places in Spain – the monasteries of Las Huelgas and Huerta and the cathedral church of Toledo (Manrique 1642–59, 3: 564).

The royal family of Aragon also favored Huerta. Alfonso II, king of Aragon and count of Barcelona, took it under his protection in 1166 (García Luján 1981: charter 6), and was received into its brotherhood in 1180 (charter 39). After the king's death in 1196, García, bishop of Tarazona, exempted Huerta in the king's name from the payment of tithes on a vineyard situated in Ateca (García Luján 1981: charter 60), where the monastery already had properties (García Luján 1981: charter 55). Pedro II of Aragon visited Huerta in 1197, the year after he succeeded his father on the throne, and later took the monastery under his protection and exempted it from the payment of *portazgo* and *herbazgo* on its flocks, an act recorded at Calatayud in the presence of Alfonso VIII of Castile (García Luján 1981: charter 61). He returned to Huerta in September of the year 1200, when Alfonso VIII mediated a dispute between him and his mother, Queen Sancha, at Ariza (Miret 1905–08, 3: 245–6), an event that will be discussed at greater length below (pp. 88–9). Finally, according to Manrique (1642–59, 3: 310), in a document written at Ariza in February of 1208, Pedro took pains to praise Huerta and the Cistercian Order in general although the king's presence in Huerta at that time is not recorded by Miret in his "Itinerario del rey Pedro I de Cataluña, II en Aragón" (1905–08, 3: 441–2). Pedro's last visit to Ariza occurred in August 1213, shortly before his death (Miret 1905–08, 4: 103).

Huerta also counted among its patrons the branch of the powerful Lara family that held the lordship of Molina. In 1167, shortly after her husband's death, Ermesinda, countess of Narbonne and Molina and wife of Manrique de Lara, gave the town of Arandilla to Huerta for the purpose of having an abbey built (García Luján 1981: charter 7). Her first-born son Aimerico, viscount of Narbonne, and his brother Count Pedro Manrique de Lara, commonly known as Pedro de Molina – also lord of Atienza and San Esteban de Gormaz, governor of Cuenca, Toledo (from 1173), and Huete, and husband of the Infanta Sancha who was the great-granddaughter of Rodrigo Díaz of Vivar – assisted at the laying of the first stone and sold the monastery half of the *salinas* of Terceguela in 1172 (charter 16). The following year Pedro de Molina and his wife granted the monastery the other half of the same *salinas* in exchange for a horse (charter 22). Manrique de Lara and his wife Ermesinda, their sons Aimerico and Pedro, Pedro's wife Sancha, and Gonzalo Pérez, his successor as count of Molina, were all buried at Huerta (Aguilera y Gamboa 1908: 200–1).

Other patrons of the monastery include Benito de Garasa and his wife Eva, who gave the estate of Terrer to Huerta in June 1172 (charters 17 and 18), and a certain Domingo, who gave an estate in Ariza (charter 21). But the group of patrons most intimately associated with the early history of Huerta was the family of one of the most influential churchmen of the period, Martín de Finojosa.

A native of Hinojosa del Campo, which is situated between Gómara and Agreda in the province of Soria, Martín was of noble lineage, the son of Miguel Muñoz of Hinojosa and Sancha Gómez of Almazán, who exercised dominion over Deza in the king's name.[1] His sister Eva, married to Jimeno Pérez de Rada, was the mother of the great Rodrigo Jiménez de Rada "el Toledano," primate of Spain, bishop of Toledo, and author of *De rebus Hispaniae* (Minguella y Arnedo 1910–12, 1: 155; Romero 1966: 86), who also endowed Huerta with numerous gifts, including money toward constructing the dormitory (Zamora 1962a: 27; Aguilera y Gamboa 1908: 261) and, in 1235, the donation of his own library (Romero 1962: 104n). Another of Martín's sisters, Teresa, was married to García Pérez de Molina (Romero 1966: 86), the son of Count Pedro Manrique de Lara. Martín de Finojosa's brother Muño Sánchez was married to a woman named Marquesa, who appears to have been the sister of the great *alférez* of Castile and lord of Vizcaya Diego López de Haro; they had two children, Martín, obviously named for his maternal uncle, and Adán (Romero 1966: 86). Muño Sánchez and Marquesa both died in 1206, and were buried at Huerta (Aguilera y Gamboa 1908: 42), as was Martín's mother Sancha (Zamora 1962a).

Martín de Finojosa passed his early monastic life, which began in April of 1158, at Cántavos, moving with the community in 1169 to *Horta Farizae*, Huerta de Ariza. In 1174 he became abbot of Huerta and he supervised the construction of the abbey from 1179. Under his direction Huerta flourished: Angel Manrique points out that the monastery acquired much property during Martín's abbacy and later when he returned there to live as a monk, but nothing in the seven years during which he was absent as bishop of Sigüenza (Manrique 1642–59, 3: 157), an office to which he was elected probably in 1184 and which he held from 1186 to 1192, when he renounced his episcopal status to retire to Huerta (Romero 1962: 105–6). Sigüenza was a *señorío*, and its bishop ruled not only the town itself but Monsalud, Quinqueyuga, the castle of Riba near Atienza, and the village of Tena near Hita (González 1960, 1: 453–5). Martín died in 1213, while returning from a visit to the Cistercian monastery of Ovila on the river Tajo, which he had protected during his term

Geography and history

as bishop. He was buried at Huerta and was revered as a saint. The remains of his renowned nephew Rodrigo Jiménez de Rada, who died in 1247 but had chosen Huerta for his tomb in 1201 when he was still a student in Paris (García Luján 1981: charter 71), were also to rest at the monastery.

St. Martín played a key role in the relations between Alfonso VIII and the Cistercian Order. He was a friend to the king, who in a charter of 18 October 1189 speaks of him as "dilecti et familiaris amici mei qui inmensa mihi cum omni sedulitate et fidelitate exhibuit obsequia" (Minguella y Arnedo 1910–12, 1: 153; Romero 1966: 90). He was active in the process by which in 1189 Las Huelgas of Burgos was founded and became the chief women's Cistercian monastery in Castile and Leon, undertaking missions in 1187 and 1188 from Alfonso VIII to the Chapter General of the Cistercian Order which was held annually at Cîteaux (Rodríguez López 1907, 1: 57–69).

During his tenure as abbot of Huerta, Martín was militant in channeling the zeal of fighting men into the struggle against the Moors. Angel Manrique, referring to documents of Huerta that he had at his disposal, reports that nobles who were about to depart against the Saracens flocked to the saint to obtain his blessing and solicit his prayers. After celebrating the Mass of the Holy Trinity, Martín would assign burial places to the nobles, then harangue them to return either dead or victorious, making them swear to emulate the deeds of those already buried in the cloister (Manrique 1642–59, 3: 23–4).

Martín was succeeded in the lordship and see of Sigüenza by his nephew Rodrigo, who had been archdeacon of Sigüenza and was consecrated bishop on 1 November 1192. Rodrigo was perhaps present at the Battle of Alarcos and certainly took part in the preparation for war against the Muslims in 1196, borrowing 1700 *maravedíes* for the purpose from the chapter of Sigüenza, for which he had to mortgage properties in Pelegrina and Romanones (Minguella y Arnedo 1910–12, 1: 178–9). Later Rodrigo participated in the Battle of Las Navas de Tolosa (González 1960, 1: 420–1).

In 1158 Martín de Finojosa's mother Sancha gave the village of Boñices to the community of Cántavos in connection with her son's entry into that monastery (García Luján 1981: charter 4). Muño Sánchez, St. Martín's brother, donated 300 *maravedíes* annually (half of it from a source in Molina) to build the dormitory of Huerta, and in addition a tenth of the sums devolving to him from his military activities (charter 34). He later substituted for that gift a property in Albaladejo near Cuenca on the river Júcar (charters 65–6, 69–70). Muño Sánchez also defined the limits of the estate of Valera near Cuenca with a monk of Huerta named Pedro López prior to the king's confirmation of Huerta's possession (charter 52). St. Martín himself endowed Huerta with part of the town of Deza (García Luján 1981: no. 45). Even taking into account the later history of the monastery of Huerta, most of the donations made to it either came from the family of St. Martín or are imputable to his influence (Alvarez Palenzuela 1978: 162).

Alfonso VIII's attachment to the Cistercian Order went beyond his concern to further the cause of Christendom. On 15 December 1199, he

The *Cantar de mio Cid*

pledged that, if he ever decided to enter the religious life, it would be as a Cistercian (Serrano 1935, 2: 150); in 1203 he exempted the Order from all taxes it owed to the crown (Manrique 1642–59, 3: 409).

Alfonso VIII visited Huerta on two occasions in the period during which Berenguela's marriage to Alfonso IX of Leon and the Pope's opposition to it were topical issues. Both visits occurred while Martín de Finojosa was living there in retirement, during the term of Abbot Jimeno.

On 10 April 1199 the Castilian court visited Huerta, on which occasion Alfonso VIII confirmed the monastery's possession of its various properties (Garcí Luján 1981: charter 62). Present were Alfonso, Queen Leonor, the Infante Fernando, and Alfonso's aunt Queen Sancha of Aragon, as well as the following prelates, officials, and courtiers who served as witnesses to the document of confirmation: the primate of Spain and bishop of Toledo Martín of Pisuerga; Bishops Martín of Burgos, Arderico of Palencia, Martín of Osma, Rodrigo of Sigüenza (Martín de Finojosa's nephew), Gonzalo of Segovia, Jacobo of Avila, Julián of Cuenca, Juan of Calahorra, and Bricio of Plasencia; Count Pedro of Molina; the *mayordomo real* Gonzalo Rodríguez Girón; the *alférez* Diego López de Haro; Alvar Nuñez de Lara – who would be the *alférez* at Las Navas de Tolosa and eventually Berenguela's enemy in the matter of custody over the young Fernando III; the former *mayordomo real* Pedro García de Lerma; Pedro González de Marañón of the family of Aza, Gómez Pérez, Lope Sánchez, Alfonso Téllez de Meneses who held Carrión in 1196, Gutierre Fernández, Guillermo González, Muño Sánchez brother of Martín de Finojosa, and the *merino* Gutierre Díaz. Probably also there was Abbot Guy of Cîteaux, since the king had written to him requesting his presence at Huerta (Aguilera y Gamboa 1908: 254), no doubt concerning the donation that Alfonso would make in December of the same year when he ceded the monastery of Las Huelgas to the Cistercian Order (González 1960, 3: no. 682). Julio González believes that Alfonso VIII was on his way to see the king of Aragon on this occasion, since from Huerta he journeyed to Almazán (González 1960, 1: 848).

Alfonso VIII probably also visited the monastery of Huerta in September 1200, since he was present in Ariza on September 26 of that year, mediating a dispute between Queen Sancha and her son Pedro II of Aragon (González 1960, 3: 861). Ariza was an appropriate place for the sovereigns to meet: it was on the border between their kingdoms and the town had initially been granted to Alfonso VIII in 1186 by Pedro's father, Alfonso II of Aragon, when the two had joined forces against Pedro Ruiz de Azagra who had set himself up as an independent ruler in Santa María de Albarracín (González 1960, 1: 823–34). Queen Sancha, who possessed Ariza (see Miret 1905–08, 3: 246n), was herself the daughter of Alfonso VII of Castile. Ariza also recalled the period in which Pedro's father and the Castilian king had joined forces in the treaty of Cazola (1179), which assigned the Muslim kingdom of Valencia to the sphere of influence of Aragon. That was before the League of Huesca (1191) which allied Aragon and Portugal against Castile, and its resulting wars (González

Geography and history

1960, 1: 830). Pedro had made a *rapprochement* with Castile early in his reign (his father died on 25 April 1196), under the influence of his Castilian mother, and had signed a peace treaty with Alfonso VIII in Calatayud on 20 May 1198 that also carved up Navarre for conquest and made quarrels between Pedro and his mother subject to Alfonso's arbitration (González 1960, 1: 844–5).

Precisely such a quarrel brought the two kings together in Ariza on 26 September 1200, where Alfonso ratified a pact between son and mother (Miret 1905–08, 3: 248) by which Queen Sancha gave Pedro the castles of Ariza (which had come to her as part of her dowry), Embid, and Epila, and income from, among other places, Calatayud (González 1960, 1: 856–7; the agreement is published in Cirot 1918: 160–3). Present were Pedro, his mother, Alfonso, and those whose names appear as witnesses, namely Bishops Raimundo of Saragossa and Gombau of Lérida; Pedro Fernández, the *mayordomo* Guillem de Castellazol, Jimeno Cornell the lord of Huesca – later to be present at Las Navas de Tolosa – Bernardo de Benavente, Martín Pérez de Vilel, Jimeno and Miguel de Lusia, Martín de Finojosa's brother-in-law Jimeno de Rada, Pedro Jiménez de Orrea, Pedro Ladrón the lord of Teruel and Belchite who was *alférez* of Aragon on 20 May 1198 (González 1960, 3: doc. 667), Lope de Valtierra, Arnaldo de Stopañano, Ramon de Castellvell, Hugo de Torreroja, Pedro de Mediano, Jordan de Pedra Alta, and Assalit de Gúdal. The document was copied by Joan de Berax, the king of Aragon's notary. The witnesses are Aragonese and Catalan magnates and officials, but also present, of course, were Alfonso VIII's courtiers. While the agreement between Pedro II and his mother was signed at Ariza, it is likely that the Castilian court, and perhaps the Aragonese too, visited Huerta.

These visits to Huerta and its vicinity take on heightened significance in view of the thematics of the *Cantar de mio Cid*. As was discussed in chapter 5, the legitimacy of offspring was a highly topical issue in the milieu of the Castilian royal family at the extreme end of the twelfth century and the beginning of the thirteenth, as a result of Berenguela's marriage to Alfonso IX of Leon and Pope Innocent III's opposition to both the marriage and the recognition of the legitimacy of its offspring. At the time of both royal visits to Huerta, Innocent had excommunicated Alfonso IX and Berenguela – who in March 1199 had already borne the first of her five children, a daughter also named Berenguela – and declared that the places they visited would be under interdiction, an extremely serious state of affairs since it entailed a prohibition against the saying of mass, the administration of the sacraments, and burial in consecrated ground wherever the couple went. In a bull of 16 June 1199, Innocent mentions having threatened the king and queen of Castile with similar punishments if Alfonso VIII did not see to it that the marriage was terminated. Already, in the bull of 24 May 1198, he had authorized the Papal Legate Rainerio to impose sanctions as he saw fit. By the time of the second visit, in September of 1200, Alfonso IX and Alfonso VIII had flouted Papal wrath by drawing up the marriage contract.

The analogy with the Cid's situation in the poem is, as discussed in the last chapter, suggestive: like Alfonso VIII of Castile, the hero is under threat from a higher authority, and the danger that hangs over those who receive him, namely that, among other things, they will lose their souls – a prohibition that would only make sense if it came from a spiritual authority – is of the same order as the menace by means of which the Pope was attempting to force the Castilian king to comply with his directives.

That Jimeno, the abbot of Huerta during Alfonso's visits, would refuse to receive the king was highly unlikely: only a few years before, in 1197, Alfonso IX of Leon had dismissed the bishop of Oviedo from his see probably for not supporting his attempt to marry his first cousin Teresa, daughter of King Sancho I of Portugal (González 1944, 1: 96; see also Serrano 1935, 2: 147).

Although the lack of precise documentation does not permit me to assert with assurance that the *Cantar de mio Cid* was performed for Alfonso VIII in April of 1199 at Huerta or in September of 1200 at Ariza or Huerta, the match between the poem's geographic scenario and the situation of Huerta is striking. The second of the two dates is perhaps the more likely because of the fact that the main military topic of the poem is the Cid's relatively minor exploits in the borderland between Castile and Aragon, to the neglect of his greatest achievement, the conquest of Valencia, and it is thus somewhat more plausible that it was composed in the form in which we have it on the occasion of a meeting between the sovereigns of both kingdoms. In the poem the Cid sends heralds out specifically and exclusively into Aragon, Navarre, and Castile to attract fighting men for the siege of Valencia (ll. 1187–8), an action that fits the political situation of the turn of the century when Alfonso VIII of Castile and Pedro II of Aragon had formed an alliance to dominate Navarre. When the Cid leaves Valencia to travel to the *vistas* with King Alfonso on the Tagus, he leaves the city in the charge of the Castilian Alvar Salvadórez and Galind Garçiaz "el de Aragon" (l. 1999), elsewhere called "una fardida lança" (l. 443b) and "el bueno de Aragon" (ll. 740, 3071). The Aragonese noble to whom the poet has given an equal share of responsibility for guarding Valencia was in history the lord of Ligüerre and Estada, who fought in the capture of Barbastro in 1100 beside Pedro I of Aragon (Michael 1978: 111n), namesake of Pedro II and historical ally of the Cid. The climax of the poem shows the Castilian Rodrigo of Vivar marrying off his daughters to the infantes of precisely Navarre and Aragon.

With two kings in the audience, the line "Oy los reyes d'España sos parientes son" (l. 3724) would take on added resonances. Alfonso VIII was a direct descendant of the Cid through his mother Blanca, the daughter of the King of Navarre García Ramírez "el Restaurador," who was the son of Cristina Rodríguez, the Cid's elder daughter. Pedro II of Aragon was not a descendant of the conqueror of Valencia, but his great-grandfather, Ramon Berenguer III "el Grande" of Barcelona, had been married to María Rodríguez, and then as a widower had married Pedro's great-grandmother Dulce of Provence. Thus while Pedro was not in direct line of descent from Rodrigo Díaz, like Alfonso he could be said to count among the Cid's *parientes* (see

Horrent 1973: 256). The indefinite plural *los reyes* could also include the king of Leon, husband of Berenguela and destined to become the father of yet another king of Castile who would be a direct descendant of Rodrigo, namely Fernando III. Horrent (1973: 253–4) makes a good case for the interpretation that *los reyes* does not necessarily include the kings of all five peninsular kingdoms, as that would entail a degree of precision that would ill fit a passage in which the poet has just asserted in the previous line, falsely, that the Cid's daughters were "señoras... de Navarra e de Aragon."

Between the possible dates of composition around the turn of the century and the date given in the poem's colophon, two extremely important events took place that would have given even greater topical relevance to the poem, with its thematic emphasis on legitimacy: Fernando's birth and the treaty of Cabreros, dated 26 March 1206, by which the boy, although perhaps still illegitimate in the eyes of the Pope, inherited from the kings of Leon and Castile and from his mother sixteen castles plus those of his mother's dowry and was confirmed as the heir to the throne of Leon (González 1960, 1: 739).

The possibility that Pedro II of Aragon was in the audience toward which the poet was pitching his performance is intriguing in light of the theme of the Cid's economic difficulties early in the poem. According to the reliable *Crónica latina de los reyes de Castilla*, Pedro had received large quantities of money from Alfonso VIII as early as 1196 when he sent an expedition into Leon in support of the Castilian king (ed. Cabanes Pecourt: 29; see Ubieto Arteta 1980: 564–8), and later had to call upon the resources both of Alfonso and of Sancho VII of Navarre in order to finance his participation at Las Navas de Tolosa (González 1960, 1: 1008). Pedro II contracted numerous debts during his reign. In the period preceding his meeting with Alfonso VIII at Ariza in September 1200, loans are documented from the Order of the Hospital in 1198 (Miret 1905–08, 3: 156, 266), from Galiana of Berguedà and her brothers in 1199 (3: 159), and from Esteve de Marimon on 7 February 1200 to pay partly for the debts contracted by Alfonso II and partly for the expenses of an embassy to the king of Morocco (3: 239, 242). Pedro continued to contract debts through his entire reign, including those documented in 1204 from Raimond V of Toulouse (3: 274, 508); in 1206 from Pedro Fernández entailing a mortage on, among other places, Ariza (3: 377), and from Berenguer and Pere Ramon de Ribera (3: 379); in 1209 from the count of Urgell (3: 499), Gaston viscount of Béarn (3: 500), Berenguer de Riera (3: 500), and King Sancho of Navarre (3: 501–2); in 1211 from Arnau de Fuxà (4: 21), Berenguer de Riera (4: 23), and Henri, abbot of Morimond (4: 25); in 1212 again from Sancho of Navarre (4: 30); and in 1213, the year of his death at the Battle of Muret, from Pedro de Navascos (4: 103). The portrayal of the Cid's penury would hardly have flattered the perennially needy Pedro II, but it may have been designed to suggest that a prince in his situation might still expect success and the allusion might well have pleased Alfonso VIII, who was the young king's economic patron at the beginning of his reign.

In enumerating in chapter 5 the choices that might reveal to us the poet's

The *Cantar de mio Cid*

motivations, I included his hostility toward Berenguer Ramon II, count of Barcelona. The life of the historical Rodrigo Díaz of Vivar was filled with resounding events that were potential subjects for the poet, who chose not only to conflate some of them (the hero's two exiles, for example) and to multiply others (the battles in defense of Valencia, for example), but excluded still others from his narrative, either consciously for artistic or political reasons or because he did not know of them. Surely there was no poetic necessity for him to recount the Battle of Tévar in which the Cid defeats and humiliates the count of Barcelona. That he was not simply receiving and passing on unchanged a traditional account of that battle that derived faithfully from the historical event is revealed by the fact that he gets the count's name wrong, calling him "el conde don Remont" (ll. 975, 987, 1009, 1018, 1028, 1059, 1066), and, with patronymic, "Remont Verenguel" (l. 998), whereas the count whom the Cid captured in history, not just once but twice – in 1082 and 1090 – was Berenguer Ramon II, "el Fratricida."

To vilify a count of Barcelona before an audience that included the reigning count – Pedro II of Aragon was also Pedro I of Catalonia – might appear to be ill-advised were it not for Berenguer Ramon II's reputation in history. Pedro was descended in direct line – through his father, Alfonso II of Aragon, I of Catalonia, his grandfather Ramon Berenguer IV, and his great-grandfather, Ramon Berenguer III "el Grande" – from Ramon Berenguer II "Cap de Estopa," who ruled Catalonia jointly with his brother Berenguer Ramon II from 1076 to 1082. In that year the quarrels that had divided the co-rulers grew in ferocity until one day "Cap de Estopa" was found dead, suspicion immediately falling upon Berenguer Ramon. The deceased count's wife Mahalda pursued the matter with the result that, fourteen years later, Berenguer Ramon was accused of fratricide before Alfonso VI and convicted by judicial duel. He was deposed, succeeded by the assassinated count's son Ramon Berenguer III, the Cid's son-in-law. The recounting of the Battle of Tévar and the humiliation of "don Remont" at the Cid's hands, then, is no obstacle to the possibility that the poem was performed before Pedro II of Aragon: on the contrary, the king's presence would explain why the poet chose to depict a scene of mockery whose victim is Berenguer Ramon II rather than, say, García Ordóñez or one of the Cid's other enemies. If the poem was indeed performed in Ariza before the two courts in September 1200, it would not only have presented favorably the *pariente* of Alfonso VIII and Pedro II, but unfavorably the murderer of Pedro's direct ancestor.

In attempting to explain why the Per Abbat text claims that the poetic Cid's daughter Sol, the María of history, married the Infante of Aragon, whereas her husband actually was the count of Barcelona, Menéndez Pidal (1961: 176–7) embroidered upon a solution first proposed by Ferdinand Wolf, who conjectured that the poet must have lived in the time of Count Ramon Berenguer IV of Barcelona (1131–62), who was regent of the kingdom of Aragon from 1150 as husband of Petronila, the daughter of King Ramiro II "el Monje" of Aragon. The poet would have associated Barcelona with Aragon because of

Geography and history

the political situation current in his own time rather than in that of Rodrigo Díaz. Menéndez Pidal proposed a historical misunderstanding of a similar nature: García Ramírez, grandson of the Cid, inherited the lordship of Monzón in Aragon from his father, and was later elected king of Navarre. The poet would have transformed this association of Aragon and Navarre into double marriages with the infantes of Aragon and Navarre. Both Wolf's and Menéndez Pidal's hypotheses raise a formidable problem, however: during the lifetimes of both Ramon Berenguer IV of Barcelona and García Ramírez (or, in other terms, in the period around the middle of the twelfth century when Menéndez Pidal's poet of Medinaceli would have completed his reworking of the poem), the union of the kingdom of Aragon and the county of Barcelona (1150) and the election of García Ramírez as king of Navarre (1134), both striking developments, were quite recent occurrences and are unlikely to have misled the poet into committing anachronisms. I do not deny that the identity of a count of Barcelona and a king of Aragon was responsible for the mistake concerning the status of Sol's (i.e. María's) husband, but the person in whom the poet observed those two offices meeting was much more likely to have lived far enough after the events in question for their nuances to have been blurred: that is to say, is much more likely to have been Alfonso II (r. 1162–96) or Pedro II (r. 1196–1213).

As I have had occasion to mention more than once, Lacarra has pointed out that two of the most powerful clans in late twelfth-century Castile, the Laras of Molina and the Castros, were descended respectively from Rodrigo Díaz of Vivar and the counts of Carrión, a state of affairs that leads her to hypothesize that the *Cantar de mio Cid* was composed by a poet favorable to the Laras and to Alfonso VIII and inimical to the Castros. She has conjectured further that the poet must have come from the region bounded by San Esteban de Gormaz[2] and Calatayud on the north and by Guadalajara and Albarracín on the south, and that the choice of the Muslim lord of Molina, Avengalbón, as the poetic Cid's ally was motivated by the fact that the Laras ruled in Molina (Lacarra 1980a: 200–1).

The attachments between Huerta and the Laras of Molina is of considerable interest in the light of those ideas. Pedro of Molina was the son of Manrique Pérez de Lara who was killed by Fernando Rodríguez de Castro at the battle of Huete in 1164. Pedro was married to the Cid's great-granddaughter, the Infanta Sancha, from 1173 until her death in 1177, and he was present at Alfonso's visit to Huerta in April of 1199. Although his name does not appear in the agreement concluded at Ariza in September 1200 between Pedro II of Aragon and his mother Sancha – an Aragonese document – it is quite likely that he was present on that occasion as well, since he was the most prominent member of the most powerful local dynasty.

The son of Pedro of Molina and the Infanta Sancha, García Pérez, who was married to Teresa, sister of St. Martín de Finojosa (Romero 1966: 86), inherited half of Molina from his grandmother Ermesinda. The lordship proper of Molina passed to another of Pedro Manrique's sons, Gonzalo

Pérez, who held it until 1221, when he ceded it to the diocesis of Toledo, whose archbishop at the time was Rodrigo Jiménez de Rada, reserving for himself and his descendants the right to rule it as vassals of the archbishop (González 1960, 1: 281).

Manrique de Lara and his successors shared a characteristic with the poetic Cid, and perhaps also with his historical model, in that all three were independent rulers of the cities that they governed. Lacarra has made a convincing case for the Cid's independence from Alfonso VI as lord of Valencia in the poem (1980a: 41–3) and in history (1980a: 109), and both Manrique de Lara and his successors as counts of Molina, Pedro and Gonzalo, unlike other vassals of the king of Castile in this period, styled themselves counts "by the grace of God" (Salazar y Castro 1696–97, 1: 147, 150, 238). Manrique's successors ruled with the trappings of royalty, granting exemptions and staffing their courts with officials entitled *alférez mayor* and *mayordomo mayor* (Salazar y Castro 1696–97, 1: 6, 116–17).

The daughters of the historical Rodrigo Díaz of Vivar were named Cristina and María, but the poet names them respectively Elvira and Sol, usually in the same formulaic hemistich "doña Elvira e doña Sol." Intent on demonstrating the poem's historicity, Menéndez Pidal attempted to recuperate this discrepancy by pointing out that medieval noblewomen often bore two names, the one "official," the other perhaps familiar, although as Louis Chalon emphasizes (1967: 220) it is not a question here of each daughter bearing two names but rather of a need to reconcile two traditions, the one attested in history, the other poetic. "Sol" in particular, absent from the canonical saintly nomenclature, is an affectionate name, Menéndez Pidal observed, preceded occasionally by a possessive adjective as in the "mea Sol domna Marina" attested for the year 1116 (Menéndez Pidal 1954–56, 2: 857) and Misol, abbess of Las Huelgas at the time when St. Martín de Finojosa helped to establish it as the premier women's monastery in Castile and Leon (Rodríguez López 1907, 1: 333–6). Looking in the late twelfth and early thirteenth centuries rather than in the period in which Menéndez Pidal situated the poem's composition, one finds Sol, wife of Domingo Sánchez of Belena, in a charter confirming a donation that the parents of St. Martín de Finojosa made in 1175 (García Luján 1981: no. 31), and, closer in time and place to the milieu in which I think the poem was composed, Sol, wife of Domingo Martín, *mayordomo* of the Infante Fernando, in a royal charter from 1202 (see J. González 1960, 3: no. 717).

But while "Sol" may well be an affectionate name, masking the name by which the *Cid* poet's model is known to history, what of "Elvira," which obviously perplexed Menéndez Pidal since in contrast to "Sol" he only devoted five lines to the entry for that name in this *Vocabulario* (1954–56, 2: 636)? It is interesting to note that "Elvira" was a traditional name in the house of Lara for more than a century preceding 1207.

A daughter of Count Gonzalo Núñez de Lara III, governor of Osma, was the first of these Elviras; she was married to Pedro Núñez, lord of Fuentear-

Geography and history

megil and San Esteban de Gormaz (Salazar y Castro 1696–97, 1: 90). In the following generation, her niece Elvira, the daughter of Count Pedro González de Lara – royal *alférez* under Alfonso VI and later the lover of the king's sister Queen Urraca – and the sister of Manrique de Lara, first lord of Molina, became successively, through her two marriages, countess of Trava and Risnel. She begins to appear in documents in 1117 and was apparently Urraca's daughter (Salazar y Castro 1696–97, 1: 101; Reilly 1982: 36, 216).

Ermesinda, viscountess of Narbonne, bore five daughters to Manrique de Lara, named María, Mayor, Sancha, Hermengard, and Elvira. The last-named married Armengol VIII of Urgell, and then, after his death in 1208, Guillem de Cervera. Widowed for the second time, she retired to the Cistercian abbey of Santa Maria de Poblet (Salazar y Castro 1696–97, 1: 128–30). Her daughter Aurembiax married Alvar Pérez de Castro, son of Pedro Fernández "el Castellano," a union that lasted at least until 1225 (Salazar y Castro 1696–97, 1: 129). This Elvira was a contemporary of Per Abbat and perhaps of the Cid poet.

Finally, to Pedro of Molina may have been born a daughter named Elvira (González 1960, 1: 622). Luis Salazar y Castro, historian of the Laras, claims, however, that the Elvira in question was the daughter of a Pedro Alfónsez rather than of Pedro Manrique, in which case she would not have belonged to the house of Lara (1696–97, 1: 155–6). What is not clear either is whether this Elvira, if indeed Pedro of Molina was her father, was the daughter of the Infanta Sancha, great-granddaughter of Rodrigo Díaz of Vivar, or of Pedro's second wife Margarita, whom he married in 1177 (Salazar y Castro 1696–97, 1: 144), or even of his third wife Mafalda.

In any case the name Elvira was decidedly the favorite for female offspring in this line of the house of Lara during the twelfth century, including the period before the Cid's lineage married into the family of Lara. The *Cid* poet may have named one of the hero's daughters "Elvira" because of the name's popularity in the family of Lara, one of whose members, Pedro of Molina, had married a descendant of Cristina Rodríguez, precisely the historical daughter whom the poet calls "Elvira."

The poem's Alvar Salvadórez was in history the younger brother of Gonzalo, count of Lara (Smith 1972: 165–6). Another character in the poem is undoubtedly a member of the Lara clan. Yeñigo (or Yñego) Simenez (Ximenez), who appears in ll. 3394, 3417, and 3422 as the messenger of the Infante of Aragon, was identified by Menéndez Pidal as a younger contemporary of Rodrigo Díaz of Vivar. This Iñigo Jiménez served Alfonso "el Batallador" and was the lord of Calahorra, Cameros, Grañón, Segovia, and Sepúlveda, and the governor of Calatayud (Menéndez Pidal 1954–56, 2: 718). In 1110 he married María González de Lara, daughter of Gonzálo Núñez, the aunt of Manrique de Lara (Salazar y Castro 1696–97, 1: 90).

Is there any indication of a connection between St. Martín de Finojosa, who was residing at Huerta from 1192 to 1213, and the poem? Two characters who figure in the *Cantar de mio Cid* are of particular relevance in this regard:

The *Cantar de mio Cid*

Martín Muñoz and Félez Muñoz. The saintly abbot of Huerta's father was, as I have mentioned, Miguel Muñoz de Finojosa, lord of Hinojosa in the province of Soria. Miguel could trace his ancestry through his father to Fernando Muñoz, a knight of some stature who lived in the reigns of Alfonso VI and Alfonso VII of Castile. Fernando Muñoz had served as *mayordomo* of Castile under Alfonso VII "el Emperador"; his parents were Muño Sanchez, whose relations with the Moor Aboabdil were the subject of legend (Aguilera y Gamboa 1908: 37–41), and María Palacín. The family's traditional burial-place until the period of St. Martín was the Romanesque cloister of the monastery of Santo Domingo de Silos (Romero 1962: 94), where the saint's father was buried.

The saint had a nephew named Martín Muñoz, as I have mentioned, who succeeded his brother Muño Sánchez as lord of Hinojosa in 1206 (Aguilera y Gamboa 1908: 42). Martín Muñoz confirmed documents of Alfonso VIII from 1211 to 1216 and occupied the posts of *mayordomo real* and *procurator regni curiae regis* under Enrique I (Romero 1966: 86, 91) from January 1217 until the king's death five months later. He fought at both Alarcos and Las Navas de Tolosa, where he was one of the three knights who captured the pass of Muradal and the castle of Ferral on 11 July 1212 prior to the battle (Huici Miranda 1956: 248–9).[3]

The Martín Muñoz of the *Cantar de mio Cid*, characterized as "que en buen punto naçio," l. 3068, and "el que mando a Mont Mayor," l. 738, has been identified as the historical governor of Coimbra and later of Arouca, verified as present in Montemayor in a document of 1091. A Martín Muñoz, who may or may not be the same person, led a contingent of Aragonese against the forces of Queen Urraca on behalf of Alfonso "el Batallador" in 1111; the fact that he was operating in the sphere of influence of the Aragonese king suggests that he might be an otherwise unidentified member of the Finojosa clan, perhaps the brother of Fernando Muñoz, although there is no written evidence for that conjecture. In any case "Martin Muñoz el que mando a Mont Mayor" only fills the role of a bit player in the poem.

Félez Muñoz, on the other hand, is the nephew of the poetic Cid and the cousin of his daughters, and accompanies them when the Infantes de Carrión lead them away from Valencia. Later he finds them abandoned in the Robledo de Corpes and takes them to San Esteban de Gormaz, a role of capital importance since otherwise, one can presume, the two women might have died.[4] His name does not appear in historical documents nor is it clear to whom his patronymic refers.

The poet may have included as characters two knights with the patronymic "Muñoz" in order to flatter the Finojosa clan, one of whom, St. Martín, the uncle of a contemporary Martín Muñoz who had obviously been named after him, was a monk at Huerta from 1192 to 1213. That same Martín Muñoz's father was present at Alfonso VIII's visit to Huerta in April 1199.

The Robledo de Corpes itself, as identified by Menéndez Pidal, is south of the present town of Castillejo de Robledo (1954–65, 1: 50–7; Criado de Val

1970 defends the identification of Robledo de Corpes de Cañamares). The closest town of any size to Castillejo de Robledo is Valdanzo, one of the places in question in a dispute that opposed the bishoprics of Sigüenza and Osma concerning jurisdiction over Ayllón, Caracena, and Berlanga de Duero in the second half of the twelfth century. The people and clergy of those towns had attempted to secede from the diocese of Sigüenza in favor of Osma, and the controversy grew until both the Papacy and the Castilian monarch were involved. It was settled to Sigüenza's advantage in 1165, with the provision that the bishop of Osma had to pay a thousand *áureos* in compensation for the income that Sigüenza had lost during the dispute, but he refused to surrender the specified amount and controversy flared up again. Alfonso VIII intervened, and on 1 April 1191, the bishops of Burgos and Segovia imposed a settlement of which one of the provisions was that the diocese of Sigüenza would cede the church of Valdanzo to Osma. Martín de Finojosa was bishop of Sigüenza until 1192, and Valdanzo, within three kilometers of the Robledo de Corpes, was thus under his care for most of the time during which he occupied the episcopal office.

A third link between the poem and Martín de Finojosa, this time through the family of his nephew Rodrigo Jiménez de Rada, is the Cid's sword Tizón. Two figures who lived in the early twelfth century and about whom Ubieto Arteta (1973: 121–8) has collected information bore the sobriquet "Tizón." The first was Pedro, lord of Monzón from 1113 to 1125 or 1127, nicknamed "Tizón," who may have died at the Battle of Fraga in 1134. Rodrigo Jiménez de Rada reports that he lost Monzón through the treachery of the count of Barcelona, that is to say Ramon Berenguer III, who ruled from 1097 to 1131:

Montionem Titio quidam nobilis ex Aragonia acquisivit, et ei castrum illud proditione sublatum Comiti Barcinonae deditione provenit.
(*De rebus Hispaniae* IV, 11; ed. Cabanes Pecourt 1968: 84)

The sword Tizón, which the Cid acquires in the poem in his victory over Búcar, and which is referred to in a pact between Armengol, count of Urgell, and Berenguer Ramon I, count of Barcelona, from around the year 1030, recorded in the *Liber feudorum* (see Pérez de Urbel 1955: 634–6), is known to have been in the castle of Monzón, whence, according to the *Crònica de Jaume I*, it was acquired by Jaume I of Aragon, son of Pedro II:

E haviem nos aduyta una espaa de Monso que havia nom Tiso, que era molt bona e aventurosa a aquels qui la portaven. (ed. Casacuberta 1926–62, 3: 96)

Pedro Tizón's predecessor as lord of Monzón and Buil was the Infante Ramiro Sánchez, who, as we have seen, had married the Cid's daughter Cristina (the poem's Elvira), and he was succeeded by the son of the same Ramiro Sánchez, García Ramírez, grandson of the Cid, soon to be the king of Navarre. Since Aragonese tenancies in the early twelfth century were transmitted within the same family, Ubieto Arteta has conjectured that Pedro

Tizón was related in some way to the Infante Ramiro and to García Ramírez, the grandson of Rodrigo Díaz.

The second Pedro Tizón was the governor of Estella (1124–35), Monteagudo de Navarra (1132–37), Pedrola (1135), Cervera del Río Alhama (1123–32), and Valtierra (1134). Rodrigo Jiménez de Rada also mentions this Pedro Tizón (VI, 2, ed. Cabanes Pecourt 1968: 118) in connection with the attempt of Pedro de Atarés to usurp the throne of Aragon from Ramiro II "el Monje." After 1137 he disappears for a time from the historical record, emerging in 1155 as a Templar, in which capacity he was *comendador* of Novillas. There is no trace of him after 1168.

Ubieto hypothesizes that the second Pedro Tizón was the son of the first. He conjectures that the sword Tizón may have been part of the dowry of Cristina Rodríguez and that Pedro Tizón the elder took his nickname – later converted into a proper name – from the sword. Both Pedros in question would, then, be descendants of Rodrigo Díaz of Vivar, as would their progeny. Of great interest to us here, then, is a genealogical link passed over by Ubieto Arteta. As has been mentioned, the great chronicler and primate of Spain Rodrigo Jiménez de Rada "el Toledano" was the nephew of St. Martín, who was the brother of his mother Eva. On his father's side, however, Rodrigo Jiménez may have been a descendant of the Cid, since his paternal grandfather was precisely Pedro Tizón the younger (Aguilera y Gamboa 1908: 30). The monks of Fitero disputed Huerta's claim to the body of "el Toledano," maintaining that they should have the right to inter him since his grandfather Pedro Tizón had been a patron of their monastery (Gorosterratzu 1925: 398).

In the poem the swords Colada and Tizón are passed on to Martín Antolínez and Pero Vermúdez respectively after the Cid receives them back from the Infantes. The duel between Pero and Fernando González ends when the latter admits defeat upon realizing that his adversary is about to attack him with Tizón. Diego González loses his duel by stepping outside the boundaries of the battlefield in his haste to escape from Colada, but Tizón is represented as an even more powerful weapon since the very sight of it forces an admission of defeat, and concomitantly of guilt. The poet may have conferred this almost numinous quality[5] upon the sword Tizón in an attempt to appeal to Jimeno de Rada (son of Pedro Tizón the younger), who, it will be recalled, was present in Ariza on 26 September 1200, when Alfonso VIII of Castile ratified the treaty between Pedro II of Aragon and his mother.

According to Salazar y Castro, Gonzalo Pérez de Lara, who, as we have seen, succeeded Pedro de Molina as lord of Molina, was the offspring of that lord's marriage with the Infanta Sancha (1696–97, 1: 236), but Julio González cites a document of 3 February 1202 that speaks of the Countess doña Mafalda and Gonzalo Pérez, her son by Pedro de Molina (1960, 1: 280 and 3: 261). Gonzalo's daughter Mafalda married the Infante Alfonso, one of the offspring of the marriage of Berenguela and Alfonso IX of Leon, in 1222 (Salazar y Castro 1696–97, 1: 238). Gonzalo was the last of his line to govern Molina without encumbrance, since he gave the town to the bishop and church of Toledo to be held by himself and his descendants (González 1960, 1: 281). He was the lord of Molina at the time when Per Abbat copied the poem.[6]

It will be recalled that García Pérez, Pedro de Molina's son by the Infanta doña Sancha, owned with his mother half of Molina, with the exception of a few properties that were given to the Order of Calatrava (charter in Salazar y Castro 1696–97, 4: 11). García and his father donated Cogolludo to the same order for the repose of Sancha's soul in 1183, which is the last mention of him in the historical record (Salazar y Castro 1696–97, 1: 154; text in 4: 16). He was married to Teresa, the sister of St. Martín de Finojosa.

St. Martín, then, was ideally situated, both socially and geographically, to serve as a link among the various figures of late twelfth-century Castile and perhaps also of Aragon who would have had an interest in the performance and preservation in writing of a poem with the themes, qualities, and characters of the *Cantar de mio Cid*. He was not only the brother-in-law of Alfonso VIII's *alférez* but a close personal friend of the monarch. He was also the uncle of Rodrigo Jiménez de Rada, soon-to-be-named primate of Spain and perhaps a descendant of the Cid, and brother-in-law of García Pérez de Lara, who was unquestionably descended from the hero of Valencia. Martín de Finojosa's social relationships were such that he might well have persuaded the abbot of Huerta, where he passed the final years of his life as a no doubt imposing influence, to have the *Cantar de mio Cid* performed in honor of Alfonso VIII – who was, after all, the great-great-grandson of Rodrigo of Vivar – and perhaps also in honor of Pedro II of Aragon.

If Huerta's association with the poem were to be accepted, the poet's choice of a fictitious place-name, in this instance "Spinaz de Can," for a town that was called something else in history would be illuminated. Menéndez Pidal mentions that a number of places on the Iberian Peninsula bear that name, but that none is situated in the region in which the poet locates "Spinaz de Can." The town one does find in that place, however, is Huerta del Rey (Menéndez Pidal 1954–56, 1: 41). The homophony of the two toponyms would have been confusing for an audience hearing the poem recited at Huerta on the Jalón, so the poet would have substituted "Spinaz de Can," perhaps chosen gratuitously, for the correct place-name.

Ubieto Arteta notes (1973: 134) that the name of the Muslim king "Fáriz" (ll. 654, 760, 769, 773, 841) reflects the phonetic contours of "Fariza" (= Ariza), and the name "Galve" is shared by towns in the province of Guadalajara, jurisdiction of Atienza, and in the province of Teruel. What Ubieto fails to mention is that the Galve near Atienza is only a few kilometers from the route that the Infantes de Carrión follow on their way to the Robledo de Corpes. Michael (1978: 126) refers to a Papal document of 1157 that mentions both Fariza and *Castellum de Galbe*, which may indicate that Galve was also a toponym in the area with which the poet shows the most intimate familiarity.

A third detail, the celebration of the Mass of the Holy Trinity on two occasions in the poem, namely before the Cid and his men leave Jimena, Elvira, and Sol behind at Cardeña (l. 319) and before the battle with Búcar (l. 2370), might have been suggested by St. Martín's practice of preparing knights for the struggle against the Muslims in a ceremony preceded by the celebration of the Mass of the Holy Trinity (Manrique 1642–59, 3: 23–4). Pérez de Urbel (1955: 637–8) mentions the saint in this connection, but only by way of example since, in the wake of Menéndez Pidal's dating of the poem to the mid-twelfth century, he did not link St. Martín with its composition.

Another detail that has long puzzled scholars might be clarified to a certain extent should one accept the hypothesis that the *Cantar de mio Cid* was composed in the Transierra, namely the identity of "Alcocer," a town on the river Jalón that the Cid and his men capture through a stratagem after camping above it "en un otero redondo fuerte e grand" (l. 554). As a result of this victory, the Cid is able to send his first set of gifts to Alfonso, launching the process of gift-giving that will eventually allow him to be recognized as the equal of his former lord. As I have mentioned, no "Alcocer" is found in the valley of the Jalón, and the town has probably been invented, although Criado de Val and Ian Michael have suggested that it may represent Castejón de las Armas. While the poet, who had already described the taking of Castejón de Henares in the episode immediately preceding this one, might well have wanted to use Castejón de las Armas as the town that the Cid captures, the designation "Castejón" used a second time would be confusing, and one is justified in asking whether another collocation of the place-name "Castejón" and "Alcocer" might not have suggested the latter name to him. Eighteen kilometers east of Sacedón, near the present-day Mar de Castilla, is the town of Alcocer, and about the same distance to the southeast of Alcocer is yet another Castejón. Perhaps significant is the fact that Monsalud, one of the southernmost Cistercian monasteries in Spain and an establishment that shared with Huerta the privilege of deriving revenues from the *salinas* of Atienza (Alvarez Palenzuela 1978: 199), is located between Sacedón and Alcocer.

The poet's attachment to a well-defined area of Transierran geography would obviously be illuminated by an association with Santa María de Huerta. The monastery owned properties in Ariza, Ateca, Cuenca, Medinaceli, and Terrer, and derived revenues from the *salinas* of Atienza, all towns named in the *Cantar de mio Cid*. I do not mean to imply that the poet delved into the monastery's archives (see chapter 8); rather I take the mention of these toponyms to indicate that he places his hero in a field of action familiar to his audience, one which would not only appeal to the local pride of inhabitants of the Jalón valley but would perhaps convince visitors that they were passing through a heroic ambiance.

Who was the abbot of Santa María de Huerta in 1207? The early history of Huerta has been poorly known until recently. The monastery's archive was badly damaged in 1707 (Romero 1962: 78n), and knowledge of its twelfth- and thirteenth-century activities was accessible mostly through the work of

Geography and history

the seventeenth-century historian of the Cistercian Order Angel Manrique, himself a monk of Huerta and later bishop of Badajoz. The publication of the *Cartulario del monasterio de Santa María de Huerta* in 1981 by José Antonio García Luján thus represents a major step forward in knowledge of the twelfth- and thirteenth-century history of this very important monastery.

Angel Manrique includes in his monumental *Annales Cistercienses* a section entitled "Series Abbatum Ecclesiae Regalis Sanctae Mariae de Horta" (Manrique 1642–59, 2: Appendix, 15–33) in which he gives the sequence of abbots of Huerta for the late twelfth and early thirteenth centuries as: Martinus (i.e. St. Martín de Finojosa), 1164–85; Armenius, 1185–92; Gerardus, 1192–95; Semenus or Egimenus, 1196–1203; and Bernardus I, 1203–17. Manrique's account is, however, sprinkled with *creditur*'s, and he was obviously at a loss to come up with a definitive list of the early abbots of Huerta.

The cartulary of Huerta published by García Luján allows greater precision. St. Martín was abbot from 1174 until he left in 1186 to become bishop of Sigüenza, and retired to Huerta after resigning from his episcopal office (González 1960, 1: 514). He was succeeded as abbot by the "Armenius, abbas Orte" who concluded the undated agreement between the monastery and the *concejo* of Montuenga (García Luján 1981: charter 56). The abbot from at least May 1195 (charter 58) to 1201 (see charter 72) and perhaps 1203 was Jimeno (Semenus, Eximinius), who was followed by Bernardus (charter 75). Finally, in the last charter in the cartulary of Huerta (see the facsimile in García Luján 1981, fol. 84v), which its editor dates to between 1208 and 1210, the abbot's name is Petrus, abbreviated as "P." (charter 76). The charter in question attests that Brother Johan de Calatayuf (*sic*), under the direction and with the consent of Petrus the abbot and the whole monastic community of Huerta (*precepto et consensu dompni P. abbatis tociusque conventus de Orta*), bought various properties in Belimbre.

When did this Pedro's abbacy begin? The marquis of Cerralbo appends an extract from the *Memoria cronológica de los abades y varones illustres del imperial y real monasterio de Huerta, sacada fielmente de los papeles del archivo, por el P. Fr Constantino Cordón, monje hijo de dicha casa*, much of which is based on still unpublished sources, to his work *El Arzobispo D. Rodrigo Ximénez de Rada y el monasterio de Santa María de Huerta* (Aguilera y Gamboa 1908: 283–348). Constantino Cordón was abbot of Huerta from 1707 to 1710. After Abbot Martín I "el Santo," Cordón lists Armenio I, Gerardo I (1191–94, according to him, although Gerardo is not represented in the cartulary), Jimeno I, Bernardo II, and Pedro I. Bernardo II is only represented in the cartulary by a survey of Albalate and Zuero that is undated. Cordón notes that Diego López and his wife Toda gave a property called "la Torre de Zafra" to the abbot Pedro in 1210, the year in which it is believed Pedro died and in which, according to Cordón, he was succeeded by Abbot Juan Gonzalo. Although Cordón gives Abbot Pedro's period in office as 1208–10, then, the earlier of these two dates is actually uncertain and he may have begun his abbacy as early as 1203, the last date attested for Jimeno.

Thus in May of 1207, the month in which Per Abbat finished writing a manuscript of the *Cantar de mio Cid* in the line of descent of the extant fourteenth-century manuscript, a monk of the same name may have been abbot of Santa María de Huerta. Can one assert that Per Abbat and Pedro I, abbot of Huerta, are one and the same? In the state of our historical knowledge it is impossible to do so. Nevertheless I believe that Pedro I of Huerta is one of the prime candidates for the identity of Per Abbat.

He is not, however, the only candidate in the entourage of St. Martín de Finojosa. The contemporary abbot of the monastery of Santa María de Ovila, a house that was situated on the river Tagus within the jurisdiction of the *concejo* of Medinaceli (Millares Carlo 1933: charter 10 of 25 February 1214), was also named Pedro. Ovila was linked to Huerta in that both were granddaughter houses of Morimond and both were located in the diocese of Sigüenza.

Santa María de Ovila was founded in the late twelfth century. On 12 August 1181, Alfonso VIII and Queen Leonor gave the town of Quinqueyuga to the bishop of Sigüenza in exchange for Muriel, a site on which a monastery was to be founded. Muriel's mother-house was Boulbonne in the Haute-Garonne, daughter-house in turn of Morimond (Maur Cocheril 1964: 237). Five years later the Muriel community was displaced to Ovila, a site five kilometers to the west on the Tagus upstream from Trillo, near the castle of Las Peñas de Alcalatén (now called Tetas de Viana), where a monastery dedicated to the Virgin Mary was built. The location, along with Muriel and its four granges and other property, was donated to the Cistercian Order on 29 June 1191 by the king.[7]

One of the smallest Cistercian monasteries in Castile (Alvarez Palenzuela 1978: 218), Ovila never attained the level of influence of Santa María de Huerta or the great houses to the north, nor did its later development fulfill the promise of its propitious beginnings (Manrique 1642–59, 3: 26, 181), but it was no mere cell or priory since Cistercian policy was to establish only full and self-sufficient abbeys, and it is obvious that Ovila was prospering in 1191 when Alfonso VIII confirmed its properties. The normal population of each Cistercian establishment was between twelve (the number of monks required initially) and sixty, and the abbey had to include within its precinct everything that was necessary for the monastic life (access to water, mills, ovens, workshops, farmland) and for the observance of the Rule of St. Benedict, including the appropriate books (Maur Cocheril 1964: 220, 224).

A charter of 26 June 1205 (Millares Carlo 1933: charter 4), issued at Riba near Sigüenza, is apparently the first in which the Abbot Pedro of Ovila is mentioned, his predecessor having been a certain Esteban. He also appears in charters dated 29 April 1206 and 20 December 1208, both acts of Alfonso VIII (Millares Carlo 1933: no. 5 and 6). He may also be the *abbas Petrus* mentioned in another charter that is undated (Millares Carlo 1933: no. 24); in any case he must have died or relinquished his post by 15 February 1215, as a charter of that date gives the abbot's name as Martín.

Geography and history

Ovila was situated in the Transierra oriental, almost midway between Zorita, which the *Cid* poet mentions as having been governed by Alvar Fáñez (l. 735), and Medinaceli, within whose jurisdictional boundaries it fell. Its bishopric was Sigüenza, which covered much of the area that is best known to the poet. On the east–west axis Ovila was located between Guadalajara, around which the poetic Alvar Fáñez conducts raids (446), and Molina de Aragón (867, 1463, 1476, 2647, 2880), ruled by Avengalbón (1464), the Cid's tributary (867). From 1191 it owned an estate in Padilla del Ducato (Millares Carlo 1933: no. 1), which is only seven kilometers south of Anguita near which were situated the Cuevas d'Anquita mentioned in l. 544 of the poem, and about nine kilometers southwest of the Luzón, which gives its name to the mountains that the Infantes de Carrión and the Cid's daughters cross in l. 2653 in the company of Avengalbón. Its monks would, then, have had a general interest in the poem's scenario.

Martín de Finojosa assumed his episcopal office in the same year as the transfer of the Muriel community to Ovila, and protected the new establishment during its early years. Later, on 18 August 1190, while he occupied the see of Sigüenza, a dispute between the diocese and Ovila over the payment of tithes on properties donated to the monastery was settled in a manner favorable to Ovila (Layna Serrano 1932: 85–7). It is certain that Martín kept up his contacts with Ovila during his retirement at Huerta, since he died while on the way back to Huerta from a visit to Ovila (Minguella y Arnedo 1910–12, 1: 167; Layna Serrano 1932: 90). St. Martín was thus an important link between Ovila and Huerta. It is not inconceivable that Abbot Pedro of Ovila would have made for the saintly and no doubt still influential[8] monk of Huerta a copy of a *Cantar de mio Cid*, perhaps one that had been presented before Alfonso VIII at Huerta in the year 1199 or, as is more likely, at either Huerta or Ariza in the year 1200 and taken down shortly thereafter.

The lack of a mention of either Huerta or Ovila in the poem is no obstacle for the hypothesis that it was performed at Huerta or Ariza or that it was copied at Huerta or Ovila: a poet who was intent on pleasing the monks of Huerta, or of Ovila, for that matter, could never go so far as to have the Cid visit either monastery, for the simple reason that everyone knew both Cistercian communities had only come into existence late in the twelfth century. In fact, Cîteaux itself was only founded the year before the death of Rodrigo Díaz of Vivar. On the other hand the Cid's association with Cardeña was well known by this time, and no abbot of either Huerta or Ovila was likely to object to the poet mentioning the Cid's devotion to the Virgin Mary even though he represents the material results of that devotion as benefitting the cathedrals of Santa María in Burgos and Valencia and the now less influential monastery of San Pedro de Cardeña.

Alfonso VII had transferred Cardeña to the Cluniac Order in 1142 in compensation for freeing himself from the obligation of donating two thousand *áureos* annually to the Burgundian abbey. At that point Cardeña's status fell from that of an abbey to that of a priory. Its abbot, Martín, resisted the

Cluniac takeover, leading his monks into exile and attempting to prove that his monastery needed no reforming since it was already obeying the Benedictine Rule in accordance with its Cluniac interpretation. After three and a half years of struggle, the Papacy restored the monks of Cardeña to their abbey, although in the meantime the Cluniacs had made off with the monastery's treasure.[9] A bull of 1150 established Cardeña as a direct dependency of the Holy See, with the purpose of guaranteeing it against further depredations; nevertheless the bishop of Burgos subsequently attempted more than once to give Cardeña to Cluny. San Pedro de Cardeña had entered into a period of decline, and it never regained the power it had exercised in the reign of Alfonso VI. In fact, a general characteristic of Castilian monasticism in the second half of the twelfth century is that the new establishments, such as Las Huelgas and Santa María de Huerta, become centers of influence at the expense of the older monasteries (Moreta Velayos 1971: 195–8).

A poet aiming to please an audience consisting of patrons who favored the Benedictine Order, and of Benedictines themselves as well, would perhaps be favorably inclined toward the Benedictine monastery Cardeña, and Cistercians would be even more receptive of the attitude of such a poet because of the history of Cardeña's struggle against Cluny. The rivalry between Cistercians and Cluniacs had reached its high point around the middle of the twelfth century (Alvarez Palenzuela 1978: 20), but resentment between the two Benedictine observances continued at a less acerbic level into the late twelfth century. In this regard it is noteworthy that the Cluniac who played the most important role in the Cid's life, Jérôme of Perigord, the poem's don Jerónimo, is never identified by the poet as a Cluniac.

When the Cid of the poem journeys to Toledo for the *cortes*, he and his men do not lodge in the city itself but rather stay across the Tagus in the castle of San Servando (ll. 3047, 3054, 3102), a monastic fortress that had been destroyed by the Arabs but was rebuilt by Alfonso VI, who donated it to the Holy See in 1088. San Servando was again destroyed in 1110, and when the Christians under Alvar Fáñez repulsed the Moors, Queen Urraca donated the castle to the archbishop and cathedral chapter of Toledo. Before the disaster of 1110, San Servando was inhabited by monks coming from the Benedictine abbey of St. Victor in Marseille, but those who populated it after that date were not from St. Victor (see Fita 1906: 281, 286). In the poem, the Cid passes the night at San Servando praying before the altar and consulting with Alvar Fáñez and his other men: "acordados fueron quando vino la man" (3059). They assist at the recitation of the canonical hours of matins and prime, hear mass, and make their "ofrenda ... muy buena e [a sazon]" (3062), exemplary conduct that could only have fallen well on the ears of a monastic audience which might have rejoiced as well at the fact that the hero's successful strategy in the court scene that follows was hatched in a monastic environment, perhaps inspired by Divine Providence. After mass the Cid picks the men who will accompany him, including the *sabidor* Malanda, then dresses himself in the ostentatious garb discussed in chapter 2 and rides off to the court. The Cid

Geography and history

is thus shown praying in two monasteries, Cardeña and San Servando, both Benedictine establishments.

The objection has been raised that if San Pedro de Cardeña were the monastery at which the poem was copied, one might expect the text to reflect the cult of St. Peter (see Menéndez Pidal 1954–56, 1: 39–40), whereas in fact the Cid shows a particular devotion not to the apostle of Rome but to the Virgin Mary, promising her a thousand masses at San Pedro de Cardeña, paying off the debt after the capture of Alcocer, and naming the cathedral of Valencia after her. While the poet recounts the hero's demise, he fails to mention that he was eventually buried at Cardeña, hardly a likely omission for a partisan of that monastery to make. On the other hand, like all monasteries founded by the Cistercian Order, Huerta was under Mary's patronage, as were Ovila and the cathedral church of Sigüenza.[10]

The Bishop of Sigüenza, Rodrigo, under whose jurisdiction the monasteries of Huerta and Ovila were flourishing from 1192 to 1207, had taken an active role in the war against the infidel, to the point of borrowing money to do so. Like the Cid's bishop Jerónimo and his own contemporary Martín of Pisuerga, archbishop of Toledo, he was a battling cleric. In 1208, during the first mass that a new archpriest was celebrating in the cathedral of Sigüenza, the crowd in attendance was so boisterous that Rodrigo had to strike out at it with his crozier; when one of those who were present died several months later, apparently as the result of an unnecessary surgical intervention, Rodrigo was accused of causing his death. He renounced saying mass until the Pope declared him pardoned. Rodrigo may have participated in the Battle of Alarcos and was later to play a role at Las Navas de Tolosa (González 1960, 1: 420–1).

Just as in the case of Pedro, abbot of Huerta, the points in favor of identifying Pedro, abbot of Ovila, as the scribe of the *Cid* manuscript are circumstantial. The monastery of Ovila benefitted greatly from Alfonso VIII's protection. He gave the land on which it was established and endowed it with donations. On 26 June 1205, at Riba near Sigüenza, he confirmed the donation of a certain Gil (Egidius) to the monastery of Ovila. More important than the mere fact of royal patronage, however, is the relationship of Ovila with Martín of Finojosa.

If either Abbot Pedro of Huerta or Abbot Pedro of Ovila was indeed the scribe who copied in May of 1207 a poem that had been performed in the presence of Alfonso VIII in 1199 or 1200 at Huerta or Ariza, such a copy might have been intended for the use of some patron or simply for the monks, among whom was Martín de Finojosa. One might also consider the possibility that it was designed as a gift to the most illustrious living descendant of Rodrigo of Vivar, Alfonso VIII himself. Was there an occasion on which Martín de Finojosa or either abbot might have shown or even presented the copy to him? An abbot could have visited the royal court practically at any time, of course, and in this regard one might think of an occasion such as 20 December 1208 on which Alfonso VIII made a donation to Abbot Pedro of

The *Cantar de mio Cid*

Ovila at Alfaro (González 1960, 3: no. 833). But the king traveled extensively in the Transierra oriental in the winter, summer, and autumn of 1207, on three separate trips.

No localized documents are available between 25 November 1206, when the king was at Palencia (González 1960, 3: no. 791), and 3 February 1207. On that date, however, he issued privileges at Alarcón concerning the cathedral of Santa María in Toledo (no. 792) and the *concejo* of Toledo (no. 793). Sometime during the winter of 1206–07, then, Alfonso had traveled to the south of the region with which the Cid poet appears to be most familiar. Later in February he moved northwest to Huete, 80 kilometers south-southeast of Ovila and about twice that distance from Huerta (22 February, no. 794), Guadalajara (6 March, docs. 795 and 796), and Hita (8 March, no. 797). He continued toward the north to Penilla de Atienza on 9 March (González 1960, 3: 871) and Atienza itself on 14 and 16 March (González 1960: no. 798), and then left the Transierra, doubling back on the path of the Cid's journey into exile, since the next documentation of his whereabouts is at Burgos in April (González 1960: 871). On 29 April he was still in the vicinity of Burgos at Belorado. He traveled southeast briefly again to San Esteban de Gormaz on 3 May (no. 801); on 12 May he was again in the north, at Carrión (no. 802) and from 25 May to 2 June at Burgos. Alfonso remained in the north until July, when he descended as far as Riaza (no. 809 of 20 July).

Alfonso's whereabouts are unknown until 7 September, when he was in Burgos. Again toward the end of September he traveled south, stopping at San Esteban (docs. 810, 811), Fresno de Cantespino near Sepúlveda (11 October; González 1960, 3: 872), and, on 24 and 25 October, Brihuega (González 1960, 3: 872; also no. 812). This last stop, only twenty kilometers west of the monastery of Ovila, would have offered an excellent opportunity for Pedro, abbot of Ovila, or Pedro, abbot of Huerta, for that matter, to show a manuscript of the *Cantar de mio Cid* to his king. After Brihuega, the royal court visited Guadalajara on 29 October (no. 813), and then Buitrago (no. 814), before returning north to Palencia. Alfonso's presence in the southeast is not documented again until December of the following year, when he was in Cuenca.

On 20 December 1208 Alfonso gave estates in Barajas, Palmiches, and Salmerón to Ovila in a charter localized at Alfaro (González 1960, 3: no. 833). He was again in Cuenca on 16 and 31 May of 1210, and must have passed close to Sigüenza on his way to San Esteban, where he is documented on 29 June.

Thus if a Per Abbat of Huerta or Ovila did make his copy of the poem in order to present it to the king, there would have been ample local opportunities in 1207 and 1208 to do so.

I suggest that the *Cantar de mio Cid* may have been performed at Huerta in the year 1199 or, more probably, at Huerta or Ariza in the year 1200 and then copied in May of 1207 by either Pedro, abbot of Huerta, or Pedro, abbot of Ovila, within the sphere of influence of Martín of Finojosa. Martín was a friend of Huerta's patron Alfonso VIII, great-great-grandson of Rodrigo of

Geography and history

Vivar, and no doubt also intent on pleasing another patron of the monastery, Pedro II of Aragon, one of the Cid's *parientes* as well. The kinsmen and descendants of Count Pedro de Molina and his wife the Infanta Sancha, great-granddaughter of the hero of Valencia, they too patrons of the monastery in which Martín had been abbot and in which he was a monk in the year in question,[11] would also have been potential interested parties, as would Jimeno de Rada, the descendant of two nobles named Pedro Tizón and perhaps of the Cid himself. Both Pedro de Molina and Sancha were buried at Huerta. Among their descendants was García Pérez de Lara, Martín de Finojosa's brother-in-law. Pedro de Molina's son by Mafalda, Gonzalo Pérez de Lara, who was lord of Molina in 1207 and made a donation to the monastery of Huerta along with his wife Sancha Gómez in 1238 (Romero 1966: 84), would no doubt also have been interested in the preservation of the hero's exploits on parchment, as would Pedro de Molina's sister Elvira.

This hypothesis does not necessarily affect proposals about the town or region of which the poet was a native. A poet born in or having grown up in San Esteban de Gormaz, given to praising its inhabitants as "siempre mesurados" (l. 2820), and laconically evoking local legends concerning the enigmatic "Alamos" and "Elpha" (ll. 2694–5), might well, of course, find himself in a position to sing about the Cid's exploits before distinguished visitors in the valley of the Jalón, and in that case there would be nothing strange about his combining his own loyalties with what he perceived as the interests of his audience. I consider it likely, however, that the importance accorded in the poem to San Esteban de Gormaz, "una buena çipdad" (l. 397) near which the oak-wood of Corpes is situated, is also linked to the fact that Pedro of Molina was the lord of San Esteban.

I realize the inferential nature of these proposals. Any attempt to place the poet or the scribe of the *Cantar de mio Cid* in a particular historical milieu is, however, bound to be inferential. They are intended as a contribution toward explaining, on the basis of the poet's geographical preferences and the distortions he makes in the historical record of Rodrigo Díaz of Vivar, the circumstances under which the poem was composed and preserved in writing.

7

The *Cantar de mio Cid* and the French epic tradition

The poet's place in society must be inferred from details found in the poem itself, since history has provided us with no other access to him. If the *Cantar de mio Cid* can be shown to owe something to foreign literary models, a strong case might be made that he belonged among the small number of individuals who were literate in this period of Castilian history. Foremost among hypotheses of this type is the idea that he had access to French models, which might imply also that he traveled to France. This issue thus has implications for establishing the poet's social context. It was first raised in the nineteenth century by Andrés Bello and François Génin (for a bibliography of studies see Horrent 1973) and it has come to the fore in recent years in the writings of British Hispanists. Colin Smith has defended the idea that the *Cid* poet was a learned man – schooled in Latin, able to read French – and that he resided in France for part of his life, and others have supported Smith's hypotheses with further arguments in the same direction. In this chapter I shall review the arguments of those who have perceived French influences in the *Cantar de mio Cid*, evaluating them and placing them in perspective.

Menéndez Pidal (1963: 27–8) expressed the opinion that weeping as a manifestation of grief, and in particular expressions of the type *llorar de los ojos* (cf. OFr. *plorer des eulz*), revealed imitation of the French epic in the *Cantar de mio Cid*; but the constructions could just as easily have developed in parallel fashion from Vulgar Latin. Menéndez Pidal did not think French influence was immediate, as would have been the case, for example, if a particular French work could be shown to have inspired a given passage in the Spanish text; rather he recognized in the poem "un fondo de tradición poética indígena y una forma algo renovada por la influencia francesa" (1963: 30).

In a study first published in 1953, Martín de Riquer proposed that the name of the Cid's horse, Bavieca, was derived from the French *balçan*, *bauçan*, "dapple-grey," used substantivally as a horse's name in the *chanson de geste* and specifically, as a proper noun, as the name of Guillaume d'Orange's horse. The phonological difficulties of such a derivation would be explained thus: either the Cid himself or the poet heard the word *bauçan*, used either generically or as the name of a horse, and, not comprehending, equated it with the OSp. *bavieca*, both words having the connotation "silly." Recourse to literary influence was necessitated by Riquer's (and perhaps also Menéndez Pidal's) puzzlement over the use of a seemingly pejorative designation as a

Cantar de mio Cid and the French epic tradition

hipponym, "tan improprio del corcel de un heróico guerrero y tan poco de acuerdo con los detalles que sobre este animal nos da el *Cantar del Cid*" (Riquer 1968: 227). The adjectival *bavieca*, "slobberer, drooler" and "silly, foolish" (for examples from early Spanish texts see Menéndez Pidal 1954–56, 2: 500–1) is a reflex of OSp. *bava*, "drivel, slaver, slobber" from V.L. *BABA with the same meanings (see Meyer-Lübke 1935, 67–8). In fact there is nothing strange about *bavieca* in an equine context: when a horse exerts itself it tends to slaver, a phenomenon so well known that it has become a commonplace in the iconography of cavalry warfare. The name *Bavieca*, understood as an epithet, was originally complimentary rather than pejorative, signifying that the horse is spirited, readily exerting itself in battle. The extension of the primary meaning to "silly, foolish," attested for reflexes in other Romance languages, is, of course, just as easily explained: one of the classic poses of an imbecile is to gape and drool, thus "drooler" came to signify "fool." Since an etymological solution is available, the necessity of proposing an analogical one is obviated: *Bavieca* owes nothing to the *chanson de geste*.

Roger M. Walker proposed in 1977 that it was "at least possible" that, for the scene of the *afrenta de Corpes*, the *Cid* poet was inspired by an episode found in the early thirteenth-century *chanson de geste* entitled *Florence de Rome*. The eponymous heroine of the French work is married to Esmeré, Emperor of Rome. While Esmeré is absent his brother Milon tries to take over the empire. After a series of events in which Florence and Esmeré triumph over their treacherous kinsman, Milon manages to spirit Florence away on the pretext that her husband has sent him to fetch her. Once he has managed to transport Florence into the forest, he attempts rape, unsuccessfully, but first is forced to kill an attacking lion and murders a hermit who lives in the forest. Walker sees a series of parallels between the plots of the French and Spanish works that he treats under seven rubrics.

Preparations for the assault In each case the assault is planned in advance. The Cid's daughters are married to their assailants, however, and the pretext that they are to be taken to Carrión, their husbands' ancestral home, is perfectly plausible. Milon, on the other hand, has shown himself to be aggressively perfidious, and Florence's naiveté in believing him lacks verisimilitude. In order to get Elvira and Sol away from the rest of their entourage, the Infantes send their followers on ahead, while Milon gallops along with Florence faster than those accompanying them. In *Florence de Rome* the heroine expresses at this point in the tale her apprehension at Milon's actions. This is not the case with Elvira and Sol, however. Walker downplays this difference by stating that "the Cid's daughters must feel a similar apprehension," but the poem is, after all, a work of imaginative fiction and, whatever one thinks would be a plausible effect in such a situation if it were to occur in real life, the critic can only perceive that the poet does not have the two women express any fear at being alone with their husbands at this point in the journey.

The *Cantar de mio Cid*

Setting for the assault   In both poems the forests in which the assaults take place are characterized, according to Walker, as "terrifying" but he only cites in *Florence* lines that describe the forest's dimensions and depth and in the *Cid* a line that emphasizes the tree-covered mountains' height. In fact in *Florence* the scene does not take place in a mountainous terrain at all. Wild beasts figure in both settings, it is true, but in entirely different capacities: in the *Cid* one is merely *told* that after the attack the Infantes leave their victims at the mercy of mountain birds and fierce beasts, but the animals do not materialize; in *Florence*, on the other hand, a lion – and, in one of the three manuscripts, a serpent – attacks Milon and he is frightened by the appearance of two monkeys. Among the myriad differences between the two scenes, the fact that in *Florence* the beasts are threatening to the aggressor rather than to the victim is of capital significance; it will also be noted that none of the animals is common to the two poems. Walker claims that in each the setting is "a kind of *locus amoenus*," and I agree, but the commonplace nature of the two milieus is all that they share: in *Florence* the action takes place in a meadow, in the *Cid* in a forest glade.

Reasons for the assault   Milon intends to rape Florence because he has been humiliated by being beaten and sent into exile, but he is prevented from succeeding by a magic stone that the lady wears on a fastener attached to her cloak. The Infantes have also been shamed, but not punished; it must be pointed out too that, unlike Florence, the Cid's daughters have played no direct role in inflicting humiliation on their assailants. Prior to the attacks, the villains undertake to murder characters who have shown them hospitality, but while Milon *acts* on his impulse, the Infantes are prevented from killing Avengalvón by the discovery of their intention. Walker asserts that in both poems the assaults have "strong overtones of sexual perversion." While this might be true for *Florence de Rome*, there is no evidence in the *Cantar de mio Cid* to support it. In fact line 2703, referring to the night before the assault, reads: "Con sus mugieres en braços demuestran les amor." Since the poet certainly did not expect his audience to understand that the duplicitous pair actually loved their wives, the reference is most likely to sexual activity. Walker's suggestion that the Infantes are meant to be taken as impotent and that the assault was "for the purpose of arousing and satisfying their perverted sexual desire" is thus misplaced.

Behavior of the victims   Both Florence and the Cid's daughters plead with their tormentors to decapitate them rather than submit them to further indignities, and both insist that the aggressors will not escape punishment for their crimes. But surely these are psychological commonplaces, not just in the Middle Ages but in narratives from all periods of European literature. The study by John K. Walsh (1970–71), for example, to which Walker refers, demonstrates effectively that the request to be killed is a standard motif of saints' lives.

Behavior of the villains   Milon and the Infantes beat their victims, but while the Castilians use cinches, the French traitor cuts a thorny branch from a nearby tree. The villains all use their feet, but while Milon kicks Florence, the Infantes dig their spurs into Elvira's and Sol's flesh. It is true that Milon, in a prior passage, threatened to use his spurs on Florence, but such a threat is hardly so implausible as to make one assume the poet had recourse to a literary source, any more than is the "unreasoning and unreasonable violence" of the attackers. Milon is prevented from killing Florence by the approach of her rescuer, Thierri, and his dogs; unlike the Infantes he does not leave his victim for dead.

Aftermath of the assault Walker claims that the descriptions of the victims' battered bodies and torn clothing are similar in the two texts. As a matter of fact, however, the only details of either type concern flesh and blood: the *Cantar de mio Cid* does not mention "flanks" or "sides" or "purple silk cloth" in this scene as does *Florence de Rome*, nor does the latter text include shifts or mantels as does the *Cid*. The reader can judge the degree of resemblance between the sets of lines in question:

> Par flans et par coustez l'a tant forment foulee
> Que sa blanche char fu trestote ensanglantee
> Et la poipre de soie deroute et desiree ...
> Sa blanche char en fu sanglante et derompue;
> Le sanc vermeil en chiet desus l'erbe menue.
> (*FR* 4097–9, 4127–8)

> Ronpien las camisas e las carnes   a ellas amas a dos;
> linpia salie la sangre   sobre las çiclatones ...
> Tanto las majaron   que sin cosimente son,
> sangrientes en las camisas   e todos los çiclatones.
> (*CMC* 2738–9, 2743–4)

It is not as if the Spanish counterparts of the words used in the two French passages did not exist: if the *Cid* poet were borrowing from the French, he could have used those words. In fact the descriptions share nothing except the most commonplace of elements in a passage of this type, for which a poet need have recourse only to the experience of everyday life, namely references to flesh and blood.

Rescue and recovery Florence is spared because of the chance arrival of a certain Thierry who takes Milon and her to his castle, the name of which, Chatel Perdu, is redolent of fantasy; the Cid's daughters are saved by Félez Muñoz, who goes looking for them and takes them to the town of San Esteban de Gormaz, where Diego Téllez cares for them. Walker, following a suggestion of Colin Smith, maintains an "undeniable similarity" between "Thierry" and "Téllez." To start with, however, "Thierry" is a baptismal name, "Téllez" a patronymic. But even if one uses the form "Tierriz," as is admissible, the orthographic resemblance between the two names is confined to the first and last letters. Furthermore they are accented on different syllables, and I do not have to insist on the role of the accent in linguistic correspondences. Finally, the Cid's daughters are not rescued by Diego Téllez, but by Félez

Muñoz: Diego only saw them after they arrived in San Esteban under Félez's protection. One could no doubt change the proposition and claim that "Thierry" resembles "Félez," but in fact neither the name "Thierry" nor the role he plays have their counterparts in the *Cantar de mio Cid*. Walker's further contention that in both poems the women recover quickly, with no mention of scars, raises yet another banal parallel for which he gives an alternate explanation in citing Walsh's hypothesis (1970–71) to the effect that this detail recalls similar events in hagiographic literature.

In summary, the episode of the abduction and beating of the heroine in *Florence de Rome* differs from the *afrenta de Corpes* in essential ways, while resembling it in banal and superficial details which the poet not only could have, but is quite likely to have, derived from observations within the ambit of his own experience or from thematic conventions of the hagiographic tradition (Walsh, 1970–71; Nepaulsingh 1983).

What is at stake here is not merely the issue of literary influences at work on the *Cid* poet, but the very nature of literary resemblances. In order to posit influence, one needs more than simply a set of superficial traits: the details in question must be couched in language that is beyond a reasonable doubt similar in vocabulary or in peculiarities of expression or in unusual thematic collocations. This problem surfaces constantly in literary studies, and must be dealt with time and again. In this case the proposition can be shown to be groundless, on the basis of internal evidence alone.

The external evidence that Walker presents has been examined by Alan Deyermond and David Hook (1981–82), who conclude that the assertion that the *Florence de Rome* now extant in *chanson de geste* form could have been composed prior to the *Cantar de mio Cid* is highly dubious and that the earlier version of *Florence*, referred to in *La Naissance du Chevalier au cygne* (Elioxe version) and thus chronologically acceptable for Walker's argument, was in all likelihood sufficiently different from the extant version as to weaken seriously any possible conclusions of influence. In fact, *Florence de Rome* was probably composed after 1207, the latest date one can plausibly posit for the Spanish poem's composition. Smith's riposte to the effect that a lost version of *Florence* may have been available to the *Cid* poet (1983: 163) is insufficient because we have no indication of what that version contained.

Deyermond and Hook also point out parallels between the *Cantar de mio Cid* and the tale of Procne, Tereus, and Philomela as told in Ovid's *Metamorphoses*, concluding that the details in question in both *Florence* and the Spanish epic "are to be situated within a tradition which had already produced a literary manifestation in Ovid" (1981–82: 26).

In his treatment of the relationship between the French epic and the *Cantar de mio Cid* Colin Smith considers Walker's conclusions to be convincing (1977: 127), and articulates a proposition only implicit in Walker's final paragraph: that the *Cid* poet (whom Smith takes to be Per Abbat) was able to read French. He could also read Latin and in fact used Latin sources, according to Smith, a hypothesis based on a theory of literary resemblance

Cantar de mio Cid and the French epic tradition

similar to Walker's and no more solidly grounded that his (see Chalon 1978 and the reply in Smith 1983: 151–2).

As indicated above, *Florence de Rome* was probably composed in its extant form after the *Cantar de mio Cid* that we have in the Per Abbat manuscript; nevertheless one should examine Smith's claim that additional passages show influence from *Florence* because it has a bearing on the theoretical issue alluded to above, the nature of cogent literary resemblances.

The alleged likenesses are of three types: uses of a particular word or phrase, of a motif, and of a scene. The words and phrases are:

çendales d'Andria, *CMC* 1971	cendaus d'Andre, *FR* 451
cavallos en diestro, *CMC* 2010, 2573	cheval en destre, *FR* 169
espessa, *CMC* 1615	espesse, *FR* 3676
romanz, *CMC* colophon	romanz, *FR* 20, 3312

The silk cloth known as *cendal d'Andre* is mentioned in a number of *chansons de geste*, only one of which is likely to be anterior to 1207, namely *Fouque de Candie*. It also figures in *Florence de Rome*. But is the mention of a term in two works sufficient to argue influence? If it were, influence studies might as well be written off because one would soon be faced with an impossibly intricate network of connections characterized by innumerable inconsequences and contradictions. What one needs is a set of criteria by which to discriminate the significant from the aleatory. A striking or unusual formal parallel might lead one to consider that the later of two poems was influenced by the earlier, provided of course that the prior work was accessible. Smith writes that he has perceived a "parecido estructural...muy notable" between "de pennes et de drais, de riches cendaus d'Andre" (*FR*) and "mantos e pielles e buenos çendales d'Andria" (*CMC*). *Drais*, Central French *dras*, is a general term for textiles, and *penne* is a silk material with long fibers. Neither corresponds to *mantos* or to *pielles*. The Spanish terms are objects of the verb *vio* occurring five lines previously, whereas the French nouns belong to prepositional phrases that are attributes of *avoir* used substantivally in the preceding line. The expressions in question, *cendaus d'Andre/çendales d'Andria*, occupy the same syntactic niches in the second hemistich positions: in the French the phrase is modified by "riches," but the Castilian poet has employed "buenos" rather than the ready Spanish counterpart of that word. The "very noteworthy structural resemblance" is thus reduced to this and only this: the two phrases occur in the same position in their respective lines. That is to say that there is no reason whatsoever to think that the expression found in the *Cantar de mio Cid* is based on, or was influenced in any way by, the phrase from *Florence de Rome*. Although Deyermond and Hook (1981–82) refuted this "parallel," on the basis of other arguments, Smith has continued to insist on a "structural similarity" (1983: 238). Even if one were to consent to the parallel, it would not remain likely that Per Abbat drew on *Florence* for other materials, as Smith asserts on poor methodological grounds.

The other signs of influence that Smith perceives are similarly unconvincing. The line "riche cheval en destre de Sulie ou d'Espaigne," *FR* 169 bears no more of a "noteworthy structural resemblance" to "e buen cavallo en diestro que va ante sus armas," *CMC* 1548 than was forthcoming in the previous comparison. The occurrence of single words, such as "espessa" or "romanz," in the two works is so trivial – in the absence of any corroborating evidence – as to require only a denial as gratuitous as the original affirmation that they are evidence of borrowing. Likewise it should be obvious that, contrary to Smith's judgment, "que donc veïst abatre et paveillons et trez," *FR* 2529 and "tanta cuerda de tienda i veriedes quebrar,/ arancar se las estacas e acostar a todas partes los tendales," *CMC* 1141–2 have nothing in common lexically except the main verb, which is not even in the same form. The grounds for Smith's remark, "Aquí sorprendemos a Per Abad casi con la pluma en la mano" (1977: 133), are difficult to perceive. In the light of all these non-correspondences the fact that Jimena, like Florence de Rome, views the spectacle of an enemy army from a window and has to be reassured by her husband (1977: 133; 1983: 163) is of no consequence whatsoever for the question of influence.

These deviations from what reasonable observers take to be the criteria of resemblance do not augur well for Smith's further investigations into the relationship between the *Cantar de mio Cid* and the *chanson de geste*. He has identified as influential certain passages, above all from the *Chanson de Roland*, Oxford version, but also from *Berte aus grans piés*, *Girart de Roussillon*, *La Prise de Cordres et de Sebille*, and *La Chevalerie Ogier*. As one might expect, all of the comparisons are of the same nature as the parallels put forward between the *Cantar de mio Cid* and *Florence*, although here at least the relative chronology does not vitiate Smith's efforts in advance.

No one would deny that the phrase "adtores mudados," *CMC* 5, is similar to "hosturs müers," *Chanson de Roland* 31, 129, 184, but molted hawks, more reliable than those which had not yet undergone the process of shedding their first feathers, were widely prized for hunting. Why should one posit that a poet who had access to the concept of "molted hawk" in his own ambiance would need to undergo literary influence from a trans-Pyrenean work in order to include such a phrase in his own composition? The same argument applies to the ideas, all invoked by Smith apropos of the *Chanson de Roland*, of pursuing the enemy to a city, kissing on the mouth as a form of greeting, calling the sea salty, dismounting from horseback, referring to vassal and lord in the same line or to a character's alacrity, describing a hero or king, or saying that he is manly. I use the word "ideas" with hesitation, for nothing in these *rapprochements* would lead an objective reader to admit a significant verbal correspondence when only individual and quite predictable words or common expressions are in question.

That drums should be played in preparation for or during battle is viewed by specialists in French epic as a sign of influence from Iberian life, and the presence of this detail in the *Roland* (l. 3137) is considered proof that the

Oxford version must have been composed after 1086 when at the Battle of Sagrajas the sound of Moorish drums contributed to the defeat of Alfonso VI's forces (Riquer 1957: 75f). The Spanish poet would have had no need to leave his own milieu in order to pick up such a typically Iberian detail for *CMC* 696 and 1658.[1] The "cierto parecido" between the enumeration of the Cid's conquests and movements in *CMC* 1087–93 and Roland's recalling of the victories he has accomplished for Charlemagne in *CR* 197–200 is barely perceptible, reduced as it is to the words for "lands" and "to conquer." Enumeration of conquests is hardly unusual in epics, and the absence of those words in such a passage would perhaps be more worthy of remark than their presence. That the Cid's followers should be referred to as having pulled out tufts from the captive García Ordóñez's beard need owe nothing to the scene in which Charlemagne's kitchen boys remove Ganelon's beard and mustache, since mutilation of an enemy's facial hair was an established way to convey disdain in Spain as well as north of the Pyrenees (see Menéndez Pidal 1954–56, vol. 2, s.v. "barba"). Finally, does Smith really expect his readers to believe that the three enumerations of a list of the Cid's captains owes anything to the three evocations of the Twelve Peers in the *Roland*? If such obviously aleatory "counterparts" are to be considered worthy of mention, to what exiguous dimensions is the role of chance to be reduced? Smith admits (1983: 165) that the absence of verbal parallels between the Cid's dressing and Charlemagne's or Baligant's arming does not deter him (the single supposed verbal parallel Smith invokes is not one at all).

One can only conclude that if a gleaning of the texts turned up such a negligible harvest of correspondences, the two poems must belong to remarkably independent literary traditions and the *Cid* poet owes little to the Oxford *Roland*.[2]

Smith claims to have found two passages in Adenet le Roi's *Berte aus grans piés* that point to possible French models for the *Cid* poet. In the first passage, Peppin, at court, kills with a spear a lion that has escaped from his cage and caused Charles Martel and his wife to flee; the famous lion episode of the *Cantar de mio Cid* shows the hero, unarmed, leading an escaped lion back to his cage while the Infantes de Carrión cower. Obviously killing a lion and pacifying one are not the same: if the *Cid* poet was influenced by an early version of *Berte aus grans piés*, then why did he not have the Cid kill the lion?

In addition, insuperable problems of chronology mar Smith's hypothesis. He admits that Adenet le Roi's *Berte*, in which the lion episode occurs, could not be the source in question, since it dates from the late thirteenth century (between 1274 and 1278), but he conjectures that an earlier version that would have given rise to a summary found in the *Chronique saintongeaise* might have furnished the scene to the *Cid* poet. The trouble is that the lion episode is not in the *Chronique saintongeaise* (Bourdillon 1897: 53–5; Henry 1963: 34–5). While this does not by itself mean the passage must have been absent from the chronicle's source, the various versions of the *Berte* legend differ so widely that it is impossible to say what any given lost version contained. Smith takes pride in working "in a positivist spirit" (1983: 1) but in spite of having taken a hypersceptical stance toward lost versions of Castilian epics whose plots have survived in chronicle form, he has recourse in this instance to a lost French epic concerning an episode for the existence of which, in that lost version, there is no evidence.[3]

While the parallels between the *Cantar de mio Cid* and *Berte aus grans piés* are at least sufficient to be taken into serious consideration,[4] in the absence of evidence for the lion episode in an early French *Berte* that would have been available to the Spanish poet one is prevented from concluding that the supposed source, if indeed it was a work about Berte, was in French. There are other possibilities. Smith mentions that the earliest known version of Peppin's encounter with the lion is found in the Monk of St. Gall, whose account is "of the kind which one might reasonably expect to find in a medieval monastic library" in Spain (Smith 1976: 523; 1977: 140). In the anecdote told by the Monk, Peppin kills a lion and a bull in order to prove to his men that he was brave enough to be a good king. In addition, according to Serlo of Wilton (d. 1181), a poem composed by a certain Robert about *pedem Berte* was circulating in the twelfth century. The *Gran conquista de Ultramar* includes the story of Berte and Peppin, and there is a fourteenth-century Catalan version (Elliott 1980–81), suggesting the possibility of earlier Peninsular sources. Most decisively, however, the lion episode is not integral to the legend of Berte: it occurs in Adenet at the beginning of *Berte aus grans piés*, before the heroine is introduced into the tale, and Adenet himself recognizes its peripheral value when he writes immediately afterward:

> En cesti ci matere ne vueil plus demorer,
> Parmi la vraie estoire m'en vorrai tost aler.   (ll. 81–2)

These considerations render the hypothesis of a French source for the lion episode not merely tenuous but unverifiable and, ultimately, otiose.

In that light the claim Smith makes to the effect that the scene in which Jimena looks out from the *alcázar* of Valencia (ll. 1610–17) is based on the famous view of Paris as seen through the eyes of Berte in Adenet's poem (ll. 1959–75) is dubious. Smith tells us that "los especialistas parecen no dudar que figuraba un panorama de París en el lugar correspondiente de la *chanson de Berte perdida*," but a statement about the lack of doubt concerning a lost plot is hardly acceptable as convincing evidence. Even if it were, however, why would the *Cid* poet need the *Berte* passage, with its enumeration of nine toponyms associated with Paris, on which to base his short and undetailed scene of the viewing of Valencia when he only had to have recourse to his own experience – not of seeing Valencia in particular but of looking out from a tower over any town? The same remark applies, *mutatis mutandis*, to the passages from *Girart de Roussillon*, *Amis et Amile*, *La Prise de Cordres et de Sebille*, and *La Chevalerie Ogier de Danemarche*. For Smith's reasoning (1977: 142–6) to be valid, the Spanish poet would have had to be so deficient in imagination that he would have needed inspiration from *chansons de geste* in order to describe how a character is dressed, how he tells his men to prepare for battle, and other banalities of noble life.⁵ The Spanish poet would not even have realized that he could divide his poem into parts without basing himself on French models (1977: 151–4): they too are divided into parts.

The conception of literary creation underlying Smith's hypotheses about the possible filiation of words, lines, and episodes in the *Cantar de mio Cid* is unworthy of the text, which is, after all, one of the major literary works of the Middle Ages. One would naturally then expect that the poet would not be so utterly lacking in imagination as to have to seek out in foreign models the means of expressing simple notions whose *signifiés* were present all around him. It is with all the greater surprise, then, that one reads, in "Further French Analogues and Sources for the *Poema de mio Cid*," an article that Smith published in the same year in which his *Estudios cidianos* appeared, the opinion that "oralist and traditionalist approaches ... virtually exclude the possibility of learned written sources and diminish the role of the individual poet-creator" (1977–78: 14). On the contrary, if a writing poet had been forced to carry the burden of the mechanistic and depreciatory theory of poetic talent that Smith's hypotheses entail, his reputation as a creator would indeed be tainted. In addition Smith seems to be laboring under the false impression that all traditionalists and oralists share the same idea of the oral poet's creativity. In any case, the mode of composition affects the types of creativity available to the poet, but not the quality of his creativity.

The supplementary hypotheses contained in this second study are of the same nature as those Smith advances in his *Estudios*. The most banal phrases are taken as highly significant: "una buena çipdad" (*CMC* 397), as the laudatory epithet for a town, would derive from "une bone cité" in *Parise la duchesse* (787, 793), for example, as if such an obvious and innocuous phrase could not have occurred independently to two poets working in cognate languages. In the same French poem the collocation "li traitres provez" (ll. 432, 442) is said to be the model for "traidor provado" (*CMC* 2523). This is an instructive example, for Smith admits that an explanation for the phrase as a legal formula is available in Peninsular materials, noting, after Menéndez Pidal, that it occurs in the *Poema de Fernán González* and the *Fuero de Navarra*; but, says he, "I think the *Cantar de mio Cid* usage a literary imitation from French rather than a native term from legal phraseology" (1977–78: 17). Nevertheless the simpler of the two explanations is preferable because it does not necessitate either the supposition of influence, which is the point at issue, or the construction of what I believe to be a debilitating theory of poetic creation.

Jimena's prayer (*CMC* 330–65) bears certain resemblances to the "epic prayer," also called the "epic credo" or "prayer of greatest peril," that is so common in the *chanson de geste*. As in the case of the lion episode, the parallels in this instance are at least close enough to deserve scrutiny, and other critics, notably J. Gimeno Casalduero (1975, first published 1957–58) and Menéndez Pidal (1963: 25–7) have expatiated on them (see also Gerli 1980).

The *Cantar de mio Cid*

The motif of the "epic prayer" varies widely from poem to poem in the French corpus, but the basic schema is this: a character, usually in a moment of great danger or heightened emotion, prays to God that he or she be saved from peril just as figures of sacred history were delivered in their moments of need. Among those whose examples are invoked one of the most common is Longinus.

The Longinus element in Jimena's prayer is one for which Smith posits French influence (1977–78: 14–15). Now one will concede, I think, that the legend of Longinus would be robbed of its essence if the person telling it were to omit that the centurion was blind, that he struck Christ with his lance, that the blood ran down the lance to his hands, that he rubbed his eyes with the bloody hands, that his sight was restored, and that he converted to Christianity. But these are precisely the elements that Smith picks out as having been imitated from "French sources," namely *Fierabras* and *Parise la duchesse*. In fact the Longinus legend is found in so many *chansons de geste* not because each succeeding author read it in the work of the previous author, but because it was a stable element in the stylized motif of the "epic prayer," an element that audiences expected to hear and that poets included regularly in their technical repertoires. They could not mention the miracle of Longinus in any detail without summoning up the words for "blind" or "lance" or "side" or "blood" or "hands," and one is only justified in positing the influence of one text on another when the motif is actualized in both texts through a rare combination of words, or expanded in unusual ways. Such is definitely not the case with Jimena's prayer and the alleged French sources, which, for the legend of Longinus, only share the essential vocabulary. Subsequently (1983: 160) Smith proposed that Jimena's prayer might be based on that of the character Aalais in *Raoul de Cambrai*, since each is uttered in an abbey church, but the circumstance of praying in such surroundings is so natural that it cannot be considered valid grounds upon which to base a proof of influence.

Smith's discussion of another element in the prayer that he identifies as deriving from a French source, the names of the three magi as mentioned in *CMC* 337, is confused. The names appear, with only a minor modification (Gaspar instead of the *Cantar de mio Cid*'s Caspar), in the twelfth-century *Auto de los reyes magos*, but Smith thinks it unlikely that the *Cid* poet knew that work. The point is, however, that the play shows that the names were available in Spain in the late twelfth century. The fact that Jimena calls the incense given as a gift to Christ *tus* rather than using some form of *acenso* as in the *Reyes magos* has no bearing on the matter, since *tus* is the word used in the Vulgate version of Matthew's gospel and would thus have been available to any Christian inhabitant of Spain in the Middle Ages. These conclusions should be related to those of Gimeno Casalduero (1975), who holds that while the presence of the "epic prayer" in the poem may be assignable to a general climate of French influence, Jimena's prayer is of a form that, along with other prayers of the same type found in Spanish and Portuguese texts, derives from a prayer attributed to St. Cyprian in the early centuries of Christianity that was well known in the Iberian Peninsula. For Gimeno Casalduero this opens the possibility that the prayer entered Castilian literature through popular and native channels (1975: 28). P. E. Russell leans toward the hypothesis that the poet's memories of the liturgy enabled him to create a form of prayer that was new but at the same time suggestive of authentic prayers (1978: 153).

Smith makes the hypothesis that the poet draws on French models one of the centerpieces of his 1983 book *The Making of the Poema de mio Cid*, taking up again a supposed parallel with *La Chevalerie d'Ogier le Danois*. Menéndez Pidal and others postulated, correctly in my opinion, that the story of the Cid's journey on behalf of Alfonso to collect tribute from the king of Seville had originally begun the poem as it was found in the complete fourteenth-century manuscript. As the story is reconstructed from chronicles, Count García Ordóñez, in league with the king of Cordoba, attacked Seville while the Cid was still there and was captured by the hero, who humiliated him by pulling out tufts of his beard. "By a strange coincidence," Smith writes, "*La Chevalerie d'Ogier* began in much the same way." In that poem Charlemagne dispatches four knights to collect tribute from Gaufrois, king of Denmark; when they return he sees that Gaufrois has insulted them by shaving their heads and faces, and determines to avenge himself on the Danish king's son, Ogier, who is a hostage at his court. In the Spanish prosifications of the *Cantar de mio Cid*, it is the protagonist himself who is sent to collect tribute; in the *chanson de geste*, Charlemagne sends four messengers whom the text does not even deign to name. In the Spanish the king's envoy insults an ally of the enemy; in *Ogier* the king's envoys are themselves insulted. In short, while it is a matter of tribute and insults involving the cutting or pulling of hair in both poems, the situations are reversed and all the details are different. Such dissimilar treatments cannot serve as evidence for imitation, but Smith has given us another example of what he considers to be narratives beginning "in much the same way."

In the category of gratuitous false parallels fall Charlemagne's pursuit of Ogier le Danois (apropos of the Cid's pursuit of Búcar), the mistreatment that Parise la duchesse suffers while in her shift and her plea to be decapitated (same for the Cid's daughters), a duel in *Parise la duchesse* ("having a general air of similarity to some aspects of duels in the *Poema*"), the phrase used in the same poem to admit defeat (1983: 163–5), and the uncle–nephew relationship in the *Chanson de Roland* (supposedly analogous to the relationship between the Cid and Alvar Fáñez).[6]

The positing of influence is a delicate matter, not to be undertaken in the absence of well-defined principles. The most obvious of these is, of course, that the source must precede the target text and, as in other matters of literary history, dating should be established beyond a reasonable doubt. Recourse to lost versions of existing works is at best undesirable, at worst unacceptable when one is treating details that are minor or peripheral to the main plot. Parallels that can be accounted for in the normal course of human experience as the author might be presumed to have lived it should be avoided, taking into consideration, naturally, the limitations of time and ambiance: one does not have to consult Virgil to know that the sun rises in the east. Expressions and combinations that are out of the ordinary carry far greater weight than those that may derive from common linguistic origins or cognate poetic traditions. In cases in which the resemblances involve formulas, David Hook has commented wisely:

> Unless we are dealing with a formula found in only one French text from the entire French epic tradition in existence at the time of the composition of the *PMC*, or unless one particular French version is marked by some peculiarity common only to it and the *PMC*, there can be no question of identifying specific sources for formulae in the Spanish poem ... Even where a single French text contains a large number of formulaic parallels for the *PMC*, this does not constitute proof that the Spanish poet knew that text. (1982: 108)

Finally, the occurrence of words and expressions whose presence is to be expected in any treatment of the subject at hand is without import for source studies.

Certain points of resemblance between the Spanish epic and the *chanson de geste* can be posited with greater validity. The most obvious, of course, is that both the *cantares de gesta* and the *chansons de geste* are organized in strophes of varying length whose unifying principle is assonance. This similarity could well derive from a common origin shared by the two bodies of epic.

Another is the enumeration of a series of actions on the battlefield – governed by the verb "to see" and introduced by the indefinite adjective *tanto* or *tant* – that are carried out by the commonality of the combatants. This stylistic device is also found in the *romancero* and in the *Mocedades de Rodrigo* and is extremely common in the *chanson de geste*. Horrent (1956) points out that its use in the *Cantar de mio Cid* is somewhat different from its function in the *Roland*, but such stylistic adaptation would not be surprising. Note that I refer here to the stylistic device rather than to any particular example of it.

Another point of contact is the "epic prayer." While the details of Jimena's prayer that are not simply assignable to similarity of theme differ from those one finds in the *chanson de geste* (see Gimeno Casalduero 1975; Russell 1978), the existence of the motif of the "epic prayer," of similar configuration in the two bodies of poetry, may be indicative of a literary relationship of some kind.

In an article marked by critical acumen, Michael Herslund (1974) deploys various types of stylistic device that are shared by the *chanson de geste* and the *cantar de gesta*: the introduction of a new character through the epideictic particle (*ez*, *afé*); description of battle by means of the verb "to see" (*la veissiez*, *veriedes*; *qui donc veist*, *quién vido*); introduction of new material by a form of the verb "to hear" (*orrez*, *odredes*); change of topic through verbs signifying "to cease, leave off" and "to speak" or "to sing" (*lairons* ... *dirons*; *dexémonos* ... *fablemos*); omission of an element of plot signaled by the verb

Cantar de mio Cid and the French epic tradition

"to recount" (*ne sai compte tenir, non quiero contar*); invocation of God's name in exclamations; segmentation of the performance into parts for ease of presentation; division of the narrative into strophes of unequal length (*laisses* or *tiradas*); verbal echoes in the linking of successive strophes (Rychner's *enchaînement*: 1955); parallel constructions in succeeding strophes; lines of intonation and conclusion to define the topic of the strophe; parataxis; repetition of lines in the relaying of messages; motifs for the attack with lance or sword, the description of armed knights, wealth, and horses, the journey, joy, pain, separation, the "epic prayer," the priest's prayer before battle, and the assembling of troops; formulas for actions accomplished in haste, the passage of time, the depiction of a leader with his followers, the praise of heroes, willingness to act, rising to one's feet, weeping, and comparisons; binomial formulas; and both simple and developed epithets for persons, places, horses, arms, eyes, and battle. Herslund also gives examples of lexical similarities between the two bodies of texts (1974: 115–17). These resemblances, which fall under the categories of jongleur's interventions, the composition of and relationship between strophic divisions, the structuring of narrative, and linguistic and rhetorical expressivity lead Herslund to conclude not that the Spanish epic was influenced by the French on a text-to-text basis, but rather that the Spanish singers learned the *art* of jongleresque composition and performance from French jongleurs (1974: 72).

Herslund's case for similarity of technique is convincing. But to conclude that one body of literature resembles another does not settle the problem of directionality. Herslund lays out the possibilities early on in his treatment: (1) the French and Spanish epics have a common (Germanic?) ancestor; (2) French jongleurs learned from their Spanish counterparts; (3) the identity of technique is fortuitous, deriving from resemblances perceivable in any oral literature; (4) the Spanish learned their art from the French. In the absence of evidence for directionality, when one perceives parallels in two medieval literary works the natural tendency is to think that, if one of them is in Latin and the other in a Romance language, the Latin must have influenced the Romance. A classic case of this type is the eleventh-century Occitanian "contrafactum" from St. Martial de Limoges, "Mei amic e mei fiel," which was always assumed to be based on its Latin counterpart until Peter Dronke showed that the reverse was true. If Spanish and French are involved, one inclines to speculate, in the absence of other evidence, that the French influenced the Spanish. Even David Hook, whose approach to source studies is enlightened by well-articulated principles, assumes without argument that the direction of influence is French to Spanish (1982: 108). In the case of both Latin and French, the presumption derives from the enormous cultural prestige and chronological precedence of those literatures in the Middle Ages, but in individual instances the direction of influence might be from the Spanish to the French or the Latin.

Jules Horrent (1956) points to three unusual and specific elements shared by the *Cantar de mio Cid* and the Oxford *Roland*. In both poems the fleeing enemy drowns in a river (*CR* 2465–74, *CMC* 1229), the protagonist's nephew is called his "right arm" (*CR* 1195, *CMC* 753, 810), and the angel Gabriel announces the future by means of a dream (*CR* 2529–69; *CMC* 405–9; Smith also adduces this similarity [1983: 161]). In this final instance, Horrent notes that the role of Gabriel in the Gospels could explain his appearance in both epics, but of the French and Spanish works in which Gabriel plays a role only in the *Roland* and the *Cid* does he appear in a dream.

Three considerations condition any conclusion concerning influence. The first is that even when one takes into account the broad similarities enumerated by Herslund and the techniques and passages cited by Menéndez Pidal and Horrent, the *Cantar de mio Cid* is still quite different from each of the more than one hundred *chansons de geste* whose texts we have. The second is that the differences in detail that come to the fore in the examination of Smith's claims make it unlikely that a text-to-text influence was operative in the period in which the extant written evidence was copied. The third is that no hard evidence for the directionality of influence is available. In that light the wisest course, it seems to me, is to posit that contact between the two bodies of epic took place well before the end of the twelfth century: either the corpus of epic in both languages derives from a common source or influence took place early enough that the *chanson de geste* and the *cantar de gesta* were able to develop into genres with discrete qualities by the period in which the extant texts were written down.

This opinion should not be taken to imply assent to a belief shared by Smith that "there is no reason to postulate a Spanish version of the *Roland* ... [in the early thirteenth century]" (1983: 157). In fact, unlike the case for the lost *Florence de Rome* or for the lion episode in the lost pre-Adenet version of *Berte aus grans piés*, there are very good reasons to think that a *Roland* in Spanish circulated before 1207 and in fact as early as the eleventh century. The *Nota Emilianense* (Alonso 1953), dated to before 1086 (Gonzalo Menéndez Pidal 1958), summarizes a poetic *Roland* composed in Spanish, as is shown by the forms of proper names and the fact that they are provided with the paragogic *-e* peculiar to the tradition of Castilian epic (see also R. Menéndez Pidal 1960: 412–13). This form of the *Roland* was probably known to the author of the *Poema de Almería* in the mid-twelfth century.

Some of the features for which I am willing to grant the possibility of French influence are present, although always in a different form, in the Oxford *Roland*. We know nothing, however, about the details passed on in the Spanish *Roland* tradition as the *Cid* poet might have known it, since the *Nota Emilianense* and the reference in the *Poema de Almería* inform us only about general characteristics, and certainly do not tell us enough to say whether it contained an assortment of elements potentially significant for the question of influence. But there is nothing in the *Cantar de mio Cid* to justify the opinion that its poet knew French, much less that he visited France, and least of all that he resided there for a substantial period of time or was a student there.

Cantar de mio Cid and the French epic tradition

The *cantares de gesta* and the *chansons de geste* are cognate genres, sharing certain features of technique. In both, heroic ideals are portrayed, although again for distinct purposes and by different means (see chapters 3 and 4). The two corpuses were, however, as far as we can tell from the surviving texts, quite different in character. So different were they from one another, in fact, that the resemblances – most of which are on the level of general characteristics and stylistic devices – suggest a link long enough before the early thirteenth century as to allow ample time for the processes of generic individuation to produce the discrete qualities that mark the extant poems. The *Nota Emilianense*, with its summary of a French epic subject in Castilian dress, allows us to date the link at least as far back as the last quarter of the eleventh century, but the differences between the genres are so great, in my opinion, that the connection must go back to a much earlier period. What little the two bodies of epic share seems likely to have derived largely from a common origin, although incidental direct influences are not to be excluded entirely since Spanish audiences and *juglares* were obviously exposed to *chansons de geste* along the *camino de Santiago*, where French travelers, settlers, and jongleurs must also have come into contact with *cantares de gesta*.

8

Mode of composition

Like the issue of the poet's possible debt to *chansons de geste*, the manner in which he composed the work is a literary question whose resolution holds the potential of shedding light on the social context in which he moved – but positively rather than negatively. As a prelude to discussing mode of composition, I will take up the matter of the tradition in which he was working and, once again but from a different point of view, the date of the *Cantar de mio Cid*.

The poem's distortions and outright contradictions of history and its unexpected silences about the attributes and achievements of figures who are known to have acted in history, when coupled with its inclusion of themes that have their greatest relevance at the very end of the twelfth century or the beginning of the thirteenth, accord well with a dating of the extant version to shortly before the year 1207 that is mentioned in its colophon. Was the poem created in that period by a poet who made it up virtually *ex nihilo*? The presence of a series of names of persons who were the Cid's historical contemporaries creates problems for this hypothesis that are insuperable.

That some of these names were borne by people of relative obscurity who are not mentioned in chronicle treatments of the period increases the probability that the poet derived them from an historical tradition of some kind. This group includes Pero Vermúdez, Martín Muñoz, Alvar Salvadórez, Diego Téllez, Galín García, Iñigo Jiménez (attested only after the historical Cid's death), Alvar Díaz, Gómez Peláyet, Muño Gustioz, Alvar Alvarez, Diego and Fernando González of Carrión and their father Gonzalo Ansúrez. Major figures are Alfonso VI, Jimena Díaz, Alvar Fáñez, and Counts García Ordóñez, Enrique of Portugal, Remont of Galicia – who was to be the father of Alfonso VII – and Froila of León.

An "archival hypothesis" has occasionally been offered to explain the poet's knowledge of the names of the minor historical figures (see, for example, Smith 1983: 166–79, who makes Per Abbat "a frequenter of archives" [178]): the supposition is that the poet had access to documentation in the form of collections of charters, from which he took the names of those associated with the Cid as witnesses to transactions and in other capacities. This suggestion runs counter to what is known about the intellectual mentalities of the twelfth and early thirteenth centuries in which other works of literature were not based upon archival material. But even assuming for the

Mode of composition

sake of argument that some were, one would have to explain why a poet who was drawing upon archives called the abbot of Cardeña "Sancho" instead of Sisebuto, named the Cid's daughters "Elvira" and "Sol," had them marry the Infantes de Carrión, and so on.

In this context I will take up once again the question of dating. Various studies have been based upon the classic method of determining the date of a medieval literary document, namely linguistic analysis. The most systematic is Menéndez Pidal's, incorporated into his three-volume edition of the poem published in 1908, to which, in the 1946 edition, he added a number of remarks ("Adiciones y enmiendas"; see 1954–56, 3: 1165–1224). I will take up each of Menéndez Pidal's arguments, adding to them the findings of other commentators.

(1) Latin short *o* diphthongizes to *ue* in words not found at the assonance, as it does in modern Castilian, but the occurrence of this diphthong in line-final position in *tiradas* whose assonances are in *ó* (ll. 1330, 2007, 2676 [?], 2691, 2696, 2700, 2774, 2843, 2920, 3468, 3641, 3688, 3706) shows that, although the fourteenth-century scribe assimilated the graphies in accord with his own linguistic habits, the poet apparently still pronounced *ó* (1954–56, 1: 117, 142–6; 3: 1191–7).

On the analogies of Italian and early Old French, Menéndez Pidal observed that Latin short *o* must have passed through the stage *uó* before arriving at *ué*, and conjectured that this sound was the one represented by the original *o*'s. In popular speech and in charters, the sound in question had already developed into *ué* by the mid-twelfth century, while the more archaic pronunciation *uó* was preserved by literate speakers and is found in the *Auto de los reyes magos*, the *Fuero juzgo*, and other texts.

In 1908 Menéndez Pidal ascribed the poem's retention of the *uo* sound to either literary usage or the archaism of the dialect of Medinaceli, but inclined later toward the second of these hypotheses (1954–56, 3: 1192). In this article on double authorship, he calls the language in which the poem was composed "un dialecto literario ilustre" (1961: 178).

Pellen (1976: 248) considers the presence of *o* and *uo* as derivatives of Latin short *o* to be an indication that the poem was written in the Aragonese dialect area rather than the Castilian, but Rafael Lapesa refutes this claim with abundant examples and supports the second alternative set forth by Menéndez Pidal in 1908, namely that the phenomenon is a literary archaism (1985: 21). Marcos Marín (1985: 29) calls attention to the similarity between the poem's treatment of the phoneme /o/ and that found in a document of 1155 from the region of Soria, the infeudation of the castle of Alcózar, which betrays traces of Aragonese dialect.

(2) Menéndez Pidal called attention to the presence of the paragogic *-e*, that is to say the etymologically justified post-tonic *-e* preserved in words from which it had disappeared in ordinary speech, a trait that is typical of certain types of line and that has been preserved in the *romancero* to the present day. By analogy, the *-e* was also added to many words in which it is

The *Cantar de mio Cid*

not etymologically correct. In addition to the two attested forms with paragogic *-e, alaudare* (335) and *Trinidade* (2370), the presence of such forms as *van* (326), *altar* (327), *veluntad* (334), *far* (1388) in assonance with *sabe* (328), *madre* (333), *fagades* (1386), *iffantes* (1391), and *Criador* (237), *Carrion* (3130), *son* (3557) in assonance with *albores* (235), *cortes* (3129), *Ordóñez* (3553) shows that the poet must have conceived of them as *vane, altare, veluntade, fare, Criadore, Carrione, sone* (Menéndez Pidal 1954–56, 1: 120–2). The preservation of the paragogic *-e* is also a feature of the 100-line epic fragment *Roncesvalles*, in which it is indicated graphically. Marcos Marín remarks (1985: 30) that the reading "en traua" in a *tirada* in the *o-e* assonance supposes an original reading not of "entrove," as Menéndez Pidal at first suggested, but "entrode" (see Menéndez Pidal 1954–56, 3: 1183–4), with conservation of the dental from the ending of the Latin third person singular of the preterite, a feature corresponding to the middle of the twelfth century but also reflected in the *Fuero de Madrid* of 1202.

(3) The patronymic *-oz*, as in *Gustioz*, which is in the *ó* assonance all twelve times that it appears under that graphy in the poem, and *Munnoz*, seven times at the assonance, is characteristic of Castilian texts in the eleventh and twelfth centuries, but not in the thirteenth (Menéndez Pidal 1954–56, 3: 1166; see also 3: 1200), a conclusion confirmed by Lapesa (1985: 23). Menéndez Pidal saw this feature as an archaism typical of the epic (1954–56, 1: 245), and proposed correcting the poem's form *Vermuez* to *Vermudoz* (the intervocalic *d* being supported by the poet's pun on *mudo*, l. 3302) with stress on the final syllable to conform to the assonance of the *tiradas* in which it appears eight times in line-final position. That this *Vermudoz corresponds to Castilian usage before 1150 is also supported by Lapesa (1985: 24), who rejects with copious documentation Pellen's claim (1976: 249) that *-oz* is a typically Aragonese form of the patronymic.

(4) The general predominance of apocopated forms (e.g. *mont, fuert, Toranz*), over those maintaining word-final vowels (e.g. *monte, fuerte, Torançio*) was taken by Menéndez Pidal (1954–56, 1: 159; see also 193–6) to be an archaic trait. Lapesa finds analogous treatment of apocopated forms between ecclesiastical documents of the twelfth century and the *Auto de los reyes magos*, the *Disputa del alma y el cuerpo*, and the *Cantar de mio Cid* (1985: 183). Rather than an archaism, however, the poem's apocopated forms may simply reflect the influence in the Transierra oriental of Aragonese dialect, in which they were widespread (1985: 179). Marcos Marín (1985: 31) notes that the document of infeudation from Alcózar contains extreme examples of apocopation. He conjectures that at least part of the original copy of the poem may have been made from hearing or that an intermediate copy may have been partially dictated.

(5) Phenomena such as the fusion of vowels in *cabel* (*cabe el*), *antel* (*ante el*), *del, della*, and other similar forms (*de* plus forms of the pronoun), *cuestayuso* for *cuesta ayuso, dio* for *di yo*, etc., assure the poem's chronological primacy over other Castilian narrative texts (Menéndez Pidal 1954–56, 1: 199).

Mode of composition

(6) The metathesis *toveldo* for *tuve te lo* is found in no other text, and the epenthesis *nimbla* for *ni me la* in only one other, the oldest part of the *Estoria de España* (Menéndez Pidal 1954–56, 1: 203; 3: 1166). Lapesa takes these forms as an indication that the original copy of the poem was taken down from a jongleur's oral version (cited by Marcos Marín 1985: 32). Both forms assume apocopation of atonic personal pronouns. Neither phenomenon was current by the thirteenth century (Marcos Marín 1985: 32).

(7) The atonic personal pronoun in the singular number apocopates as the enclitic of a word ending in a vowel, as in *quisol besar, quel sirven, nol diessen, privadol, quandol, feridal, aquis, diot*, etc. The apocope of *le* is obligatory, while that of *se, me*, and *te* is so only after a verb but also occurs frequently in other positions in the text, especially in the case of *se*. In its treatment of *se, me*, and *te* after verbs and in the predominance of *s'* over *se*, Menéndez Pidal found the *Cantar de mio Cid* to be more archaizing than any other of the texts known to him except the *Disputa del alma y el cuerpo*. Under this same rubric another archaic feature is the transformation of *-m* and *-t* into *-n* and *-d* in apocopated forms, as in *sin salue Dios, quen (que me)*, etc. (Menéndez Pidal 1954–56, 1: 254).

(8) Marcos Marín (1985: 34) observes that the maintenance of a series of masculine forms of the possessive (*mio, to, so*), distinct from the feminine (*mi(e), tu(e), su(e)*) as a regular and general system is a twelfth-century characteristic.

(9) *Ser* and *aver* used as auxiliaries never begin a proposition (Menéndez Pidal 1954–56, 1: 412–13), a practice in conformity with the usage found in the *Auto de los Reyes Magos*, which probably dates from the late twelfth century, but more archaic than that followed by Berceo.

(10) The form of the definite article is still not set, *esse* and *aquel* being used with the force of articles as an epic archaism (Menéndez Pidal 1954–56, 1: 329–30). The article derived from Latin *ille* preserves its initial vowel (*elas, ellos*), as in the archaizing Leonese dialect (1954–56, 1: 232–3).

(11) Nouns in apposition are joined by the copulative conjunction: *a Dios e al padre que esta en alto* (l. 2456; see also ll. 300, 372, 1633, 2342, 2626), a practice found otherwise only in tenth- and eleventh-century texts (Menéndez Pidal 1954–56, 1: 313; 3: 1166).

(12) Menéndez Pidal took the graphy of the anthroponym *Oiarra* for *Ocharra* as a clue that the original copy of the poem was made in the twelfth century or at the very beginning of the thirteenth. The *i* as a representation of the sound that is normally written *ch* in Old Spanish is found in documents from the eleventh to the beginning of the thirteenth century such as the *Fuero de Madrid* of 1202, and was preserved only because the name in question was very rare (1954–56, 3: 1219–20).

D. G. Pattison (1967) maintained that the state of suffixation in the poem – and in particular the suffixes *-ada, -ida* and *-ura* in deverbal formations with certain meanings – corresponded to the development of the Old Spanish language around the beginning of the thirteenth century, but Lapesa (1985:

11–13) has found examples of the use of these suffixes with the meanings in question in notarial documents and *fueros* of the twelfth century, and in some cases of the eleventh and tenth centuries. Pattison's findings are thus in keeping with a dating toward the beginning of the thirteenth century, but they do not exclude an earlier date (see also his reply [1985–86] to Lapesa).

Andrés Bello had taken the archaic forms of pronouns and verbs to indicate that "la composición del *Mio Cid* puede referirse a la primera mitad del siglo XIII, aunque con más inmediación al año 1200 de la era vulgar que al año 1250" (1883: 15). Menéndez Pidal's control of the data of linguistic change incomparably surpassed Bello's, of course, but it must be stressed that dating on the basis of linguistic traits allows us only to approximate the period in which the text was composed. What is at issue, after all, is the distance between the middle and the end of the twelfth century, the lifespan of a single person.

The major piece of external evidence that has a bearing on the chronology of the tradition of songs about the Cid is the mid-twelfth-century *Carmen de expugnatione Almariae urbis* or, as it is more commonly known, the *Poema de Almería*, dated by Ubieto Arteta (1957) to the period 1147–49, which praises Alvar Fáñez, compares him to other heroes, and emphasizes his relationship to Rodrigo Díaz:

> Tempore Roldani si tertius Aluarus esset
> Post Oliuerum, fateor sine crimine uerum,
> Sub iuga Francorum fuerat gens Agarenorum
> Nec socii cari iacuissent morte perempti,
> Nullaque sub celo melior fuit hasta sereno.
> Ipse Rodericus, Meo Cidi semper uocatus,
> De quo cantatur quod ab hostibus haud superatur,
> Qui domuit Mauros, comites domuit quoque nostros,
> Hunc extollebat, se laude minore ferebat.
> Sed fateor uerum, quod tollet nulla dierum:
> Meo Cidi primus fuit Aluarus atque secundus.
> Morte Roderici Ualentia plangit amici
> Nec ualuit Christi famulis ea plus retineri.
>
> (ed. Gil 1974: ll. 228–40)

Certain considerations have led various readers as far back as Andrés Bello (1883: 4) to believe, correctly, that the phrase *de quo cantatur quod ab hostibus haud superatur* refers to epic tradition concerning the Cid. First, the designation "meo Cidi," found repeatedly in the *Cantar* as "mio Çid," contrasts with the titles given to the hero in other texts – *campidoctor* in the *Carmen Campidoctoris*, *campidoctus* in the *Historia Roderici*, and *campiator* in the *De rebus Hispaniae* of Rodrigo Jiménez de Rada – and places the source to which the *Poema de Almería* refers squarely in the tradition of the extant poem. The line *Meo Cidi primus fuit Aluarus atque secundus*, associating the renowned hero Alvar Fáñez with the Cid in a relationship of subordination that does not correspond to the historical record but does fit the situation

Mode of composition

portrayed in the *Cantar*, also leads to the conclusion that the phrase *de quo cantatur* must refer to a contemporary poem or poems on the Cid in the tradition of the text that Per Abbat copied. That it should be a specific reference to that text itself does not follow, however, since many other indications, outlined in chapter 1 and here, point for that text to a date of composition at the end of the twelfth or the beginning of the thirteenth century. I agree with Menéndez Pidal (1954–56, 1: 23–31; 3: 1169–70), Jules Horrent (1973: 263–9), Rafael Lapesa (1985: 35–7), and Diego Catalán (1985: 816) in taking the passage in the *Poema de Almería* as testimony that a version of the *Cantar de mio Cid* was in existence before the middle of the twelfth century, although I do not assent to Lapesa's assertion (approaching Menéndez Pidal's position) that it was a text "tal como hoy lo poseemos ... sin alteraciones" (1985: 42).

What would such a text have contained? Jules Horrent, following Menéndez Pidal, sees the poem's reference to the king of the Montes Claros as only making sense in a mid-twelfth-century version. The inhabitants of Valencia, besieged by the Cid's army, seek relief from the king of Morocco:

> Por el rey de Marruecos ovieron a enbiar;
> con el de los Montes Claros avien guerra tan grand
> non les dixo consejo nin los vino huviar. (ll. 1181–3)

The king of Morocco is undoubtedly Yusuf ibn Teshufin, the great Almoravid emperor, to whom the Valencians did in fact send for help during the siege of Valencia, and the Montes Claros are, according to Menéndez Pidal (1954–56, 2: 764–5) who cites references to them in medieval texts, the mountains south of the Atlas in North Africa. Yusuf was not preoccupied by any king of the Montes Claros, however, and Menéndez Pidal saw the passage as an anachronistic reference to the battles that, beginning in 1122, pitted the Almoravids against the Almohads, who did indeed come from the area south of the Atlas. This struggle culminated in the death of the Almoravid King Teshufin in 1145, the year before the Almohads invaded Spain from Morocco. Horrent remarks that it would make no sense to include such a reference in a late twelfth-century version of the *Cantar*, when the Almoravids had long passed from the scene, and sees the lines as the remnant of the mid-twelfth-century text (1973: 267). Lapesa (1985: 36) concurs. The reference to a king of the Montes Claros, however, appropriate as it might be in a mid-twelfth-century version, tells us little about the larger meaning of that state of the poem.

The development by which the Cid's deeds were transformed from what occurred in history to their depiction in the poem must have involved, fairly early on, a process of localization in which his campaigns were narrowed down and displaced geographically by poets of the Transierra who invented or emphasized tales that ascribed some of the exploits of his exile to the valleys of the Henares and the Jalón and joined them to the narration of his historical presence in the valley of the Jiloca.

The *Cantar de mio Cid*

Earlier versions, from which the reference to the king of the Montes Claros and the general Transierran locale of the Cid's campaigns may have survived, would presumably not have included the "familial" themes – the implication of bastardy and the transmutation of the values of wealth into values of lineage that entailed the invention of the Cid's daughters' first marriages, the *afrenta de Corpes*, the deliberative trial in Toledo, Ansur González's intervention, the trials by combat in Carrión, and the daughters' second marriages. These would have been late additions, motivated by the marriage of Berenguela with Alfonso IX of Leon and by Papal opposition to the recognition of their offspring as legitimate. Memories of the events of the Cid's life would have been too vivid around the middle of the twelfth century for the poet to have gotten away with distorting the lives of important historical characters as he does so egregiously in the second half of the poem. Contemporaries of the Cid's daughters and of Diego and Fernando González of Carrión would still have been alive at that time. The *Poema de Almería* does not mention the Infantes de Carrión or the Cid's judicial triumph, and while an argument from silence is by no means sufficient, that consideration coupled with the analogies between the legal situation of the Cid and his daughters and the interests of the Castilian royal family at the end of the twelfth century lead me to think that most of the episodes in the second half of the Per Abbat text were absent from the poem (or the tradition) to which the author of the *Poema de Almería* refers. I suspect that the themes of legitimacy and the acquisition of wealth were set in place by one and the same poet.

I do not agree that a betrothal of the Cid's daughters with the Infantes de Carrión, which Menéndez Pidal saw as the first stage of what was later developed into the marriages by a poet of Medinaceli, was ever a part of the tradition.

It may well be that the unhistorically close association between the Cid and Alvar Fáñez was already present in mid-twelfth-century versions, as the *Poema de Almería*'s reference suggests.

I believe then, that the first *cantar*, even though it too appears to be based on fictitious conquests, contains material that was developed earlier than that found in the second and third *cantares*. The fictions found in them represent later developments in the process of change that characterizes the *Cid* tradition.

This model accords well with what is found in another heroic epic composed in a Romance language. The historical kernel of the *Chanson de Roland* was the battle of AD 778 in which the *Wascones* defeated Charles the Great's rearguard in a Pyrenean ambush. Looking at the whole tradition of the *Roland*, one finds after the episode in which Charlemagne returns to Roncevaux to find the body of his nephew a proliferation of episodic developments and a much greater textual diversity than before it: the expansions of the episode of Aude, the two flights of Ganelon, the addition in the Venice 4 manuscript of the narration of the capture of Narbonne by Aimeri, the double tradition of the trial of Ganelon, and the deliberations over the traitor's

Mode of composition

punishment. These later episodes are typically not found in all the texts, whereas the Battle of Roncevaux and Roland's death, the essential ingredients of the drama, are.[1]

Beyond the precinct of heroic epic composed in the Romance languages, one finds another analogous situation in the Serbo-Croatian epic, in regard to which Albert B. Lord has noted that the beginnings of songs tend to be more stable in the tradition than their later episodes. Lord ascribes this phenomenon to the fact that songs are not always sung to the end: thus the poet will begin his song more frequently than he will end it, and these repeated starts will lead him to sing the beginning in the same way. In addition the progress of a performance depends very much on the audience's stability and willingness to listen, and on preferences that can be made known to the poet on the spot, allowing him to add or eliminate pertinent episodes.

This model also accounts for the fact that, although Menéndez Pidal perceived such great differences of historicity and versification between the first and the third *cantares* that he was led to posit two authors for the poem as we have it – the second one revising, especially in its last half, a poem created by the first – the links and resemblances between the two halves are many. Jules Horrent (1973: 248–51) has identified a number of them, among which are that the Cid expresses the wish to marry his daughters as early as line 282; that the couples Elvira and Sol Rodríguez, and Diego and Fernando González, are characterized in the second and third *cantares* with the same lack of individualization as Rachel and Vidas in the first; and that the Cid dominates the action from beginning to end, a trait which relegates both his allies and his enemies to the role of bit players in the drama. It is not a matter of discrete lines or episodes of the poem being created by different poets, but rather of a poet appropriating what was handed on to him by previous poets, "making it new," and composing another version of the poem, using what served his purposes and abandoning what did not. The tagmemic model of a poet retaining discrete segments is inadequate in this instance.[2]

The arguments that Menéndez Pidal makes concerning differences in versification do not necessarily reveal two poets at work. He analyzes the poem's assonances (1961: 177–9) according to their degree of difficulty, pointing out that while the first and second *cantares* each employ eleven different assonances ranging through the entire spectrum of difficulty, the third *cantar* uses only six, none of which falls into the most difficult category. In the final *Cantar de Corpes*, 73 percent of the assonances are in the easy *ó-e*, a preference that cannot be accounted for on thematic grounds. Furthermore, this is over double the rate at which the easiest assonances occur in the first two *cantares*. The average length of *tiradas* increases from 17 lines in the first *cantar*, to 25 lines in the second, and 35 lines in the third (1961: 180–1). In addition, the third *cantar*, in contrast to the first two, contains no *tiradas* of less than five lines, and has fewer of less than ten lines than either of its counterparts. *Tiradas* of more than fifty lines account for only 6 percent of those in the first *cantar*, 12 percent of those in the second, but 25 percent of those in the third including four of the seven *tiradas* in the poem that number over 100 lines. On this basis, Menéndez Pidal concluded that his poet of San Esteban favored a varied versification, with frequent changes of assonance and the use of both difficult and easy assonance, while his later poet of Medinaceli, reworking the second *cantar* "a medias" (182) and the third *cantar* extensively, tended toward a versification of great simplicity, suppressing difficult assonances, eliminating short *tiradas*, and lengthening the longest ones (181–2).

Without challenging Menéndez Pidal's factual analysis, I prefer to account for the data he presents with a hypothesis that is simpler because it allows one to posit that a single poet is responsible for the evolution in versification that is observed in the course of the poem. This hypothesis is that an oral poet, a *juglar*, performing the *Cantar de mio Cid* in a single day, grew more tired as time passed, using fewer different assonances and easier ones, as well as longer *tiradas*, as the day progressed. This fatigue might also have contributed to the poet's failure to tell about the liberation of Alvar Salvadórez, captured in line 1681 but inexplicably free again in line 1719, and perhaps also about the repayment of the loan the Cid received from Rachel and Vidas.

The hypothesis that a single poet was responsible for the features of the text as we have it from beginning to end, with the exception of scribal modifications, is strengthened by the fact that Menéndez Pidal perceived no linguistic differences between the poem's various sections. Both Franklin M. Waltman (1973) and John S. Geary (1980: 13–14) have concluded on the basis of relative formulaic densities in different parts of the poem that a single poet produced the text. But if this poet reworked the tale at the end of the twelfth century, what of the notion that the linguistic traits support a dating to the middle of the century? The patronymic in *-oz*, which the fourteenth-century manuscript preserves in the forms "Munnoz" and "Gustioz" but which is also required by the assonance in the form "Vermuez" which for the poet must have been "Vermudoz," does not survive in Castilian into the thirteenth century. The pronunciations *muort, fuort, fuont, aluon, despuos, puode,* and *puoden,* assured by the assonance although written "muert," "fuert," "fuent," "aluen," "despues," "puede," and "pueden," may be ascribable to the dialect of a poet living in the Extremadura castellana, as Menéndez Pidal came to believe (1954–56, 3: 1192; 1961: 177–8), or they may constitute an archaism preserved in epic language, as Lapesa maintains (1985: 21). Other archaic linguistic traits include phonosyntactic phenomena such as the fusion of vowels in adjacent words, the metathesis "toveldo," the epenthesis "nimbla," and the apocope of personal pronouns; the use of the auxiliaries *ser* and *aver* exclusively in non-initial position, the treatment of the definite article, the use of the copula with nouns in apposition, and the graphy "i" for the sound *ch*, as discussed above. While the phonological and syntactic characteristics isolated by Menéndez Pidal undoubtedly point to the twelfth century, all of them may have survived in the dialects of the Transierra well into the second half of that century. The period in which each had transmuted into a practice identified with a slightly later stage of the language is uncertain.

Mode of composition

Some of them may, in addition, be analogous to the paragogic *-e* that is found in Spanish epic, ballad, and lyric traditions for centuries after the time in which it arose, in defiance of the course of normal linguistic development but in conformity with the expectations of genre. Their preservation may also have been reinforced by their prosodic usefulness. As Lapesa remarks concerning the preservation of the sounds *o* and *uo* at the assonance, "es natural que la recitación o salmodia de los juglares épicos conservara la variante fonética más tradicional, por lo menos en finales de verso, donde les era útil para las rimas" (1985: 21). Their presence in the text provides only a possible *terminus a quo* for the tradition rather than a *terminus ad quem* for the Per Abbat text.

As Menéndez Pidal noted, the lines and scenes in which these traits are found are scattered in random distribution throughout the text. In any case it would be a mistake to think that the late-twelfth- or early-thirteenth-century poet retained all the individual lines and passages in which they are preserved from an earlier version of the poem characterized by archaisms. He probably passed on some lines as he received them, but many passages marked by the older linguistic features are found in episodes that must have been composed long after the middle of the twelfth century.

The preservation of archaic linguistic features is, however, precisely a characteristic of orally transmitted heroic epic. The Homeric epics preserve linguistic traits that are much older than one would normally expect considering the period in which they were written down, such as the effect of the digamma, a sound that had passed out of the Greek language by the end of the Bronze Age but still played a role not only in the versification of the *Iliad* and the *Odyssey* but also in that of Hesiod and of the Homeric hymns (for this and other phonological and morphological archaisms in Homer, Hesiod, and the Hymns, see, among many treatments, Janko 1982, especially chapters 3 and 4). In fact the *Iliad* and the *Odyssey* are both preserved in a language that mixes dialect traits in such an artificial way that it must never have been spoken in ordinary discourse but rather was only used for the performance of heroic and mythological tales (see, for example, Heubeck 1981, esp. p. 73). One might object that the Homeric hexameter, a highly bound type of versification, is exceptional in its conservation of older forms, but the phenomenon is attested also in the Romance languages.

The *Chanson de Guillaume*, for example, a poem transmitted orally in its early stages of development (Rychner 1955), is extant in a single manuscript copied around 1225, but the text from which that copy descends has been dated by its editor Jeanne Wathelet-Willem to around the middle of the twelfth century (1975: 187). Nonetheless it retains the archaic final dental of the present tense of verbs in *-er* (183), and of perfects in *-i*, *-a*, and *-u*, reflecting a sound that had disappeared in the late eleventh century (218–19).

P. E. Russell adumbrated the thesis that the language of the *Cantar de mio Cid* is a *Kunstsprache* (1958: 70) and Ian Michael supported his theory in the introduction to his edition of the poem (1978: 56), but J. M. Aguirre (1968) was the first to see that the phenomenon was corroborated by the analogy of other traditions of orally composed epic.

The archaic linguistic features of the *Cantar de mio Cid*, then, may be evidence not that the text as we have it was composed around the middle of the twelfth century, but only that a poet was participating in the conventions of an oral tradition of songs about Rodrigo Díaz of Vivar that stretched back at least to the middle of the twelfth century and perhaps beyond, the same tradition referred to in the *Poema de Almería*. In the recent history of *Cid* scholarship many of those who have argued on a historical basis for a dating toward the end of the twelfth century or the beginning of the thirteenth, in opposition to Menéndez Pidal's hypothesis of the period around 1140, have also argued for the individual authorship of a writing poet. In fact, however, the arguments for the later dating support the thesis of oral transmission, which is the most plausible means of accounting for the presence of linguistic archaisms in a relatively late text. It is perhaps relevant to note that the problematics of the Homeric language were the primary impetus for Milman Parry's development of the theory of oral poetry in the 1920s (see Parry 1971).

Jules Horrent (1973: 308–11) has posited three stages in the development of the *Cantar de mio Cid*. Sometime in the late 1120s, that is to say shortly after most of the poem's protagonists had died, there would have been a version in which the facts of history were retold in a fairly faithful way but took on a poetic form designed to highlight the hero's exploits. A second version, between 1140 and 1150, would have introduced the mention of Alfonso VII "el Emperador." Finally, after 1160, a version whose *sustancia épica* would have differed little from that of the 1120s, would have introduced features best explained as arising during the reign of Alfonso VIII. That third version, according to Horrent, was copied in 1207 and has been passed down to us in the fourteenth-century manuscript.

I believe that Horrent is correct in seeing the tradition as developing gradually toward the Per Abbat version during the course of the twelfth century, but I am not so confident about the state of our knowledge of the various layers of the text as to posit such a definite series of steps. It is more likely, in my view, that a large number of songs concerning the Cid's exploits existed and that the singers who performed them influenced each other's versions constantly. Some of the changes effected in the tradition were no doubt great and sudden, but others must have been small, on the level of the individual line or even the individual word, and most have been lost to us permanently.

The choice of Carrión as the geographical seat of the Cid's enemies is no doubt in part due to the fact that, as Lacarra has shown, the Castro family, enemies of the Laras and also of Alfonso VIII, was descended from the Beni-Gómez, the comtal family of Carrión in the poem, as well as from García Ordóñez. But the poet could have chosen ancestors of the Castros other than Diego and Fernando González de Carrión as his villains – villains for fictitious reasons, after all – and I believe that the choice of the family of Carrión in

Mode of composition

particular was partly to be ascribed to an extremely important incident in the political relationship between Leon and Castile in the late twelfth century.³ In 1188, at the first solemn court of Alfonso VIII's reign, the fifteen-year-old Alfonso IX of Leon was knighted by his cousin the king of Castile, kissing his hand in a gesture of homage (González 1960, 1: 705-6).

Although this resounding event was in harmony with the accord that had been drawn up in 1158 in Sahagún between Fernando II of Leon and Sancho III of Castile, to the effect that if the ruler of either kingdom died without a legitimate heir, the other would inherit his realm (González 1960, 1: 670), Alfonso of Leon felt it deeply as a humiliation. The Leonese king was also supposed to marry one of Alfonso VIII's daughters, either Blanca or Urraca, but that part of the agreement was never carried out and two years later when Alfonso IX married Teresa, daughter of the king of Portugal – a union that, as we have seen, was in the same year declared incestuous – he is thought to have renounced and annuled the homage (710). The *Crónica latina de los reyes de Castilla* ascribes Alfonso IX's hostility toward Castile after the Battle of Alarcos (1095) partly to his rancor over the *cortes* of Carrión:

Rex vero Legionis, qui ibat in auxilium regis Castelle, venit Toletum; et consilio quorundam satellitum Sathane, conversus est in arcum pravum, querens occasiones quibus discederet ab amico; et de amico factus est crudelissimus inimicus. Nempe manebat alta mente repositum quod ei contigerat in curia, de qua supra facta est mentio, in Carrione celebrata.   (ed. Cabanes Pecourt 1964: 31)

In the campaign that Alfonso IX, in company with Almohad troops whose collaboration was arranged by Pedro Fernández de Castro, waged against Castile in 1196, he reached Carrión and cleansed himself of the dishonor done to him there eight years before:

... Pervenit autem usque Carrionem ubi visus fuit purgare dedecus quod sibi credebat illatum quando manum regis Castelle fuit osculatus.   (32)

At the end of the twelfth century, then, Carrión was for Alfonso IX of Leon a symbol of shame, and for Alfonso VIII of Castile a symbol of hegemony.

Although the *Cantar de mio Cid* reflects, as I have argued, the state of hostility between Castile and Leon at the end of the twelfth century, and one might suspect, as have many historians, that the Beni-Gómez of Carrión were Leonese, Lacarra has proven that in fact they were Castilians (1980: 146). Ubieto Arteta has further shown that Carrión was not in Leonese hands until 1196 (1980: 573). Nevertheless the poetic Cid's enemies reside in Carrión. The symbolism of Carrión for partisans of Alfonso VIII must have played a role in that choice, allowing the ancestor of Alfonso VIII, Rodrigo Díaz of Vivar, to triumph over his enemies, the ancestors of the hated Pedro Fernández de Castro, in judicial combats held in the same town in which the king had triumphed over his Leonese rival and in which that rival had attempted to rid himself of the resulting stigma.

That the process by which the poem was recomposed over several generations occurred in oral tradition rather than in writing is reinforced by a statistical analysis that I published over a decade ago (Duggan 1974).[4]

In his classic treatment of orality in the *chanson de geste*, Jean Rychner (1955) concentrated on ten twelfth-century poems which he studied from a variety of points of view: the manner in which they were presented in medieval society, the state of their preservation in manuscripts, and their compositional characteristics, including strophic structure and formulas. Basing himself on Milman Parry's and Albert B. Lord's publications on Homeric and Yugoslavian epic, on Marcel Jousse's cross-cultural study of oral performers, and on the research of other scholars working mostly in Slavic literatures, Rychner studied the characteristics of the twelfth-century French epics, concluding that, with the sole exception of the *Chanson de Roland*, they were orally composed and orally transmitted.[5] A prime piece of evidence in his analysis was the technique of composition by formula (stock phrase) and theme (stock scene).

Milman Parry had defined the formula as "a group of words used under the same metrical conditions to express a given essential idea," and most subsequent work has been based upon that definition despite efforts to revise it (see, for example, De Chasca 1970). One of the most important considerations for Parry and for Albert Lord, whose book *The Singer of Tales* (1960) remains the most cogent statement of the theory, was formula density, the proportion of formulas that a poet employed. Parry, Lord, and a number of other researchers have considered a relatively high proportion of formulas as a sign the poem in question was orally composed, whereas a low formula density would be an indication that it was composed in writing.

In several publications (Duggan 1973, 1980–81a, 1980–81b), I have attempted to work out a controlled and consistent statistical approach to this question. Taking the ten *chansons de geste* that Rychner treated and three other works that are presumed to have been created by writing poets, I counted the hemistichs that were repeated within each text (a practical approach to isolating a corpus of the "groups of words used under the same metrical conditions to express given essential ideas") on the basis of computer-generated data, mostly in the form of concordances. I found that, on the average, while the *chansons de geste* contained 30.3 percent formulas, the works presumed to have been created in writing contained only 16 percent repeated hemistichs. Furthermore, in the sequence of works laid out according to formulaic density, all of the *chansons de geste*, including the *Chanson de Roland* at 35 percent, were situated above the level of 22 percent, while the other three works were below 18 percent, leading me to suggest 20 percent as a threshold above which the probability would increase that a work was orally composed (Duggan 1973: 21–30). This thesis was later attacked by William Calin and defended by me in a series of articles appearing in the journal *Olifant* (see Calin 1980–81a, 1980–81b; Duggan 1980–81a, 1980–81b), in the last of which a proof of the statistical aspect of the argument is offered.

Mode of composition

The method I employed by no means yields a listing of all of the semantic formulas in a poet's repertory, since it does not record as a formula any phrase that the poet employs only once in the work under examination but might use habitually in composing *other* poems. Nor does it include syntactic formulas, that is to say what Lord calls "formulaic expressions," repeated patterns in which different words occupy the same syntactic slot. Its advantage, however, is that it allows comparative studies to be carried out on a valid basis, since the limitations in our perceptions of repeated phrases apply equally to all of the texts under scrutiny. It is preferable to Edmund de Chasca's procedure (1972) of counting only phrases that occur three or more times in the poem, since De Chasca's method eliminates over a third of the hemistichs that are repeated within the poem; in addition, his results cannot readily be compared with those for other poems in the Romance languages, since comparable data have never been gathered. The method I developed is comparative in its essence, and the results are significant on a comparative basis.[6]

While formula density is one sign that the poem under scrutiny was orally composed, it is by no means sufficient to bear the entire burden of proof in this matter. In fact, a number of *chansons de geste* and other medieval French and Latin texts provide external evidence that would be sufficient unto itself to show that many of the French epics were composed and transmitted orally (see Duggan 1980–81b, 1986b). But the analysis of formula density provides a very important piece of evidence.

The irregularity of versification of the *Cantar de mio Cid* as it has come down to us raises a number of issues that are relevant to the analysis of formulas. The inconsistency in the number of syllables per line has been catalogued by Menéndez Pidal (1954–56, 1: 87), who found that, of the 987 lines in the poem that are free of hiatus and other features of uncertain metrical effect, the most frequently occurring measure was that of fourteen syllables, which included only 27 percent of the lines in question. The syllable counts of the other lines, taken in descending order of frequency, cluster on either side of fourteen in almost perfectly symmetrical distribution: 216 lines of fifteen syllables (22 percent), 187 of thirteen syllables (19 percent), 115 of sixteen syllables (12 percent), 93 of twelve syllables (9 percent), 37 of seventeen syllables (4 percent), 27 of eleven syllables (3 percent), 22 of eighteen syllables (2 percent), 12 of nineteen syllables (1 percent), 6 of ten syllables, the shortest, and 2 of twenty syllables, the longest. Assuming that these percentages would be fairly constant for the entire poem, one is faced with a metrical situation in which only just over a quarter of the lines conform to the most frequently found syllable count. Even greater irregularity is evident if the data are disaggregated by hemistich (1954–56, 1: 99–100): the combination of two hemistichs of seven syllables each is the most common but only makes up 15 percent of the total lines that were analyzed.

The poem as it was performed was, I believe, metrically regular. The *chanson de geste*, a genre cognate with the *cantar de gesta*, is composed in isosyllabic lines and was sung to a chant-like rhythm, the melody being repeated from line to line, possibly with variations for the beginning and the end of the laisse and for the speech of characters. The *romances*, a number of which derive from *cantares de gesta*, also consist of isosyllabic lines. Even taking into account that other Castilian poems of this period exhibit some degree of metrical irregularity (see Henríquez Ureña 1933), it is difficult to admit that a sung text should vary in syllable count from line to line to the extent that the *Cantar de mio Cid* does in a literature in which versification is based upon syllable count. No theory positing another system of versification has been able to account for the metrical anarchy (Henríquez Ureña's characterization: 12) of the poem in the Per Abbat text.

When one examines hemistichs that appear in different verses of the poem in slightly varied form, one finds quite often an additional word or two in the variation that can easily be removed with little or no change to the primary meaning of the phrase. Thus "yo" in "entrare yo del otra part" (1696), while it emphasizes the speaking subject, is easily dispensed with as is the case in line 1132, "entrare del otra part." Likewise the six-syllable "cras a la mañana" (537, 949) becomes the four-syllable "cras mañana" (3050), "una cofia sobre los pelos" (3094) is also found as "cofia sobre los pelos" (2437), and so on (for other examples and further discussion see Duggan 1975: 76–80). Variations of this type are also frequent in the *chansons de geste* that are composed in decasyllabic meter, but there they serve to adapt phrases occurring in the first hemistich position, which must be four syllables long (or five syllables, if the fifth is post-tonic) for use in the second hemistich position which is subject to the exigencies of end-rhyme and requires six syllables (or seven if one is post-tonic). Since the ability to adapt formulas to use in either position obviously constituted a very important part of the poet's technique, I did not discount, in studying the formulas of the *chansons de geste*, hemistichs that underwent such variation in their recurrences within the same text as long as they contained the same principal words – nouns, attributive adjectives, verbs – the parts of speech that carry the formula's semantic weight, convey its "given essential idea." Within the set of guidelines, change of word order was permitted ("plega al Criador," ll. 2149 and 2892, for example, was counted as a form of "al Criador plega," l. 2100), as was tense variation ("por que las dexamos," l. 3299, and "por que las han dexadas," l. 3278, for example).

In the *Cantar de mio Cid* I found 2,385 formulas, comprising 31.7 percent of the poem's hemistichs, a result that places it squarely within the range of the nine *chansons de geste* for which Rychner posited oral composition and transmission plus the *Chanson de Roland*. The Spanish poem ranks slightly above the median, which is to say that it is more formulaic than the *Pèlerinage de Charlemagne* (23 percent), the *Siège de Barbastre* (23 percent), the *Moniage Guillaume* (24 percent), *Gormont et Isembart* (29 percent), the *Charroi de Nîmes* (29 percent), and the *Chanson de Guillaume* (31 percent), and less formulaic than *Raoul de Cambrai* (33 percent), the *Chanson de Roland* (35 percent), the *Couronnement de Louis* (37 percent), and the *Prise d'Orange* (39 percent), which tops the list.

Mode of composition

John S. Geary (1980) has applied the same method to a study of the relative formula densities of the *Mocedades de Rodrigo* and the *Poema de Fernán González*, concluding that they are as formulaic, respectively, as *Buevon de Conmarchis* (15 percent) and the decasyllabic *Roman d'Alexandre* (17 percent), two of the French poems presumed to have been composed in writing. Since the *Mocedades* shows signs of clerical intervention and has been linked to the propagandistic needs of the diocese of Palencia (Deyermond 1969), and since *Fernán González* is composed in *cuaderna vía* and is widely considered to be based on both learned and popular sources, there are excellent reasons to believe that the same stylistic opposition between works composed orally and works composed in writing exists in medieval Spanish literature as has been found for medieval French.

The types of external evidence that are available for the French epic, which has survived in hundreds of manuscripts (see Duggan 1982), unfortunately do not exist for the *cantares de gesta*, but a number of the characteristics of the *Cantar de mio Cid* concord well with the theory that it was orally composed. Like the *chansons de geste*, the poem is based distantly on historical events that have been distorted for compositional and other purposes, appears to have been recomposed in successive stages over a long period of time, and is anonymous. It is also composed in a language marked by archaic linguistic features, and some of its linguistic traits are associated with oral discourse such as apocopated forms (Marcos Marín's suggestion), the metatheses, and the epenthesis *nimbla* (Lapesa's hypothesis). Although no *juglar*'s prologue is extant to provide clues to the conditions of presentation, line 1085, "Aquis conpieça la gesta de mio Cid el de Bivar," suggests that the second *cantar* represents a new beginning after a pause, and is more easily explained as a feature of performance than of writing. The poem's versification betrays signs of fatigue, another element that is easily explained in the context of performance. The *juglares* who presented the *cantares de gesta* in public, wandering singers belonging to the lowest stratum of medieval Spanish society, are unlikely to have possessed the ability to read and write, typically in the twelfth and thirteenth centuries the acquisition of the highest levels of society.

The thesis that the *Cantar de mio Cid* was not only orally composed but was orally transmitted up until the time when it was taken down in Per Abbat's manuscript in substantially the form in which we have it today provides a solution to the irregularity of the poem's versification. This solution was elaborated by L. P. Harvey (1963) who drew upon a suggestion in Lord's *Singer of Tales*. Lord had found that when Yugoslav oral poets were asked to recite their songs for the collector rather than sing them, metrically irregular texts resulted that "look very like the text of the Old Spanish *Cid*" (Lord 1960: 127), whereas when the poems were sung they were indeed in regular versification. The metrically defective versions were produced both when the songs were recited to be recorded on phonograph disks and when they were dictated to a scribe. Thus, according to Harvey, what we have in the fourteenth-century copy of Per Abbat's text is:

The *Cantar de mio Cid*

a poem which gives every appearance of being authentic, i.e. of having come from the mouth of the poet with little or no garbling, and yet defective, in that it does not give us the words we might have heard if we could have been present at an actual living *performance*. (1963: 140)

That the theory of oral composition and transmission provides a reasonable solution to an otherwise extremely puzzling characteristic is decidedly a point in its favor, as it renders unnecessary the formulation of an additional hypothesis to account for the phenomenon.[7] The irregularity of versification originated in the interface between the oral and the written, the dictated text and its first recording in manuscript.

The manner in which an oral poet passes on the text of a poem that he performs has sometimes been understood too restrictively. There is no reason to think that oral transmission is ever purely mechanical: it is seldom even largely mechanical. That the performer's intention can count for a great deal indeed is shown by an anecdote that the chronicler Lambert of Ardre, writing in the late twelfth century, tells about the nobleman Arnold of Guines, who died around 1140. Arnold had taken part in the First Crusade. One day a jongleur came by singing a *Chanson d'Antioche* in which Arnold presumably would figure, and asked him for the gift of a pair of scarlet shoes. But Arnold refused,

qui humanam nullatenus quaerens gloriam, scurrae maluit quantumcumque munusculum denegare, quam in ore scurrae et nomine indigni, licet omni haberetur laude dignissimus, in orbe terrarum deferri et cum instrumento musicari vel decantari.

In retaliation, the jongleur suppressed the narrative of Arnold's deeds in performing his song:

Et de eo in cantilena sua, in qua ficta veris admiscens, multa multorum nichilominus laudandorum gesta sub silentio intacta reliquit, mentionem non fecit.
 (Godefroy Menilglaise 1855: 311)

Whether Lambert of Ardre's anecdote is true or not – it may simply have been a stratagem for explaining why versions of the *Chanson d'Antioche* that circulated in his day did not narrate the achievements of his hero before Antioch – it demonstrates that to the eyes of a late twelfth-century observer the intentional alteration of jongleur's epic song from one performance to the next was entirely plausible.[8] I believe that just such a process accounts for the presence in a version of the *Cantar de mio Cid* taken down in or shortly before 1207 of economic and social themes that were of importance to the political situation of the Castilian monarchy and its partisans at the extreme end of the twelfth century and during the first decade of the thirteenth.

The *juglar* who dictated the poem was probably one who was active in the vicinity of Huerta. Menéndez Pidal's theory of the two poets, one from San Esteban de Gormaz and the other from Medinaceli, has not found favor with critics, although Horrent points out (1973: 274–5) that a poet from San

Mode of composition

Esteban would be in a good position to recall the raids that the historical Cid had carried out in the valley of the Henares before his first exile, raids that may be the inspiration for the activities that take place in that same area in the poem. In any case the region that the poet who is responsible for the *Cantar de mio Cid* in the form in which we have it seems to know best is located, as I have argued, between Anguita, southeast of Medinaceli, and Calatayud, as is demonstrated by ll. 542–55:

> Vansse Fenares arriba   quanto pueden andar,
> troçen las Alcarias   e ivan adelant,
> por las Cuevas d'Anquita   ellos passando van,
> passaron las aguas,   entraron al campo de Torançio,
> por essas tierras ayuso   quanto pueden andar,
> entre Fariza e Çetina   mio Çid iva albergar.
> Grandes son las gananças que priso   por la tierra do va.
> Non lo saben los moros   el ardiment que an.
> Otro dia movios   mio Çid el de Bivar
> e passo a Alfama,   la foz[9] ayuso va,
> passo a Bovierca   e a Teca que es adelant
> e sobre Alcoçer   mio Çid iva posar
> en un otero redondo   fuerte e grand;
> açerca corre Salon,   agua nol pueden(t) vedar.

All the place-names in this passage with the exception of the notorious "Alcocer" can easily be identified: the rivers Henares, Alcarria, and Jalón; Campo Taranz; the towns Anguita, Ariza, Cetina, Alhama, Bubierca, and Ateca. Elsewhere Terrer and Calatayud, to the east, are mentioned. As Ubieto Arteta recognized (1973: 85), of all the regions described in the poem, none is depicted in such detail. In the midst of this landscape, between Campo Taranz and Ariza, is situated the monastery of Santa María de Huerta.

Even "Alcocer" would be there, if one were to accept its identification with Castejón de las Armas or Peñalcázar, but as I have argued in chapter 6, Alcocer was probably invented by the poet for the purpose of locating one of the Cid's important victories somewhere in the valley of the Jalón, in the absence of local tradition supporting his fiction. The battle for Alcocer, along with the passages devoted to its occupation, its defense against the forces of Fáriz and Galve, the distribution of the booty, and the sale of the town back to the Muslims, takes up an impressive amount of narration, from l. 556 to l. 857, and constitutes the action to which the poet gives the most leisurely attention, in sharp contrast to the operation that was historically the most important achievement of Rodrigo Díaz, the capture of the great city of Valencia, narrated in only eleven lines. The motivation behind the attention given to the Cid's activities in the valley of the Jalón is palpable: local interest.

Nothing in Menéndez Pidal's remarks on the dialectal coloring of the poem's language, which he believed to be that of a *juglar* of Medinaceli, would rule out composition in the vicinity of Huerta: "Lo que sí podemos asegurar es que la región castellana donde se escribió el Cantar sufrió, poco antes de la composición de este, una fuerte influencia aragonesa y que fué territorio muy disputado por Aragón y Castilla" (1954–56, 1: 74). Aragonese influence would fit equally well a region that was in the borderland between Aragon and Castile and had belonged at one time or another to either kingdom, namely the valley of the Jalón.

9

Conclusion

The "best hypothesis" to which this analysis of the *Cantar de mio Cid* leads is as follows. In the year 1199 or, more likely, 1200, a *juglar* of the Transierra, active in the valley of the Jalón, familiar with the area circumscribed by San Esteban, Calatayud, Guadalajara, and Medinaceli, and intent on pleasing Alfonso VIII of Castile and his partisans, performed the poem at Ariza or Huerta de Ariza, in the circle of Martín of Finojosa.

The *juglar*'s motives as they can be reconstructed according to this hypothesis were, like those of most poets, complex: they included the wish to entertain, of course, but also the desire to flatter high-ranking members of the audience by evoking the exploits of their ancestors and the misdeeds of their enemy's ancestors. This evocation would have emphasized the solidarity of the Lara clan with the Castilian monarchy by displaying how the renowned Rodrigo Díaz – their kinsman through marriage as well as Alfonso VIII's direct ancestor – had regaled his king with extravagant gifts, and how his legitimacy, called into question by a popular tradition, had been confirmed in a judgment of God.

The jongleur also wanted to present fictional situations that reflected social issues of his day, involving both the political relationships of the Castilian monarchy with the other Christian kingdoms of the Iberian Peninsula and the depiction of economic incentives that would contribute toward reviving interest in the Reconquest after the disastrous experience of the Battle of Alarcos. One of the causes of this defeat was the desertion of trans-Pyrenean contingents who believed that their participation in the battle against the Moors would not bring appropriate rewards.

The poet quite likely composed in the hope of receiving recompense for his labors in the form of gifts that would be inspired not merely by the immediate performance, with its representation of the Cid's generosity, but by the interest shared by certain members of his audience that his version be propagated to attract participants in the campaign that Alfonso VIII knew he had to undertake some day soon against the Almohads. As far as the larger audience is concerned, the poet was presenting a series of characters as exemplars of the kind of conduct that was needed in those social and military circumstances.

The portrait of the poet that emerges is of a person belonging to one of the lowest levels of society – a *juglar* with little or no formal education, and probably no direct contact with French culture, but whose creative gifts in composing traditional epic rendered him useful to the nobility.

That a *juglar* should sing such a song is, unlike the hypothesis that the poet conducted archival research, perfectly in keeping with what we know about the mental structures and poetic practices of the period. Sung history was the province of jongleurs: Lambert of Watrelos recounts in the annals of Cambrai for the year 1108 the tale of a family in which ten brothers were killed in battle: "Unde apud nostrates de illis adhuc elegi versus per cantilenam mimorum recitantur" (cited in Heers 1974: 26). The poems about the Cid's exploits referred to in the *Poema de Almería* were most likely the same type of *cantilena*. Lambert of Ardre's story of the jongleur who refused to sing about Arnold of Guines in his *cantilena* because he was not receiving proper compensation is an example of the practice of popular singers appropriating historical events for their own ends.

The argument that the *Cantar de mio Cid* is of too high a quality to have been orally composed is without foundation. Both written and oral works can be ordered theoretically in an array ranging from those that best exemplify subtlety, tightness of structure and motivation, or whatever qualities of beauty one is inclined to devise, to those that worst represent those qualities. Even granting for the sake of argument that the spectrum of written works would be situated higher on such a scale than the oral, it would be wrong to assume that the worst work composed in writing would inevitably rank higher than the best of the orally composed. For that reason alone it is obvious that neither the presence nor the absence of aesthetic value is sufficient by itself to decide the issue of whether a given poem was composed orally or in writing. In fact in this regard considerations of aesthetic quality are beside the point, although the *type* of aesthetic effect that one finds in a poem is relevant because it may reveal stylistic procedures typical either of authors schooled in literacy or of the unlettered.

For scholars, who are themselves among the more advanced members of their societies in the arts of literacy, to hold that the creative ways of the educated are aesthetically superior is highly suspect (see Armistead 1986: 56). Stephen Jay Gould (1981) has shown how in the last two centuries various schemes for ranking the two sexes and the races of man according to single quantifiable indices (craniometry, I.Q. testing, and the like) were devised so as to produce results in which the investigator's group, the white male, emerged on top – in the face of data that support different conclusions entirely. Gould concludes not that the purveyors of such rankings acted in bad faith – although a few certainly did – but that scientific methods, far from attaining the objectivity to which they pretend, are the work of fallible personalities not all that much more inclined to objectivity than their nonscientific contemporaries. How much more fragile, then, are historical conclusions based on judgments of aesthetic superiority which just about everyone admits to be subjective in the first place?

Furthermore judgments of aesthetic quality are notoriously time- and

Conclusion

culture-bound. What will appear to one age or national tradition as a timeless criterion of beauty stands a good chance of being considered a defect at some other time or in some other place. While no judgment is completely immune from the effect of differences in mentality, matters of aesthetic quality are perhaps the most difficult of all to control. In the final analysis, aesthetic superiority depends to a greater extent on the personality and background of the person who judges than on objectifiable factors.

The historical record abounds with examples of Western intellectuals preferring the simple pleasure, the "unstructured" narrative, the unsophisticated tone of oral tales (among them ballads) to the products of their own lettered contemporaries. Not that they were necessarily thereby engaging in correct or incorrect conduct (in fact "correct" and "incorrect" have no meaning in this context): but their example points up the futility of assuming that what impresses the investigator as aesthetically superior poetry was necessarily produced in writing.

Finally, the *Iliad* and the *Odyssey*, cornerstones of so much that European and American readers admire in literature, were orally composed. This is a conclusion based on Milman Parry's analysis of the relationship in the Homeric corpus between meter and sense and his observation that its diction must result from a long oral tradition, as well as on the very strong probability that writing was not used for literary purposes in the period to which the Homeric poems can be dated. One can plausibly hold that high aesthetic quality necessarily reveals creation in writing only if one is willing to maintain that the epic in question is superior to its Homeric rivals.

That the *Cantar de mio Cid* was composed orally does not in the least diminish the artistic achievements of the poet whose work has come down to us, as has been shown by Edmund de Chasca's analyses of its compositional merits (1972, 1976), carried out on the assumption that the poem is an oral composition.[1] Ruth Webber has remarked recently that the acoustic patterning perceived in the poem is "the result of its having evolved intuitively by ear and then having been continually refined through performance" (1986a: 72). None of the poem's stylistic or compositional features, in fact, argues for the hypothesis that they were the product of a poet who composed according to rules accessible only to the educated or who had learned his craft by reading the *auctores*. Poetic merit was not, nor has it ever been, the exclusive domain of those who were schooled in the elements of writing or who had access to poetic theory as preserved in the arts of rhetoric.

The poem survived in a text that the *juglar* dictated, that eventually resulted in a copy made by either Abbot Pedro of Huerta or Abbot Pedro of Ovila in May of 1207, according to my hypothesis, and that has been handed down, perhaps after passing through intermediary copies, in the fourteenth-century manuscript. The inconsistencies of its versification can be ascribed mainly to the process by which it was recorded. Many medieval literary works were dictated to scribes, and most of these were taken down first on wax tablets that could be erased and reused. From the tablets texts were copied onto parchment, a more expensive medium. In taking down the poet's words the scribe would be hard put to keep pace with the rhythm of sung performance, which made it natural that the poet should be asked to speak his text rather than sing it. This deprived the poet of his normal cadence and resulted in a highly irregular text.

Two aspects of the *Cantar de mio Cid* stand out when one compares it with other epics in the Western tradition: the stress on economic exchange and the fact that so much of the narrative centers on the marriages of the hero's daughters.

Does not the representation of an acquisitive hero result in a poem of rather narrow scope in the context of the epic genre? Marcel Mauss, whose model of a gift economy provides the theoretical base for much of the analysis contained in this book, observes that the exchange of gifts constitutes one of the bases of social life (1954: 2). In focusing on the processes by which wealth is amassed and distributed, the poet is describing in an ideal state many of the functions that are the basis of the Castilian civilization to which he belongs and of which he is a partisan. With our retrospective view, we perceive the Reconquest as a continuum, a victorious flow of Christian hegemony from the north toward the south interrupted occasionally by the ebb of momentary defeat. But without that comprehensive vision, the poet no doubt entertained the possibility that a very real alternative to his own Christian, Castilian civilization could come to dominate Spain, namely the civilization of the Almohads which had recently asserted its presence so forcefully that some Castilians must have been led to doubt that their own cause would prevail. For him the Cid's exercise of power is superior not just because the hero was in the right, but because he exercised it effectively, with measure and good judgment. The Cid's gifts to Alfonso buy him peace and impose an obligation on the king to return the favors, both immediately in the form of what Alvar Fáñez requests and later in the form of the marriage alliance that the king arranges with the Infantes de Carrión. The contemporary audience's expectation that gifts would be reciprocated – a fundamental assumption in societies such as this – was reinforced by this portrayal.

Gift-giving is not merely an economic function but a moral one, and the Cid is presented as a man who heals through his gifts the wounds inflicted on society by the unjust accusations of *malos mestureros*. Portrayed as a giver rather than a receiver of gifts, he takes on a moral superiority that depends for its effect not upon the principles of Christian conduct but rather upon a system of social custom, termed by Mauss "total prestation" (1954: 6–8). He acts not as an individual but as the head of a clan, whose members, including Alfonso VIII of Castile and the Laras of Molina, constitute the most important segment of the poet's audience and participate in the prestige deriving from the hero's superiority. His enemies – and their descendants – on the other hand, demonstrate their subservience by accepting gifts that they subsequently refuse to return until the legal proceedings force them to.

In its portrayal of the process of acquiring and distributing goods, then, the

Conclusion

Cantar de mio Cid is by no means narrow; in fact, it demonstrates in more specific ways than other Western European epics the reciprocal obligations that hold society together.

The Cid's daughters' two sets of marriages are imbedded in this framework. They serve a predominantly economic purpose in that they allow the exchange of the hero's wealth first for an ephemeral prestige based solely upon the values of inherited rank, then for a lasting one that joins his lineage with the royal families of Navarre and Aragon.

As Claude Lévi-Strauss has observed, in societies characterized by gift economies the woman given in marriage is "the supreme gift among those that can be obtained in the form of reciprocal gifts" (1969: 65). The gift-giving through which the hero manifests his wealth and power in the first and second *cantares* leads directly to the king's intervention in favor of the most extravagant gift-giving, the bestowal of his daughters on the Infantes de Carrión carried out by Alfonso VI's own hand. Alfonso VIII also ventured to give one of the most cherished of the gifts at his disposal, his daughter Berenguela, to a powerful prince, Alfonso IX of Leon, in a gesture similarly fraught with dangers to his honor.

The marriages allow the poetic Cid to test the value of the reputation he has acquired during his campaigns against well-established inherited values. In the period in which the poem was composed, Alfonso VIII and the Laras of Molina belonged to an extended kin group whose interests coincided not merely on the political but also on the social level. Both the king and the Laras had an interest in maintaining the honor of their renowned ancestor Rodrigo Díaz of Vivar, which was a kind of moral capital inherited from him that they shared in common.

The invention of a lineage as a political strategy was by no means unheard of in the Middle Ages. A noteworthy example is found in the case of the kin group of Bertulf, provost of the collegial church of St. Donatian of Bruges. Several of Bertulf's nephews conspired together to murder Count Charles the Good of Bruges in 1127 and have one of their own number replace him, because the count, in retaliation for acts of private warfare committed within his jurisdiction, had destroyed a house belonging to a member of the clan. One by one Bertulf's kin, even those who had not taken part in the conspiracy, were killed by Count Charles's avengers. The notary Galbert of Bruges, writing about these events, places Bertulf's kin in a lineage that he calls the "Erembalds." He claims they were descended from a certain low-ranking knight named Boldran, a castellan of Bruges who had killed his lord by throwing him into a river after committing adultery with the lord's wife, in conjunction with whom he took over the castellany. This fictitious evil lineage was designed to justify the collective punishment of Bertulf's kinsmen, some of whom were executed by being thrown from a tower (Barthélemy 1988: 93–6). The invention of a lineage is, of course, the motivation behind the constitution of the French epic cycle of Doon de Mayence, who was purported to be the ancestor not only of Ganelon but of many of the other notable traitors whose deeds are recounted in the genre. The Cid poet does not invent lineages, but he ascribes fictional deeds to their members, and his work was inspired by the same mental structure that motivated Galbert of Bruges's revisionist history: the inheritance of social merit and blame from one's ancestors.

The *Cantar de mio Cid* was an appropriation of the Cid's fame adapted to the interests of the society in which the *juglar* lived. This view entails a model of the poem's functions in society and its relationship to the historical period it purports to represent. The poet was not an historian, but rather one who took a few historical details – that probably reached him through the tradition of songs about the Cid – and wove out of them a fictional song whose purpose was to encourage certain types of conduct. The poem is not, as Menéndez Pidal interpreted it, a faithful account of eleventh-century history marked by a few exaggerations and distortions, but rather fiction in which a very few eleventh-century details happen to be preserved.

Notes

1 HISTORICAL AND THEORETICAL FRAMEWORK

1 Is it more likely, for instance, that an epic poem was composed orally or in writing in a period in which only a tiny proportion of the population was able to read and an even smaller fraction was able to write? Furthermore, as I shall argue in chapter 5, legal knowledge was in this age largely in the custody of specialists who learned it and passed it on by oral means. From what we know of the state of twelfth-century society, an assumption of orality should take precedence over the historical accident that *one* of the Castilian epics known to have existed in the period has come down to us in writing. Among the more than 300 manuscripts that comprise the corpus of medieval epic poetry in the Romance languages, only one, the Oxford manuscript of the *Chanson de Roland*, can be dated with assurance to the twelfth century.
2 Mentions of the *Cantar de mio Cid* without further qualification refer to the extant manuscript rather than to lost versions, prosifications, or the corpus of surviving versions as a whole.
3 It is entirely possible that the *Cantar de mio Cid*, the only Castilian epic to survive substantially intact, owes its existence today partly to a perceived aesthetic superiority over its epic congeners. Certainly the appreciation lavished upon it by critics since Menéndez Pidal first published his classic edition might lead to the assumption that, if we could compare the poem to other integral *cantares de gesta* in their poetic form, it would rank toward the high end on a scale of quality.
4 The medieval title *Estoria de España* is used here and throughout in preference to the designation *Primera crónica general* under which Menéndez Pidal published the work (1955).
5 Unless otherwise noted, all quotations from the text of the *Cantar de mio Cid* are based on Colin Smith's 1972 edition.

2 THE ACQUISITION OF WEALTH

1 I am not convinced by Pardo's arguments (1972) that, while the codex lacks a folio, the poem may well have begun with the line "De los sos ojos tan fuerte mientre lorando."
2 As Resina remarks (1984: 420), the question of the Cid's guilt is never resolved:

> Diríamos que la cuestión de la culpabilidad, inserta en la cuestión de honor feudal, es desplazada por una nueva manifestación del valor de la persona cifrado en la ostentación de las riquezas adquiridas.

The displacement of responsibility for a possible economic impropriety by the acquisition of extraordinary riches is an instance of the poet's narrative irony.

3 Half of the loan is given in the form of gold: not 300 gold marks but the equivalent in gold of 300 silver marks. Russell too is puzzled by the function of the exchange, and thinks that the poet may be influenced by the fact that chests were exhibited at Cardeña in connection with the tomb cult of the Cid (1958: 77). This possibility is not to be ruled out, but it does not exclude a reason that is motivated by the plot.

4 Lacarra (1980a: 190), basing herself on Pirenne, points out that most loans were made for the term of one year, as in the poem.

5 Cipolla (1956) notes that loans to rulers were considered to be riskier than those made to private parties, and that the rates of interest charged to them were correspondingly higher. The Holy Roman Emperor Frederick II usually had to agree to 30 to 40 percent per annum. A lord in the Cid's position, however, who was putting up "security," might obtain lower rates despite his lack of an economic base.

6 The poem's economic aspects have seldom attracted attention. Nilda Guglielmi (1963–65: 52–3) sees the Cid's social mobility as the result of the acquisition of wealth, both movable and landed, deriving from military power and resulting in the acquisition of prestige. Gárate Córdoba (1967) discusses the thematics of booty. Rodríguez Puértolas (1967), Garci-Gómez (1982, 1987), and Conerly (1984) also treat the question, but from points of view different from mine. Although Garci-Gómez knew of Duby's work, he made little use of its conceptual framework and confined himself for the most part in his book to discussion of the roles of Rachel and Vidas.

7 Guglielmi (1963–65: 59–65) discusses the differences between the lax feudal practices found in the Iberian Peninsula and those associated with the stricter systems of France and Germany, with appropriate references and an analysis of certain aspects exemplified in the poem.

8 The poet's concern to show that the Cid did not pay the king his fifth may account for ll. 507–11:

> Comidios mio Çid   el que en buen ora fue nado
> al rey Alfonso   que legarien sus compañas,
> quel buscarie mal   con todas sus mesnadas.
> Mando partir   tod aqueste aver [sin falla]
> sos quiñoneros   que gelos diessen por carta.

Perhaps the *mal* that the Cid would undergo in this situation would be the king's appropriation of his *quinta*.

9 David Hook (1980: 41) quotes documents from the years 1062 (cartulary of the monastery of Vega), 1076 (cartulary of San Pedro de Arlanza), and 1205 (from Menéndez Pidal's *Documentos lingüísticos de España*), in which horses are evaluated at 200 silver solidi, 40 solidi, and 20 *maravedíes* respectively. I have preferred to use the documentation of Reyna Pastor de Togneri since it involves the period that the poet is depicting. A good war horse was unquestionably worth more than a pack horse or a plough horse, and my calculations assume that the horses acquired from Moorish armies were of considerable value.

10 Coins were, of course, often debased and varied considerably in value.

3 ECONOMY AND GIFT-GIVING

1 "Must have been" because otherwise the Cid would have no adequate source for the gift to Alfonso of 100 horses (1274); the Cid's *quinta* of 30,000 marks may well represent the value of his booty rather than a trove of coins.
2 Puns are not alien to the poem: see l. 1068 and the note to it in Michael (1978); also l. 2411.
3 Almost the entire passage is missing from the Per Abbat manuscript but its contents are paraphrased in the *Crónica de veinte reyes* (Dyer 1975: 86–7).
4 Resina (1984: 426) underscores the ironic sense of l. 2147, "Dixo el rey don Alfonsso: '¡Mucho me avedes enbargado!'": the king's status falls in relation to the Cid's as he accepts more gifts from the latter without giving any in return.

4 SOCIAL STATUS, LEGITIMACY, AND INHERITED WORTH

1 John K. Walsh (1976–77) astutely points up the discrepancy between the Infantes' cowardly behavior and their capability as fighters in the trials by combat, ascribing the latter to the poet's consciousness of composing within an epic tradition of judicial combat between worthy opponents.
2 In the scene in the *Crónica particular* in which Ansur González intervenes in court, there is no mention of either *molinera* or *molinos*, but the phrasing of Ansur's exhortation to his cousins, "dexad essas compañas villanas e derrachadas," contains a hint of the notion that their enemy is perhaps not of pure noble lineage. A masterly treatment of the legends here under discussion will be found in Samuel G. Armistead's article, "Dos tradiciones épicas sobre el nacimiento del Cid," forthcoming in the *Nueva Revista de Filología Hispánica*, of which the author kindly furnished me an advance copy.
3 I agree with Smith, Menéndez Pidal, and Huntington, against Michael, that the first hemistich of l. 3691, "vençudo es el campo," belongs to Gonzalo Ansúrez's speech. Menéndez Pidal and Smith give the whole line to Gonzalo Ansúrez, whereas Huntingdon only ascribes to him the first hemistich.
4 Nilda Guglielmi has devoted a rich study (1963–65) to social mobility in the poem, treating the Cid's rise in status within the social estate (*estamento*) of the aristocracy. Michael Harney (1987) has taken up questions of class stratification with relation to the sociological literature, concluding that the features found in the poem "imply a society of elementary ranking ... but not of finely graded class stratification" (218).

5 THE POET'S MILIEU

1 Ubieto Arteta (1973: 116–21) has made a case for María having married the infante Pedro, son of Pedro I of Aragon, who would have died in 1104 without offspring; she would then have contracted marriage with Ramon Berenguer III, count of Barcelona. Since the main source for this first marriage is the *Estoria de España*, however, its historicity is not at all certain, and Chalon (1967: 222–6) and Lapesa (1985: 34) have called its existence into question.
2 Russell (1958: 71), however, thinks that the poet may simply be attempting to win

Notes to pages 64–96

sympathy for the inhabitants of San Esteban from an audience which was remote from the town.
3 A more elaborate account of the writing down of formerly oral laws is given in the *Fuero viejo de Vizcaya*, cited in Pérez-Prendes 1978: 398.
4 Whether that is the case or not, it is perhaps of interest that the particular form that the name takes, obviously by popular etymology, recalls the character Thorhall Asgrimsson in *Njal's Saga* – a work in which Germanic customal law plays an even more prominent role than it does in the *Cantar de mio Cid* – who, although afflicted with an infection on the leg, sends crucial legal advice by messenger to the court in which the lawsuit against Njal's killers is being prosecuted. In addition to *sabidor*, the poem uses the term *coñosçedor* to designate those charged with seeing to it that the law was followed, in this case in the trial at Toledo where the term refers to, among others, counts Anrrich and Remond (ll. 3137–8).
5 See also, in regard to the status of law in the poem, the perspicacious remarks of Ruth Webber (1986a: 84–6). David Hook has pointed out (1980) what he considers to be similarities between the poem and certain contemporary documents of a legal nature. The problem with his analysis is that the phrases and practices in question ("del otra part," the valuation of swords and other property in monetary terms, the use of comprehensive binomials such as "Moors and Christians," concern for the provision of offspring, insistence on the fact of payment having been made) are not uniquely legal: they belong to the language and concerns of day-to-day existence that provided the impetus for law-making. Hook maintains that "the *PMC* has an exceptionally rich legal content" (49) but I must insist on the parallel with Marie de France, in whose *Lanval* all the major steps of what later emerges as Anglo-Norman trial procedure can be traced but who has never, as far as I know, been linked with the legal profession. Poets are word-smiths, aspiring to portray scenes in a convincing manner: it is their business to be knowledgeable about laws when they are describing trials just as they must show themselves to be familiar with weapons and military techniques when describing battles, whatever their non-poetic occupations.
6 Colin Smith has conjectured (1977: 83–4; 1980: 108) that Berenguela's abortive engagement to Conrad and her later marriage to Alfonso IX of Leon might have played a role in inspiring the poet to posit double marriages for the Cid's daughters. Smith may well be correct, and his speculation accords with the conclusions formulated later in this chapter.
7 Viewed in this light, the features of the poem that reinforce group unity take on a special significance (see Montgomery 1986–87).

6 GEOGRAPHY AND HISTORY

1 Romero 1966: 89–90. Sancha's patronymic has been called into question. See Romero 1962: 94–5.
2 Ubieto Arteta (1973: 74–81) argues that the poet knew the area around San Esteban de Gormaz by hearsay only. This reasoning is based partly on the mention of the Calçada de Quinea in the vicinity of San Esteban, l. 400, which Ubieto takes as a mistaken location, the "true" Calçada de Quinea linking Astorga with Mérida in the western part of the Iberian peninsula. This is a fragile argument, especially for a period for which knowledge of local details is often lacking.
3 As his cousin Rodrigo Jiménez de Rada tells it:

Domino autem aliter faciente, Didacus Lupi de Pharo, cui ducatus exercitus erat commissus, praemisit filium Lupum Didaci, et duos nepotes eius, Sancium Fernandi et Martinum Munionis, ut praecederent ad montis supercilia obtinenda. Verum cum illi de strenuitate confisi, aliquantulum procederent improvisi, in summitate montis iuxta castrum quod Ferral dicitur, quosdam Arabes invenerunt, qui insultum facientes in eos, fere laesissent, nisi divina gratia operante, acceptis armis, praedicti Christiani cum suis Arabes viriliter repulsissent: et summitatem montis per Dei gratiam observarunt, ita quod statim fixis tentoriis, inibi remanserunt.   (ed. Cabanes Pecourt 1968: 182)

4 Seen from the point of view of later generations, Félez Muñoz's action would have made possible the descent of the Aragonese and Castilian royal families and of the Laras of Molina from the Cid.
5 Marcel Mauss (1954: 22) describes a similar phenomenon in regard to the exchange of a certain type of gift (*vaygu'a*: armshells and necklaces "kept for the joy of having") among the Trobriand Islanders:

> All of them, at least the most valuable and the most coveted, have a name, a personality, a past, and even a legend attached to them, to such an extent that people may be named after them. One cannot say that they are actually the object of a cult, for the Trobrianders are positivists in their way. But it is impossible not to recognize their superior and sacred nature. To possess one is "exhilarating, comforting, soothing in itself." Their owners handle them and gaze at them for hours. Mere contact with them is enough to make them transmit their virtues.

6 An undated charter in which Sancha Gómez, widow of Gonzalo Pérez of Molina, grants to the monastery of Huerta the property of Buenafuente for the establishment of a monastery of women is witnessed by, among others, one Pedro Abad, the son of Blasco García (Salazar y Castro 1696–97, 4: 31). The last attestation of Gonzalo Pérez of Molina is a donation of 6 April 1238 (Salazar y Castro 1696–97, 1: 239), thirty-one years after the date given in the poem's colophon.
7 In monastic parlance, a grange is a substantial arable field with a farmhouse in which the *granjero* dwelt. See Alvarez Palenzuela 1978: 53–9.
8 See no. 74 in García Luján (1981: 116), dated by its editor to 1194–1203, in which Pedro de Vera lends 200 *alfonsinos* to Abbot Jimeno, *in presencia dompni Martini quondam Segontini episcopi*. The implication is obvious: the monastery was only able to secure the assistance of this particular patron through the good graces of St. Martín, even though he was now in retirement.
9 Colin Smith (1980) makes a case for identifying the Cluniacs who took possession of Cardeña in 1142 as coming from San Zoil de Carrión long patronized by the family of the counts of Carrión.
10 This was not necessarily true of monasteries which had been established before becoming affiliated with the Cistercian Order. See Cocheril 1964: 228. The poet does not mention the great monastery of Santo Domingo de Silos, which is squarely on the path the Cid takes into exile. His favoritism toward the Cistercian variant of the Benedictine Order would explain this notable omission.
11 The early trajectory of the Per Abbat manuscript is unknown. If it was kept at Huerta in the thirteenth century, its contents could have entered the tradition of Alphonsine historiography as the result of Alfonso X's *vistas* there in 1267 with his

father-in-law Jaume I of Aragon, who, it will be recalled, owned the sword Tizón. Diego Catalán has suggested that Alfonso X himself may have been the first to confer high historical value on the poem (1963: 305). Both Catalán (300–1) and Pattison (1983a: 121) believe that the *Estoria de España* version of the Cid's deeds is based on the extant redaction of the poem and the king may have commissioned a copy after seeing the poem in manuscript at Huerta. See Zamora 1962a: 44–5. Fernando III also met with Jaume I at Huerta, in 1234 (Aguilera y Gamboa 1908: 255). Another possibility is that the text was passed on in the lineage of Martín Muñoz, nephew of Rodrigo Jiménez de Rada, who donated funds to build the refectory of Huerta. His grandson, Juan Díaz, was *caballerizo* of Alfonso "el Sabio," and another grandson, Gonzalo of Finojosa, who died in 1319 and was thus perhaps a contemporary of the scribe who copied the extant manuscript, was bishop of Burgos (Aguilera y Gamboa 1980: 44).

7 THE *CANTAR DE MIO CID* AND THE FRENCH EPIC TRADITION

1 It should be pointed out that a supposed "parecido estructural" (Smith 1977: 135) is, in this case as well, limited to an expected and well nigh inevitable collocation of the words for "army," "drums," and "to sound."
2 The parallels culled by Smith (1977: 136–7) from previous scholarship are no more convincing, with the exception of the "epic prayer," on which more below.
3 Smith has suggested, as the reader will recall, that the *Cantar de mio Cid* may have been influenced by a lost early version of *Florence de Rome*. Another instance of the same selective positivism: In arguing that the poet must have conducted "historical investigation" (Russell's phrase) to come up with the names of so many characters who lived in the Cid's time, Smith asserts that "we have no reason to suppose their presence in some other chronicle source now lost." But why not, if he is willing to suppose the presence of an influencing episode in the lost version of a French poem even in the face of a summary of that version that lacks the episode? See also Deyermond 1985: 125.
4 Both Pio Rajna, who first took cognizance of similarities in the two lion episodes, and Menéndez Pidal, who referred to them (1963: 23–4), considered them to be too vague to form the basis for any significant conclusion.
5 I cite one detail as an example: Smith believes that the name of the French church *San Symon* could have made the *Cid* poet recall *San Servan*. The anthroponyms are both bisyllabic and share initial and final letters – hardly resemblance enough on which to base solid conclusions.
6 The uncle–nephew relationship is not mentioned specifically in the *Cantar de mio Cid*, but Alvar Fáñez calls Elvira and Sol his *primas* on two occasions: if the poet meant to draw the parallel with the Charlemagne–Roland relationship, he was certainly timid about doing so!

8 MODE OF COMPOSITION

1 Menéndez Pidal observed (1961: 177): "Los refundidores de los poemas épicos medievales suelen retocar el desenlace, dejando intacto el comienzo del Cantar." In evoking this phenomenon he had the model of only two poets in mind.
2 What I wrote in 1973 apropos of the incorporation of the Episode of Baligant into the *Chanson de Roland* is also pertinent here: "Each singer in the oral tradition is at

liberty to change any individual verse, and even to modify larger portions of the received work as he sees fit, as long as his audience does not prevent him from doing so by its protestations. We know from Albert B. Lord's testimony and analyses that a singer may alter every line of a song he has just heard sung, and still produce what is, in effect, the same song, for in the oral tradition the reproduction of a song consists not in a phrase by phrase rendering of the previous version, but in a recreation, often with quite different phraseology, of what is basically the same plot. Through this gradual process (gradual because, although the poem is in a constant state of flux, the traditional *connaissances* of both singer and audience exert a strong conservative influence), the poem comes inevitably to change. But within the tradition of any given poem there is a greater stability on the level of themes than on the formulaic level. Thus it may well be that the principal elements of *Roland*'s plot, including the Episode of Baligant, were constituted before the middle of the eleventh century, and that even some of the highly mythical themes had for hundreds of years been passed along in the same tradition as the central historical events, while others represent more recent innovations; this course of development would not necessarily be detectable as a *formulaic* variation between the different parts of the song, for the jongleurs who transmitted it during the latter part of the eleventh century would have substituted formulas of their own liking while remaining more or less faithful ... to the basic plot. This process would eventually produce the uniformity of formulas we find in the Oxford *Roland* despite the composite nature of its narrative" (102–3). The process here described is characteristic of certain oral traditions of extended narrative.

3 Pellen (1976: 88) registers 27 occurrences of the word "Carrión" in the second *cantar* and 110 in the third.

4 For an assessment of the controversy over written vs. oral composition see Webber 1986b.

5 Precisely one of the purposes of the book I published in 1973 was to demonstrate that the reasoning by which Rychner concluded that the *chansons de geste* were orally composed applied to the *Chanson de Roland* as well as to the other nine poems.

6 Margaret Chaplin (1976), analyzing samples of Berceo's *Milagros*, the *Libro de Apolonio*, and the *Libro de Alexandre*, found respectively 7 percent, 10 percent, and 12.5 percent formulas. Even if the study of samples were adequate (see Duggan 1973: 18–21), these figures would only be meaningful on a comparative basis. Chaplin merely concludes, however, that "formulae are certainly not the exclusive property of oral composers" (15). That poets occasionally repeat themselves regardless of the mode of composition they employ has never been contested, but when one is attempting to find evidence for or against orality it is the *relative levels* of repetition in oral and written works that are of interest. Chaplin also quotes Lord as maintaining, in conversation, that "anything less than 50 per cent of true formulae is unsatisfactory," that is to say indicates that the text under examination was probably not orally composed; I cannot help thinking that some misapprehension is involved, since Lord has published his view (1968: 24) that "a pattern of 50 or 60 percent straight formula or formulaic, *with 10 to perhaps 25 percent straight formula*, indicates clearly literary or written composition" (my italics). Chaplin's figures for formulaic density in the *Cantar de mio Cid* are based on samples consisting of a total of only seventy-nine lines. While I agree with her conclusion regarding Spanish epic that "at some stage an oral tradition such as that described by Parry and Lord has

played a part in the formation of the poems" (18), I do not share her view that "the epics as we have them today are learned," at least as regards the *Cantar de mio Cid*. John Miletich, in a series of studies (see Miletich 1981: 194n2), has made the case for two types of style, an "elaborate" style characterized by the recurrence of hemistichs expressing similar ideas, and an "essential" or non-recurring style. Examining the elaborate style in a body of Hispanic, South-Slavic, and Russian poetry consisting of approximately 15,000 lines, he has found that the traditional texts average 33 percent of elaborate-style repetition, while South-Slavic texts that were composed in writing, along with the *Cantar de mio Cid*, average only about 16 percent. That these categories do not correspond to formulaic and non-formulaic language explains why Miletich's figures for the *Cantar de mio Cid* are so radically at variance both with mine and with those set forth in the important study by John Geary (1980), who provides a classification of formulas and conducts an analysis of repetition in the *Mocedades de Rodrigo* and the *Poema de Fernán González*. Miletich concludes (1981: 194) that the poem "is a text composed in writing in which oral tradition has to some extent played a part, and that it was destined for oral diffusion." For a critique of Miletich's concepts and methodology, see Lord 1986: 481–91.

7 Kenneth Adams's contention (1972: 118) that dictation would not adequately account for the presence side by side of good meaning and syllabic irregularity remains to be proven. According to Harvey's hypothesis, the text would be made up of the poet's own words – with the exception of modifications introduced by the person taking the recitation down from dictation and by the scribal tradition – thus making sense, but those words would have been uttered without the rhythmic reinforcement that music would normally have provided him. He would, then, presumably have used on many occasions words and phrases other than the ones he would have uttered in an oral performance, thus the irregularity of meter. Wholesale attempts to arrive at metrically regular forms of proper names, epithets, and other formulas on the basis of the extant text are thus unlikely to succeed unless one is a poet with access to the traditional technique of epic composition in Old Spanish. Adams has elsewhere (1976) explored other anomalous features of the text that are illuminated with recourse to Lord's transcriptions of Yugoslavian materials.

8 Lambert's tale is also evidence for the existence of what Menéndez Pidal called the *canto noticiero*, since the jongleur would have been spreading word of an event in which some of his contemporaries had taken part, as well as for the sanctioning function for the medieval epic. See Duggan 1986b: 7–10.

9 Smith's text reads "la Foz." I accept Ubieto Arteta's suggestion (1973: 85) that the word "foz" should remain uncapitalized, with the meaning "narrow pass, defile."

9 CONCLUSION

1 In a similar context Samuel Armistead, in his critique of D. G. Pattison's *From Legend to Chronicle* (Armistead 1986–7: 342–3), laments "the recurrent individualist misconception that, if the poem attests to 'artistry' – if it is inventive, if it is, *in fine*, an artistic success – then, of course, it cannot possibly be popular or oral or traditional."

List of References

Adams, Kenneth. 1972. "The Metrical Irregularity of the *Cantar de mio Cid*: A Restatement Based on the Evidence of Names, Epithets and Some Other Aspects of Formulaic Diction." *Bulletin of Hispanic Studies*, 49: 109–19.
— 1976. "The Yugoslav Model and the Text of the *Poema de Mio Cid*." In *Medieval Hispanic Studies Presented to Rita Hamilton*, 1–10. London: Tamesis.
— 1978–79. "*Pensar de*: Another Old French Influence on the *PMC* and Other Medieval Spanish Poems." *La Corónica*, 7: 8–12.
Aguilera y Gamboa, Enrique de, Marqués de Cerralbo. 1908. *Discursos leídos ante la Real Academia de la Historia en la recepción pública en 31 de mayo de 1908: El arzobispo D. Rodrigo Ximénez de Rada y el monasterio de Santa María de Huerta*. Madrid: Real Academia de la Historia.
Aguirre, J. M. 1968. "Epica oral y épica castellana: Tradición creadora y tradición repetitiva." *Romanische Forschungen*, 80: 13–43.
Alamo, Juan del. 1950. *Colección diplomática de San Salvador de Oña (822–1284)*, vol. 1: 822–1214. Consejo Superior de Investigaciones Científicas, Escuela de Estudios Medievales, Textos, 12. Madrid.
Alfonso X "el Sabio." 1555. *Las siete partidas*. Glosadas por el licenciado Gregorio López. Salamanca: Andrea de Portonariis.
Alonso, Dámaso. 1953. "La primitiva épica francesa a la luz de una nota emilianense." *Revista de Filología Española*, 37: 1–94. Repr. in *Primavera temprana de la literatura europea: lírica, épica, novela*, 81–200. Colección Guadarrama de Crítica y Ensayo, 22. Madrid: Guadarrama, 1961. Also repr. in *Obras completas*, 2: *Estudios y ensayos sobre literatura*, part 1: *Desde los orígenes románicos hasta finales del siglo XVI*, pp. 225–319. Madrid: Gredos, 1973.
Alvarez Palenzuela, Vicente-Angel. 1978. *Monasterios cistercienses en Castilla*. Universidad de Valladolid.
Armistead, Samuel G. 1960. "Para el texto de la *Refundición de las Mocedades de Rodrigo*." *Anuario de Estudios Medievales*, 3: 529–40.
— 1986–87. "From Epic to Chronicle: An Individualist Appraisal." *Romance Philology*, 40: 338–59.
— Forthcoming. "Dos tradiciones épicas sobre el nacimiento del Cid." *Nueva Revista de Filología Hispánica*.
Aubrun, Charles. 1972. "Le *Poema de mio Cid*, alors et à jamais." *Philological Quarterly*, 51: 12–22.
Barceló, Miguel. 1967–68. "Sobre dos textos cidianos." *Boletín de la Real Academia de Buenas Letras de Barcelona*, 32: 16–25.
Barthélemy, Dominique. 1988. "Kinship." In *A History of Private Life*, ed. Philippe Ariès and Georges Duby, 2: *Revelations of the Medieval World*, ed. Georges Duby, 85–155. Cambridge, Mass.: The Belknap Press of Harvard University Press.

References

Bello, Andrés. 1883. "Observaciones sobre la *Historia de la literatura española* de Jorge Ticknor, ciudadano de los Estados Unidos." *Obras completas*, 6: *Opúsculos literarios i críticos*, 1: 281–436. Santiago de Chile: Pedro G. Ramírez.

Bloch, R. Howard. 1977. *Medieval French Literature and Law*. Berkeley: University of California Press.

Bourdillon, F. W., ed. 1897. *Tote Listoire de France (Chronique saintongeaise), Now First Edited from the Only Two Mss., with Introduction, Appendices, and Notes*. London: David Nutt.

Burriel, Andrés Marcos, S. J. 1800. *Memorias para la vida del santo rey don Fernando III*, ed. Miguel de Manuel Rodríguez. Madrid.

Cabanes Pecourt, María Desamparados, ed. 1964. *Crónica latina de los reyes de Castilla*. Textos Medievales, 11. Valencia: Anubar.

— 1968. Rodericius Ximenius de Rada, *Opera*. Rept. of the 1793 edn. With index of places and people compiled by María Desamparados Cabanes Pecourt. Textos Medievales, 22. Valencia: Anubar.

Calin, William. 1980–81a. "L'Epopée dite vivante: Réflexions sur le prétendu caractère oral des chansons de geste." *Olifant*, 8: 227–37.

— 1980–81b. "Littérature médiévale et hypothèse orale: Une divergence de méthode et de philosophie." *Olifant*, 8: 256–85.

Casacuberta, Josep de. 1926–62. Jaume I, *Cronica*. 9 vols. Barcelona: Editorial Barcino.

Castro, Américo and Federico de Onís. 1916. *Fueros leoneses de Zamora, Salamanca, Ledesma y Alba de Tormes*. Madrid: Centro de Estudios Históricos.

Catalán, Diego. 1963. "Crónicas generales y cantares de gesta. El *Mio Cid* de Alfonso X y el del Pseudo Ben-Alfarây." *Hispanic Review*, 31: 195–215 and 291–306.

— 1985. "El Mío Cid: Nueva lectura de su intencionalidad política." In *Symbolae Ludovico Mitxelena septuagenario oblatae*, ed. José L. Melena, 807–19. Vitoria: Universidad del País Vasco.

Chalon, Louis. 1967. "A propos des filles du Cid." *Le Moyen Age*, 73: 217–37.

— 1969. "Le Roi Búcar du Maroc dans l'histoire et dans la poésie épique espagnole." *Le Moyen Age*, 75: 39–49.

— 1976. *L'Histoire et l'épopée castillane du moyen âge: Le Cycle du Cid, le cycle des Comtes de Castille*. Nouvelle Bibliothèque du Moyen Age, 5. Paris: Champion.

— 1978. "Le poète du *Cantar de mio Cid* s'est-il inspiré de Salluste?" *Le Moyen Age*, 84: 479–90.

Chaplin, Margaret. 1976. "Oral-Formulaic Style in the Epic: A Progress Report." *Medieval Hispanic Studies Presented to Rita Hamilton*, 11–20. London: Tamesis.

Cipolla, Carlo M. 1956. *Money, Prices, and Civilization in the Mediterranean World, Fifth to Sixteenth Century*. Princeton University Press, published for the University of Cincinnati.

Cirot, Georges. 1918. "Appendices à la Chronique latine des rois de Castille jusqu'en 1236." *Bulletin Hispanique*, 20: 149–84.

Cocheril, Maur. 1964. "L'implantation des monastères dans la péninsule ibérique." *Anuario de Estudios Medievales*, 1: 217–87.

Conerly, Porter. 1984. "Largesse of the Epic Hero as a Thematic Pattern in the *Cantar de mio Cid*." *Kentucky Romance Quarterly*, 31: 281–9.

Craddock, Jerry R. 1974. "La nota cronológica inserta en el prólogo de las *Siete partidas*: Edición crítica y comentario." *Al-Andalus*, 39: 363–90.

— 1986. "Dynasty in Dispute: Alfonso X el Sabio and the Succession to the Throne of Castile and Leon in History and Legend." *Viator*, 17: 197–219.

Criado de Val, Manuel. 1970. "Geografía, toponimía e itinerarios del *Cantar de Mio*

References

 Cid." *Zeitschrift für Romanische Philologie*, 86: 83–107.
De Chasca, Edmund. 1968. *Registro de formulas verbales en el Cantar de mio Cid.* University of Iowa.
 1970. "Toward a Redefinition of Epic Formula in the Light of the *Cantar de mio Cid*." *Hispanic Review*, 38: 251–63.
 1972. *El arte juglaresco en el Cantar de mio Cid.* 2nd edn. Madrid: Gredos.
 1976. *The Poem of the Cid.* Twayne's World Authors Series, 378. Boston: Twayne Publishers.
Deyermond, Alan. 1969. *Epic Poetry and the Clergy: Studies on the "Mocedades de Rodrigo."* Colección Támesis, Serie A, Monografías, 5. London: Tamesis.
 1977. "Tendencies in 'Mio Cid' Scholarship, 1943–1973." In Deyermond, ed. 1977, 13–47.
 1982. "The Close of the *Cantar de Mio Cid*: Epic Tradition and Individual Variation." In *The Medieval Alexander Legend and Romance Epic: Essays in Honour of David J. A. Ross*, ed. Peter Noble, Lucie Polak, and Claire Isoz, 11–18. London: Kraus International Publications.
 1985. "A Monument for Per Abad: Colin Smith on the Making of the *Poema de Mio Cid*." *Bulletin of Hispanic Studies*, 62: 120–6.
 ed. 1977. *"Mio Cid" Studies.* London: Tamesis.
Deyermond, Alan, and David Hook. 1981–82. "The 'Afrenta de Corpes' and Other Stories." *La Corónica*, 10: 12–37.
Duby, Georges. 1973. *Guerriers et paysans, VIIe–XIIe siècle: Premier essor de l'économie européenne.* Paris: Gallimard. English trans.: *The Early Growth of the European Economy. Warriors and Peasants from the Seventh to the Twelfth Century.* Trans. Howard B. Clarke. Ithaca: Cornell University Press, 1974.
Duggan, Joseph J. 1973. *The Song of Roland: Formulaic Style and Poetic Craft.* Publications of the Center for Medieval and Renaissance Studies, University of California, Los Angeles, 6. Berkeley: University of California Press.
 1974. "Formulaic Diction in the *Cantar de mio Cid* and the Old French Epic." *Forum For Modern Language Studies*, 10: 260–9. Repr. in Duggan, ed. 1975: 74–83.
 1980–81a. "La Théorie de la composition orale des chansons de geste: Les faits et les interprétations." *Olifant*, 8: 238–55.
 1980–81b. "Le Mode de composition des chansons de geste: Analyse statistique, jugement esthétique, modèles de transmission." *Olifant*, 8: 286–316.
 1981. "Legitimation and the Hero's Exemplary Function in the *Cantar de mio Cid* and the *Chanson de Roland*." *Oral Traditional Literature: A Festschrift for Albert Bates Lord*, ed. John Miles Foley, 217–34. Columbus, Ohio: Slavica Publishers, Inc.
 1982. "The Manuscript Corpus of the Medieval Romance Epic." In *The Medieval Alexander Legend and Romance Epic: Essays in Honour of David J. A. Ross*, ed. Peter Noble, Lucie Polak, and Claire Isoz, 29–42. London: Kraus International Publications.
 1986a. "Medieval Epic as Popular Historiography: Appropriation of Historical Knowledge in the Vernacular Epic." In *La Littérature historiographique des origines à 1500, 1: Partie historique*, ed. Hans Ulrich Gumbrecht, Ursula Link-Heer, and Peter-Michael Spangenberg. *Grundriss der romanischen Literaturen des Mittelalters*, 11: 285–311. Heidelberg: Carl Winter Universitätsverlag.
 1986b. "Social Functions of the Medieval Epic in the Romance Literatures." *Oral Tradition*, 2: 1–39.
 ed. 1975. *Oral Literature: Seven Essays.* Edinburgh: Scottish Academic Press.
Duncalf, Frederic. 1969. "The Councils of Piacenza and Clermont." *A History of the*

References

Crusades, ed. Kenneth M. Setton, 1: *The First Hundred Years*, ed. Marshall W. Baldwin. 2nd edn. Madison: University of Wisconsin Press.

Dunn, Peter N. 1970. "Levels of Meaning in the *Poema de mio Cid*." *Modern Language Notes*, 85: 109–19.

1975. "*Poema de mio Cid*, vv. 23–48: Epic Rhetoric, Legal Formula, and the Question of Dating." *Romania*, 96: 255–64.

Dyer, Nancy Joe. 1975. "*El Poema de mio Cid* in the *Crónica de veinte reyes* Prosification, a Critical Edition and Study." Ph.D. dissertation: University of Pennsylvania.

Elliott, Alison Goddard. 1980–81. "The Emperor's Daughter: A Catalan Account of Charlemagne's Mother." *Romance Philology*, 34: 398–416.

Esteban, Luis. 1962. "Pergaminos del monasterio de Santa María de Huerta en el Archivo Histórico Nacional." *Celtiberia*, 23: 139–45.

Faral, Edmond. 1911. "Pour l'histoire de *Berte au grand pied* et de *Marcoul et Salomon*." *Romania*, 40: 93–6.

Fita, Fidel. 1906. "El monasterio toledano de San Servando en la segunda mitad del siglo XI. Estudio crítico." *Boletín de la Real Academia de la Historia*, 49: 280–331.

Fletcher, Richard. 1976. "Diplomatic and the Cid Revisited: The Seals and Mandates of Alfonso VII." *Journal of Medieval History*, 2: 305–37.

Fradejas Lebrero, José. 1962. *Estudios épicos: El Cid*. Aula Magna, 3. Ceuta: Instituto Nacional de Enseñanza Media.

Francis, E.-A. 1939. "The Trial in *Lanval*." *Studies in French Language and Medieval Literature Presented to Professor Mildred K. Pope*, 115–24. Manchester University Press.

Gacto Fernández, Enrique. 1969. *La filiación no legítima en el derecho histórico español*. Prólogo de José Martínez Gijón. Anales de la Universidad Hispalense. Serie: Derecho. No. 5.

Gárate Córdoba, José M. 1967. "A más moros, más ganancias. Los moros y la ganancia en el *Cantar de mio Cid*." *Espíritu y milicia en la España medieval*, 111–83. Claves de España, 5. Madrid: Publicaciones Españolas.

García Gallo, Alfonso. 1936–41. "Textos de derecho territorial castellano." *Anales de Historia del Derecho Español*, 13: 332–69.

García González, Juan. 1963. "Notas sobre fazañas." *Anuario de Historia del Derecho Español*, 11: 609–24.

García Luján, José Antonio. 1981. *Cartulario del monasterio de Santa María de Huerta*. Biblioteca Hortense, Serie A, Documenta: 1. Monasterio de Santa María de Huerta.

Garci-Gómez, Miguel. 1982. *El Burgos de mio Cid. Temas socio-económicos y escolásticos, con revisión del antisemitismo*. Burgos: Publicaciones de la Excma. Diputación Provincial de Burgos.

1987. "The Economy of *Mio Cid*." In *Romance Epic: Essays on a Medieval Genre*, ed. Hans-Erich Keller, 227–36. Studies in Medieval Culture, 24. Kalamazoo, Michigan: Medieval Institute Publications.

Gautier Dalché, Jean. 1979. *Historia urbana de León y Castilla en la edad media (siglos IX-XIII)*. Madrid: Siglo Veintiuno Editores.

Geary, John Steven. 1980. *Formulaic Diction in the Poema de Fernán González and the Mocedades de Rodrigo: A Computer-Aided Analysis*. Madrid: Ediciones José Porrúa Turanzas.

Gerli, E. Michael. 1980. "The *Ordo commendationis animae* and the Cid Poet." *Modern Language Notes*, 95: 436–41.

References

Gifford, Douglas. 1977. "European Folk-Tradition and the 'Afrenta de Corpes.'" In Deyermond, ed. 1977, 49–62.

Gil, Juan. 1974. "Carmen de expugnatione Almariae urbis." *Habis*, 5: 45–64.

Gimeno Casalduero, Joaquín. 1975. "Sobre la 'oración narrativa' medieval: estructura, origen y supervivencia." In Gimeno Casalduero, *Estructura y diseño en la literatura castellana medieval*, 11–29. Madrid: Ediciones José Porrúa Turanzas. Repr. from *Anales de la Universidad de Murcia*, 16 (1957–58).

Godefroy Menilglaise, le Marquis de. 1855. *Lambert d'Ardre, Chronique de Guines et d'Ardre*. Paris: Jules Renouard.

González, Julio. 1944. *Alfonso IX*. 2 vols. Madrid: Consejo Superior de Investigaciones Científicas.

— 1960. *El reino de Castilla en la época de Alfonso VIII*. 3 vols. Consejo Superior de Investigaciones Científicas, Escuela de Estudios Medievales, Textos, 25–7. Madrid.

— 1975. "La crónica latina de los reyes de Castilla." *Homenaje a Agustín Millares Carlo*, 2: 55–70. Gran Canaria: Caja Insular de Ahorros de Gran Canaria.

— 1980–86. *Reinado y diplomas de Fernando III*. 3 vols. Cordoba: Publicaciones del Monte de Piedad y Caja de Ahorros de Córdoba.

Gorosterratzu, Javier. 1925. *Don Rodrigo Jiménez de Rada, gran estadista, escritor y prelado*. Pamplona: Viuda de T. Bescansa.

Gould, Stephen Jay. 1981. *The Mismeasure of Man*. New York: W. W. Norton & Company.

Grassotti, Hilda. 1964. "Para la historia del botín y las parias en León y Castilla." *Cuadernos de Historia de España*, 39–40: 43–132. Repr. in Hilda Grassotti, *Miscelanea de estudios sobre instituciones castellano-leonesas*. Prólogo de Claudio Sánchez Albornoz. Bilbao: Editorial Nájera, 1978.

— 1969. *Las instituciones feudo-vasalláticas en León y Castilla*. 2 vols. Spoleto: Centro Italiano di Studi sull'Alto Medioevo.

Guglielmi, Nilda. 1963–65. "Cambio y movilidad social en el *Cantar de mio Cid*." *Anales de Historia Antigua y Medieval*, 12: 43–65.

Harney, Michael. 1987. "Class Conflict and Primitive Rebellion in the *Poema de mio Cid*." *Olifant*, 12: 171–219.

Harvey, L. P. 1963. "The Metrical Irregularity of the *Cantar de mio Cid*." *Bulletin of Hispanic Studies*, 40: 137–43.

Heers, Jacques. 1974. *Le Clan familial au moyen âge. Etude sur les structures politiques et sociales des milieux urbains*. Paris: Presses Universitaires de France.

Henríquez Ureña, Pedro. 1933. *La versificación irregular en la poesía castellana*. 2nd edn. Publicaciones de la Revista de Filología Española, 4. Madrid: Centro de Estudios Históricos, 1933.

Henry, Albert, ed. 1963. *Les Œuvres d'Adenet le Roi*, vol. 4: *Berte aus grans piés*. Université Libre de Bruxelles, Travaux de la Faculté de Philosophie et Lettres, 23. Brussels: Presses Universitaires de Bruxelles; Paris: Presses Universitaires de France.

Herslund, Michael. 1974. "Le *Cantar de mio Cid* et la chanson de geste." *Revue Romane*, 9: 69–121.

Heubeck, Alfred. 1981. "Zum Problem der homerischen Kunstsprache." *Museum Helveticum*, 38: 65–80.

Hinojosa, Eduardo de. 1899. "El derecho en el *Poema del Cid*." In *Homenaje a Menéndez y Pelayo*, 1: 541–81. Madrid: Librería General de Victoriano Suárez.

Holland, Michael. 1966. "*Rolandus Resurrectus*." In *Mélanges offerts à René Crozet à*

References

l'occasion de son soixante-dixième anniversaire, ed. Pierre Gallais and Yves-Jean Riou, 1: 397–418. Poitiers: Société d'Etudes Médiévales.

Hook, David. 1973. "The Conquest of Valencia in the *Cantar de mio Cid*." *Bulletin of Hispanic Studies*, 50: 120–6.

——— 1979. "The Opening *Laisse* of the *Poema de mio Cid*." *Revue de Littérature Comparée*, 53: 490–501.

——— 1980. "On Certain Correspondences between the *Poema de mio Cid* and Contemporary Legal Instruments." *Iberoromania*, N.S. 11: 31–53.

——— 1982. "The *Poema de mio Cid* and the Old French Epic: Some Reflections." In *The Medieval Alexander and Romance Epic: Studies in Honour of David J. A. Ross*, ed. Peter Noble, Lucie Polak, and Claire Isoz, 107–18. London: Kraus International Publications.

Horrent, Jules. 1956. "El *Cantar de mio Cid* frente a la tradición rolandiana." *Coloquios de Roncesvalles, Agosto 1955*. Universidad de Zaragoza, Cursos de Verano en Pamplona. Pamplona: Diputación Foral de Navarra, Institución Príncipe de Viana. Repr. in Horrent 1973: 341–74.

——— 1973. *Historia y poesía en torno al Cantar del Cid*. Barcelona: Editorial Ariel.

Huber, Victor Aimé, ed. 1844. *Chronica del famoso cavallero Cid Ruydiez Campeador*. New edition. Marburg: Bayrhoffer.

Huici Miranda, Ambrosio. 1913. *Las crónicas latinas de la Reconquista*. 2 vols. Valencia: Establecimiento Tipográfico Hijos de F. Vives Mora.

——— 1956. *Las grandes batallas de la Reconquista durante las invasiones africanas (almorávides, almohades y benimerines)*. Madrid: Consejo Superior de Investigaciones Científicas, Instituto de Estudios Africanos.

——— 1965. "Las luchas del Cid campeador con los almorávides y el enigma de su hijo, Diego." *Hesperis*, 6: 79–114.

Huntington, Archer M., ed. 1903. *Cronica del famoso cauallero Cid Ruydiez campeador*. New York: De Vinne Press.

Janko, Richard. 1982. *Homer, Hesiod and the Hymns. Diachronic Development in Epic Diction*. Cambridge University Press.

Jordán de Asso, Ignacio, and Miguel de Manuel y Rodríguez. 1771. *El Fuero viejo de Castilla*. Madrid: Ibarra.

Labande, Edmond-René. 1955. "Le Credo épique: à propos de prières dans les chansons de geste." In *Recueil de travaux offert à M. Clovis Brunel*, 2: 62–80. Paris: Société de l'Ecole des Chartes.

Lacarra, José María. 1975. "En torno a la propagación de la voz 'hidalgo'." In *Homenaje a Agustín Millares Carlo*, 2: 43–53. Gran Canaria: Caja Insular de Ahorros de Gran Canaria.

Lacarra, María Eugenia. 1980a. *El Poema de mio Cid: realidad histórica e ideología*. Madrid: Ediciones José Porrúa Turanzas.

——— 1980b. "La utilización del Cid de Menéndez Pidal en la ideología militar franquista." *Ideologies and Literature*, 3: 95–127.

Lalinde Abadía, Jesús. 1970. "Apuntes sobre lo erudito y lo popular en el derecho medieval español." *Homenaje a Elías Serra Ráfols*, 305–18. Universidad de la Laguna.

——— 1976. *Los fueros de Aragón*. Zaragoza: Librería General.

——— 1981. *Derecho histórico español*. 2nd edn. Barcelona: Ariel.

Lapesa, Rafael. 1985. *Estudios de historia lingüística española*. Madrid: Paraninfo.

Layna Serrano, Francisco. 1932. *El monasterio de Ovila*. Madrid: Nuevas Gráficas.

Lévi-Strauss, Claude. 1969. *Les Structures élémentaires de la parenté*. The Hague: Mouton.

References

Lindley Cintra, Luis Felipe, ed. 1951–61. *Crónica Geral de Espanha de 1344*. Fontes Narrativas da História Portuguesa, 2. 3 vols. Lisbon: Academia Portuguesa da História.
Lomax, Derek W. 1977. "The Date of the *Poema de Mio Cid*." In Deyermond, ed. 1977: 73–81.
— 1978. *The Reconquest of Spain*. London: Longman.
López Estrada, Francisco. 1982. *Panorama crítico sobre el Poema del Cid*. Literatura y Sociedad, 30. Madrid: Editorial Castalia.
Lord, Albert B. 1960. *The Singer of Tales*. Cambridge, Mass.: Harvard University Press.
— 1968. "Homer as Oral Poet." *Harvard Studies in Classical Philology*, 72: 1–46.
— 1986. "Perspectives in Recent Work on the Oral Traditional Formula." *Oral Tradition*, 1 (1986), 467–503.
McMillan, Duncan, ed. 1972. *Le Charroi de Nîmes, chanson de geste du XIIe siècle*. Paris. Klincksieck.
Magnotta, Michael. 1976. "Sobre la crítica del *Mio Cid*: problemas en torno al autor (1750–1970)." *Anuario de Letras*, 9: 51–98.
Manrique, Angel. 1642–59. *Annales Cistercienses*. 4 vols. Lyon: Laurence Anisson.
Mansilla, Demetrio. 1965. *La documentación pontificia de Honorio III (1216–1227)*. Monumenta Hispaniae Vaticana, Registros, 2. Rome: Instituto Español de Historia Eclesiástica.
Marcos Marín, Francisco, trans. 1985. *Cantar de mio Cid. Edición modernizada, estudio y notas*. Madrid: Alhambra.
Mateu y Llopis, Felipe. 1946. *Glosario hispánico de numismática*. Barcelona: Consejo Superior de Investigaciones Científicas, Sección de Estudios Medievales de Barcelona.
Mauss, Marcel. 1954. *The Gift: Forms and Functions of Exchange in Archaic Societies*. Trans. Ian Cunnison. Introduction by E. E. Evans-Pritchard. Glencoe, Illinois: The Free Press.
Menéndez Pidal, Gonzalo. 1958. "Sobre el escritorio emilianense en los siglos X y XI." *Boletín de la Real Academia de la Historia*, 143: 7–19.
Menéndez Pidal, Ramón. 1929. *La España del Cid*. 2 vols. Madrid: Editorial Plutarco.
— 1947. *La España del Cid*. 4th edn. 2 vols. Madrid: Espasa-Calpe.
— 1954–56. *Obras completas*, 3–5: *Cantar de mio Cid. Texto, gramática y vocabulario*, 3 vols. 3rd edn. Madrid: Espasa-Calpe.
— 1960. *La Chanson de Roland et la tradition épique des Francs*. Paris: A. et J. Picard.
— 1961. "Dos poetas en el *Cantar de mio Cid*." *Romania*, 82: 145–200.
— 1963. *En torno al Poema del Cid*. Barcelona: Editora y Distribuidora Hispano Americana.
— 1967. *España del Cid*. 6th edn. *Versión abreviada*, 3rd edn. Madrid: Espasa-Calpe.
— ed. 1955. *Primera crónica general de España, que mandó componer Alfonso el Sabio y se continuaba bajo Sancho IV en 1289*. 2nd edn. 2 vols. Madrid: Facultad de Filosofía y Letras.
Menéndez y Pelayo, Marcelino. 1903. *Antología de poetas líricos castellanos*, vol. 8. *Romances viejos castellanos (Primavera y flor de romances)*. Madrid: Perlado, Páez.
Meyer-Lübke, Wilhelm. 1935. *Romanisches etymologisches Wörterbuch*. 3rd edn, revised. Heidelberg: Carl Winters Universitätsbuchhandlung.
Michael, Ian, ed. 1978. *Poema de mio Cid*. Edited with introduction and notes. 2nd edn. Clásicos Castalia, 75. Madrid: Castalia.

References

Michaëlis, Carolina, ed. 1871. *Romancero del Cid*. New edition. Leipzig: F. A. Brockhaus.

Migne, J.-P., ed. 1890–91. *Saeculum XIII Innocentii III romani pontificis opera omnia*, 1–2. Patrologiae Cursus Completus. Series Latina, 214–15. Paris: Garnier Frères.

Miletich, John S. 1981. "Repetition and Aesthetic Function in the *Poema de mio Cid* and South-Slavic Oral and Literary Epic." *Bulletin of Hispanic Studies*, 58: 189–96.

Millares Carlo, Agustín. 1933. "Cartulario del monasterio de Ovila (siglo XIII)." *Anales de la Universidad de Madrid*, 2, 2: 1–42.

Minguella y Arnedo, Toribio. 1910–12. *Historia de la diócesis de Sigüenza*. 3 vols. Madrid: Revista de Archivos, Bibliotecas y Museos.

Miret y Sans, Joaquín. 1905–08. "Itinerario del rey Pedro I de Cataluña, II en Aragón (1196–1213)." *Boletín de la Real Academia de Buenas Letras de Barcelona*, 3 (1905–06): 79–87, 151–60, 238–49, 265–84, 365–87, 435–50, 497–519; 4 (1907–08): 15–36, 91–114.

Montgomery, Thomas. 1986–87. "The Rhetoric of Solidarity in the *Poema del Cid*." *Modern Language Notes*, 102: 191–205.

Moreta Velayos, Salustiano. 1971. *El monasterio de San Pedro de Cardeña. Historia de un dominio monástico castellano (902–1338)*. Acta Salmanticensia, Filosofía y Letras, 63. Universidad de Salamanca.

Nepaulsingh, Colbert I. 1983. "The 'Afrenta de Corpes' and the Martyrological Tradition." *Hispanic Review*, 51: 205–21.

Núñez Marqués, Vicente. 1955. "Itinerario del Cid desde San Esteban de Gormaz a Navapalos, lugar donde fueron golpeadas cruelmente las hijas del Cid." *Boletín de la Institución Fernán González*, 34: 737–41.

Otero Varela, Alfonso. 1959. "El *riepto* de los fueros municipales." *Anuario de Historia del Derecho Español*, 29: 153–73.

Pardo, Aristóbulo. 1972. "Los versos 1–9 del *Poema de mio Cid*. ¿No comenzaba ahí el *Poema*?" *Thesaurus*, 27: 261–92.

Parmly, Ruth. 1935. *The Geographical References in the Chanson de Garin le Loherain*. New York: Columbia University Press.

Parry, Milman. 1971. *The Making of Homeric Verse. The Collected Papers of Milman Parry*, ed. Adam Parry. Oxford: Clarendon Press.

Pastor de Togneri, Reyna. 1962. "Ganadería y precios: consideraciones sobre la economía de León y Castilla (siglos XI–XIII)." *Cuadernos de Historia de España*, 35–6: 37–55.

Pattison, D. G. 1967. "The Date of the *Cantar de mio Cid*: A Linguistic Approach." *Modern Language Review*, 42: 443–50.

——— 1983a. *From Legend to Chronicle: The Treatment of Epic Material in Alphonsine Historiography*. Medium Ævum Monographs, New Series, 13. Oxford: The Society for the Study of Mediaeval Languages and Literature.

——— 1983b. "The Cid and Alcocer." *Bulletin of Hispanic Studies*, 60: 49–51.

——— 1985–86. "Word Formation in the *Poema de mio Cid*: A Second Visit." *La Corónica*, 14: 86–8.

Pellen, René. 1976. "Le *Poème du Cid* étudié à l'ordinateur. Vocabulaire des noms propres. Examen de ce fichier." *Cahiers de Linguistique Hispanique Médiévale*, 1: 7–99.

——— 1977–78. "*Poema de mio Cid*. Vocabulaire réduit (vocables avec leur fréquence globale et leur fréquence par chant)." *Cahiers de Linguistique Hispanique Médiévale*, 2: 171–251; 3: 155–267.

References

1979. "*Poema de mio Cid*. Le système verbal: présentation générale de la conjugaison (de l'analyse du discours à la découverte des paradigmes)." *Cahiers de Linguistique Hispanique Médiévale*, 4: 71–135.

1980–81. "Cantares de mio Cid. Vocabulaires exclusifs (thématique et diachronie)." *Cahiers de Linguistique Hispanique Médiévale*, 5: 249–87; 6: 219–317.

Pérez de Urbel, Justo. 1955. "Tres notas sobre el *Cantar de Mio Cid*." *Boletín de la Institución Fernán González*, 34: 634–41.

ed. 1959. Fray Antonio de Yepes, *Crónica general de la orden de San Benito*. 3 vols. Biblioteca de Autores Españoles, 123–5. Madrid: Ediciones Atlas.

Pérez-Prendes y Muñoz de Arracó, José Manuel. 1978. *Curso de historia del derecho español*. 1. Introducción y parte general. Madrid: Ediciones Darro.

Puyol, Julio, ed. 1925. *Crónica de España por Lucas, obispo de Tuy. Primera edición del texto romanceado, conforme a un códice de la Academia*. Madrid: Revista de Archivos, Bibliotecas y Museos.

Ramos Loscertales, José María, ed. 1956. *Fuero de Viguera y Val de Funes*. Acta Salmanticensia, Serie de Filosofía y Letras, 7. Salamanca: Publicaciones de la Facultad de Filosofía y Letras de la Universidad de Salamanca.

Reilly, Bernard F. 1982. *The Kingdom of León-Castilla under Queen Urraca: 1104–1126*. Princeton University Press.

Resina, Juan Ramón. 1984. "El honor y las relaciones feudales en el *Poema de mio Cid*." *Revista de Estudios Hispánicos* (Alabama), 18: 417–28.

Riquer, Martín de. 1968. "Bavieca, caballo del Cid Campeador, y Bauçan, caballo de Guillaume d'Orange." *La leyenda del graal y temas épicos medievales*, 227–47. El Soto, 6. Madrid: Editorial Prensa Española. Repr. from *Boletín de la Real Academia de Buenas Letras de Barcelona*, 25 (1953): 127–44.

1957. *Les Chansons de geste françaises*. Trans. Irénée Cluzel. Paris: Nizet.

Rodríguez Fernández, Justiniano. 1966. *Pedro Ansúrez*. León: Excma. Diputación Provincial de León, Servicio de Publicaciones.

Rodríguez López, Amancio. 1907. *El real monasterio de las Huelgas de Burgos y el hospital del rey. Apuntes para su historia y colección diplomática con ellos relacionado*. 2 vols. Burgos: Imprenta y Librería del Centro Católico.

Rodríguez Puértolas, Julio. 1967. "Un aspecto olvidado en el realismo del *Poema de mio Cid*." *PMLA*, 82: 170–7.

1973. Francisco Santos, *El "No importa de España" y "La verdad en el potro"*. Colección Támesis, serie B, Textos, 15. London: Tamesis Books.

Romero, Agustín. 1962. "Hacia una biografía científica de San Martín de Finojosa." *Celtiberia*, 23: 93–116.

1966. "Doña Sancha Gómez, madre de San Martín de Finojosa." *Celtiberia*, 31: 77–95.

1976. "Huerta, pueblo y monasterio." *Celtiberia*, 51: 55–68.

Russell, P. E. 1952. "Some Problems of Diplomatic in the *Cantar de mio Cid* and their Implications." *Modern Language Review*, 47: 340–9.

1956. "Where Was Alcocer? (*Cantar de Mio Cid*, 1.553–861)." In *1930–1955: Homenaje a J. A. van Praag, catedrático de la Universidad de Amsterdam*, 101–7. Amsterdam: Plus Ultra.

1958. "San Pedro de Cardeña and the Heroic History of the Cid." *Medium Ævum*, 27: 57–79.

1978. "La oración de Doña Jimena (*Poema de Mio Cid*, vv. 325–367)." In *Temas de "La Celestina" y otros estudios (del "Cid" al "Quijote")*, 113–58. Letras e Ideas, Maior, 14. Barcelona: Editorial Ariel.

References

Rychner, Jean. 1955. *La Chanson de geste: Essai sur l'art épique des jongleurs.* Geneva: Droz.
Salazar y Castro, Luis. 1696–97. *Historia genealógica de la casa de Lara, sacada de los instrumentos de diversas iglesias, y monasterios, de los archivos de sus mismos descendientes, de differentes pleytos que entre sí han seguido, y de los escritores de mayor crédito y puntualidad.* 4 vols. Madrid: Imprenta Real por Mateo de Llanos y Guzmán.
Sánchez, Galo. 1919. *Fueros castellanos de Soria y Alcalá de Henares.* Madrid: Centro de Estudios Históricos.
Sánchez Albornoz, Claudio. 1962. "Dudas sobre el Ordenamiento de Nájera." *Cuadernos de Historia de España*, 35–6: 315–36.
Sancho Izquierdo, Miguel. 1916. *El fuero de Molina de Aragón.* Madrid: Librería General de Victoriano Suárez.
Santos, Francisco. 1671. *La verdad en el potro y el Cid resucitado.* Madrid: En la Imprenta de Lucas Antonio de Bedmar.
Serra Ruiz, Rafael. 1969. *Honor, honra e injuria en el derecho medieval español.* Departamento de Historia del Derecho de la Universidad de Murcia, Colección de Estudios y Documentos de Historia del Derecho, 1. Murcia: Departamento de Historia del Derecho.
Serrano, Luciano. 1935. *El obispado de Burgos y Castilla primitiva desde el siglo V al XIII.* 3 vols. Madrid: Instituto de Valencia de Don Juan.
Severin, Dorothy Sherman. 1985. "'El ynfante Epitus': The Earliest Complete Castilian Version of the Dialogue of 'Epictetus and the Emperor Hadrian.'" *Bulletin of Hispanic Studies*, 62: 25–30.
Smith, Colin, ed. 1972. *Poema de mio Cid.* Oxford: Clarendon Press.
　1976. "The Cid as Charlemagne in the *Leyenda de Cardeña*." *Romania*, 97: 509–31.
　1977. *Estudios cidianos.* Madrid: CUPSA Editorial.
　1977–78. "Further French Analogues and Sources for the *Poema de mio Cid*." *La Corónica*, 6: 14–21.
　1980. "The Choice of the Infantes de Carrión as Villains in the *Poema de mio Cid*." *Journal of Hispanic Philology* 4 (1980): 105–18.
　1983. *The Making of the Poema de mio Cid.* Cambridge University Press.
Spitzer, Leo. 1948. "Sobre el carácter histórico del *Cantar de Mio Cid*." *Nueva Revista de Filología Hispánica*, 2: 105–17. Repr. in *Sobre antigua poesía española*, 7–25. Universidad de Buenos Aires, 1962.
Suárez, Federico. 1942–44. "La colección de 'fazañas' del ms. 431 de la Biblioteca Nacional." *Anuario de Historia del Derecho Español* 14: 579–92.
Sumption, Jonathan. 1975. *Pilgrimage: An Image of Mediaeval Religion.* Totowa, New Jersey: Rowman and Littlefield.
Ubieto Arteta, Antonio. 1957. "Observaciones al *Cantar de mio Cid*." *Arbor*, 38: 145–70.
　1972. "El *Cantar de mio Cid* y algunos problemas históricos." *Ligarzas*, 4: 5–192.
　1973. *El "Cantar de mio Cid" y algunos problemas históricos.* Valencia: Anubar.
　1980. "El sentimiento antileonés en el *Cantar de mio Cid*." In *En la España medieval: estudios dedicados al Profesor D. Julio González González*, ed. Miguel Angel Ladero Quesada, 557–74. Madrid: Universidad Complutense.
　1982. "Otro dato sobre la cronología del *Cantar de mio Cid*." In *En la España medieval, III. Estudios en memoria del Profesor D. Salvador de Moxó*, 673–9. Madrid: Universidad Complutense.
Valdeavellano, Luis G. de. 1968. *Historia de España*, 1: *De los orígenes a la baja Edad*

References

Media. Part 2. 4th edn. Madrid: Manuales de la Revista de Occidente.
Vallerie, Josephine, ed. 1947. *Garin le Loheren, According to Manuscript A*. Ann Arbor: Edwards Brothers, Inc.
Vàrvaro, Alberto. 1971. "Dalla storia alla poesia epica: Alvar Fáñez." In *Studi di filologia romanza offerti a Silvio Pellegrini*, 655–65. Padua: Liviani.
Vicens Vives, Jaime. 1964. *Manual de historia económica de España*. With the collaboration of Jorge Nadal Oller. 3rd edn. Barcelona: Editorial Vicens-Vives.
Walker, Roger M. 1977. "A Possible Source for the 'Afrenta de Corpes' Episode in the *Poema de mio Cid*." *Modern Language Review*, 72: 335–47.
Wallensköld, A., ed. 1909. *Florence de Rome, chanson d'aventure du premier quart du XIIIe siècle*. SATF. Paris: Firmin-Didot.
Walsh, John K. 1970–71. "Religious Motifs in the Early Spanish Epic." *Revista Hispánica Moderna*, 36: 165–72.
    1976–77. "Epic Flaw and Final Combat in the *Poema de mio Cid*." *La Corónica*, 5: 100–9.
Waltman, Franklin M. 1973. "Formulaic Expression and Unity of Authorship in the *Poema de mio Cid*." *Hispania*, 56: 569–78.
Wathelet-Willem, Jeanne. 1975. *Recherches sur la Chanson de Guillaume: Etudes accompagnées d'une édition*. 2 vols. Bibliothèque de la Faculté de Philosophie et Lettres de l'Université de Liège, 210. Paris: Société d'Edition Les Belles Lettres.
Webber, Ruth House. 1986a. "The *Cantar de mio Cid*: Problems of Interpretation." In *Oral Tradition in Literature: Interpretation in Context*, ed. John Miles Foley, 65–88. Columbia: University of Missouri Press.
    1986b. "Hispanic Oral Literature: Accomplishments and Perspectives." *Oral Tradition*, 1: 344–80.
Wolf, Ferdinand, and Conrad Hofmann, eds. 1856. *Primavera y flor de romances*. Berlin: A. Asher.
Zahareas, Anthony N. 1964. "The Cid's Legal Action at the Court of Toledo." *Romanic Review*, 55: 161–72.
Zamora, Florentino. 1962a. "Mitras y coronas en el Real Monasterio de Santa María de Huerta." *Celtiberia*, 23: 7–50.
    1962b. "Obispos y cardenales que fueron huéspedes de Huerta." *Cistercium*, 5: 252–4.

Index

Abu Bakr, 60
Adams, Kenneth, 156n7
Adenet le Roi, 115
Aesthetic value, 5, 144, 149n3, 156n1; relativity, 144–5
Aguilera y Gamboa, Enrique de, marquis of Cerralbo, 86, 88, 96, 98, 101, 153–4n11
Aguirre, J. M., 133
Aimerico, viscount of Narbonne, 85–6
Alamos, 107
Alarcos, battle of, 11, 12, 28, 68, 69, 71, 79, 80, 84, 87, 96, 105, 135, 143
Albarracín, Santa María de, 11, 88, 93; neighbourhood "Búcar," 60
Alcadir of Valencia, 59
Alcalá de Henares, 82
Alcarria, 84, 141
Alcocer, battle of, 11, 21, 22, 25, 32, 60, 82, 83, 105, 141; fictitious place, 83–4; location of, 83; suggested by geographical collocation, 84, 100; value of, 23, 24
Alcózar, 125, 126
Alfonso I "el Batallador," king of Aragon, 10, 55, 95, 96
Alfonso II, king of Aragon and count of Barcelona, 70, 72, 88, 91, 92–3; patron of Huerta, 85
Alfonso II, king of Portugal, 9
Alfonso V, king of Leon, 60
Alfonso VI, 12, 16–17, 23, 24, 25, 33, 34, 40, 49, 60, 61, 65, 78, 79, 147; choice as topic, 58, 79; historical figure, 8, 11, 28, 35, 44, 59, 64, 74, 82, 92, 95, 96, 104, 124
Alfonso VII "el Emperador," 6, 8, 9, 11, 12, 28, 62, 71, 74, 78, 88, 96, 124
Alfonso VIII, 8, 11, 12, 13, 28, 29, 43, 64, 67, 68, 69, 70–2, 73, 74, 75, 76, 78, 79, 80, 84, 87, 91, 93, 96, 97, 103, 135, 143, 147; allied with Pedro II of Aragon, 89, 90, 91; and Cistercian Order, 87–8; descendant of Rodrigo Díaz of Vivar, 90, 105, 106–7, 134, 135, 146; intermediary between Pedro II and Sancha, 85, 89, 98; patron of Huerta, 84–5; patron of Ovila, 102; testament, 75
Alfonso IX, king of Leon, 9, 71–2, 74, 75, 76, 77, 80, 90; descended from Rodrigo Díaz of Vivar, 91; kissed hand of Alfonso VIII, 70, 135; marriage with Berenguela, see Berenguela, daughter of Alfonso VIII
Alfonso X "el Sabio," 67, 153–4n11; Alphonsine historiography, 80; *Siete partidas*, 44–6, 53, 55
Alfonso, son of Berenguela and Alfonso IX, 74, 75, 98
Alfonso Téllez de Meneses, 88
Al-Ghalib, son-in-law of Almanzor, 22
Alhama de Aragón, 84
Almohads, 20, 28, 71–2, 79, 80, 129, 143, 146
Almoravids, 8, 10, 12, 28, 59, 79, 129
Alonso, Dámaso, 122
Altercatio Hadriani Augusti et Epicteti philosophi, 56–7
Alvar Alvarez, 60, 124
Alvar Díaz, 43, 60, 124
Alvar Fáñez, Minaya, 6, 10, 18, 25, 26, 32, 33–4, 35, 36, 38, 39, 49, 54, 56, 82, 84, 103, 119, 130, 146, 154n6; historical figure, 10, 59, 61, 104, 124; in *Poema de Almería*, 128
Alvar Núñez de Lara, 76, 88
Alvar Salvadórez, 50, 90, 95, 124, 132
Alvarez Palenzuela, Vicente-Angel, 84, 87, 100, 102, 104, 153n7

168

Index

Amis et Amile, 116
Anguita, 84, 103, 141
Anrrich, Count, 56, 152n4
Ansur González, 45, 48–9, 51–2, 55–7, 59, 60, 77, 80, 130, 151n2
Aragon, 7, 9, 25, 55, 64, 69, 88, 90, 99, 142; united to Barcelona, 78, 92–3
Aragonese. *See* Dialect features
Arderico, bishop of Palencia, 88
Ariza, 82, 84, 85, 86, 88, 89, 91, 92, 93, 98, 99, 100, 103, 105, 106, 141, 143
Armistead, Samuel G., 144, 151n2, 156n1
Arnaldo de Stopañano, 89
Arnold of Guines, 140, 144
Assalit de Gúdal, 89
Astorga, bishop of, 73
Ateca, 83, 84, 85, 100, 141
Atienza, 85, 86, 99, 100, 106
Audience, 4
Aurovita, 55, 60
Auto de los reyes magos, 118, 125, 126, 127
Avengalbón, 6, 40, 54, 93, 103

Baldric of Dol, 26
Bani Hūd dynasty of Saragossa, 10
Barceló, Miguel, 10
Barcelona, 10, 12, 82; united to Aragon, 78, 92–3
Barthélemy, Dominique, 147
Bastardy, 2
Bavieca, 14, 42, 108–9
Bello, Andrés, 108, 128
Beltrán, Count, 59
Benedict, Order of St., 104, 153n10
Berceo, 127; *Milagros*, 155–6n6
Berenguela, daughter of Alfonso VIII, 9, 77, 79, 88, 89, 91; *carta de arras*, 73, 74; castles of dowry, 72, 73, 74, 75, 80; marriage to Alfonso IX, 70, 72, 73, 74, 76, 80, 89, 130, 147, 152n6
Berenguela, daughter of Alfonso IX and Berenguela, 74, 89
Berenguer Ramon I, 97
Berenguer Ramon II "el Fratricida," called in poem Remont Verenguel, 9, 21, 58, 60, 61; historical figure, 58, 79; name, 92; poet's hostility, 81, 92
Bernardo de Benavente, 89
Berte aus grans piés, 114–16, 122
Bertulf of Bruges, 147

Blanca, daughter of Alfonso VIII, 135
Blanca of Navarre, 7, 12, 15, 90
Bloch, R. Howard, 1, 67
Bologna, 66
Booty, 20–26, 30, 56, 68, 71; classic age of, 28, 79; clothing, 20, 27; distribution of, 20, 22, 26, 61, 62; enumeration of, 20, 26; evaluation of, 20, 23–6; and fame, 26; and honor, 26; *quinta*, 21–2, 23, 25, 33, 35, 36, 150n8, 151n1; unearned, 38; *see also* Wealth
Bricio, bishop of Plasencia, 88
Brihuega, 106
Bruges, 147
Bubierca, 84, 141
Búcar, king of Morocco, 60; army of, 38; battle against, 21, 24, 25, 37–8, 46–7, 55, 97, 100; *see also* Albarracín, Santa María de
Buevon de Conmarchis, 139
Burgos, 9, 11, 12, 18, 31, 61, 97, 103, 104, 106
Burriel, Andrés Marcos: *Memorias para la vida del santo rey don Fernando III*, 77

Cabanes Pecourt, María Desamparados, 29, 69, 70, 71, 72, 75, 91, 98, 135
Cabra, battle of, 16–17, 46
Cabreros, treaty of, 75, 91
Calatayud, 11, 61–2, 81, 83, 84, 85, 93, 95, 141, 143; treaty of, 78, 89
Calin, William, 136
Campaigns, military, 82; Henares valley, 22–3, 24, 35, 82, 129, 141; Jalón valley, 22–3, 24, 33, 60, 82, 129, 141; Jiloca valley, 129; Valencia, 21, 24
Campo Taranz, 84, 141
Cantar de mio Cid: *Cantar del destierro*, 6, 11, 130, 131, 147; *Cantar de las bodas*, 6, 11, 82, 130, 131, 147; *Cantar de Corpes*, 6, 11, 36, 61, 130, 131, 147; missing beginning, 16–17
Cantares de gesta, 120, 122, 149n3; resemblances to *chansons de geste*, 120–1, 123, 137, 139
Cantilena, 144
Canto noticiero, 156n8
Capital, 18, 22
Cardeña, 32, 100, 103–5; Cid legend of, 61, 150n3

Index

Carmen Campidoctoris, 128
Carrión, Beni-Gómez family of, 43, 45, 49, 54, 58, 60, 61, 77, 134, 135, 153n9
Carrión, 39, 51, 88, 106, 109, 135; court held at, 11, 12, 70, 134–5; frequency of word, 155n3
Casacuberta, Josep de, 97
Casalduero, J. Gimeno, 117, 118–19, 120
Castejón: abandonment of, 23; capture of, 21, 22, 35, 38, 82; identification as Castejón de las Armas, 83, 100, 141; value of, 24, 25
Castejón de Henares, 84
Castillejo de Robledo, 96–7
Castro, Américo, 52
Castro family, 43, 54, 80, 93, 134
Catalán, Diego, 7, 129, 153–4n11
Catalonia, 64
Cazola, treaty of, 88
Celestine III, Pope, 70, 72, 73
Cetina, 10, 82, 141
Chalon, Louis, 7, 12, 41, 43, 44, 60, 82, 151n1
Chanson d'Antioche, 19, 140
Chanson de Guillaume, 133, 138
Chanson de Roland: Battle of Roncevaux, 131; episode of Aude, 130; episode of Baligant, 154–5n2; flights of Ganelon, 130; non-Oxford versions, 131; Oxford version, 67, 68, 114, 119, 121–2, 130, 136, 138, 149n1, 155n5; trial of Ganelon, 67, 130; Venice 4 version, 130
Chansons de geste, 1, 19, 27, 80–1, 108, 114, 116, 117–18, 119, 120, 122, 123, 124, 136, 137–9, 146–7, 155n5
Chaplin, Margaret, 155–6n6
Charroi de Nîmes, 19, 138
Chevalerie Ogier de Danemarche, 114, 116, 119
Chronique saintongeaise, 115
Cipolla, Carlo M., 150n5
Cirot, Georges, 89
Cistercian Order, 85, 87–8, 101, 102, 104, 105, 153n10
Cluniac Order, 103–4, 153n9
Cocheril, Maur, 84, 153n10
Coimbra, bishop of, 74
Colada, 14, 21, 24, 25, 39, 40, 51, 98
Colophon, 6, 13–14, 62, 66, 91, 153n6
Compostela, bishop of, 74

Concubinage, 45–7, 49, 53–5
Conerly, Porter, 150n6
Conrad, son of Friedrich Barbarossa, 70
Consanguinity, 70, 72–3, 76, 78, 135
Consuegra, battle of, 60
Contract, 18
Cordón, Constantino, 101
Corpes, Robledo de, 96–7, 99, 107; Cid's preoccupations after, 40; French influence, 109–12; legal effect, 45; outrage of, 6, 39–40, 47–9, 58, 80, 96, 130
Cortes, 11, 66; *see also* Toledo *and* Carrión
Costanza, daughter of Alfonso IX and Berenguela, 74
Couronnement de Louis, 138
Cowardice, 46–8, 151n1
Craddock, Jerry R., 44, 80
Criado de Val, Manuel, 83, 96–7, 100
Cristina Rodríguez. *See* Daughters, Cid's
Crónica de Castilla, 50
Crònica de Jaume I, 97
Crónica de veinte reyes, 16–17, 18, 33, 151n3
Cronica geral de Espanha de 1344, 50
Crónica latina de los reyes de Castilla, 29, 68–9, 70, 71, 75, 91, 135
Crónica particular del Cid, 50, 151n2
Cuarte, battle of, 11, 55, 59
Cuenca, 64, 85, 87, 100, 106

Date of the poem, 4, 5–15, 62, 68, 84, 90, 91, 94, 100, 125–30, 132–4
Daughters, Cid's, 32, 34, 38, 39, 40, 43, 45–9, 51, 53, 54, 96, 109–12, 130, 131; Elvira, 45, 54, 78, 94, 100, 109, 111; Sol, 45, 54, 78, 92–3, 100, 103, 109, 111; endowed with Cid's wealth, 36; historical daughter Cristina, 58, 78, 90, 94, 95, 97; historical daughter María, 58, 78, 90, 92–3, 94, 151n1; husbands' names, 58, 79, 92–3; names, 58, 79, 94, 125; *see also* Marriages, Cid's daughters
Debts: Alfonso VIII's, 29; Cid's to the Virgin Mary, 23, 32, 36; Cid's to Martín Antolínez, 36; Pedro II of Aragon's, 69, 72, 91; Rodrigo, bishop of Sigüenza's, 105
De Chasca, Edmund, 136, 137, 145

Index

Descriptions, length of related to personal worth, 27
Deyermond, Alan, 62–3, 112–13, 139, 154n3
Dialect features: Aragonese, 9, 11, 125, 126, 142; Castilian, 125; of Medinaceli, 125, 141; literary, 125
Dictation, 126, 127, 139–40, 145, 156n7
Diego Laínez, 43, 49–50
Diego López de Haro, 71, 74, 86, 88
Diego Rodríguez, 60, 79
Diego Téllez, 111–12, 124
Disputa del alma y el cuerpo, 126, 127
Documents, poet's familiarity with, 62–3, 154n3; archival hypothesis, 100, 124
Doon de Mayence, cycle of, 147
Dronke, Peter, 121
Duby, Georges, 1, 30–1, 150n6
Duels, judicial, 48–9, 51, 55, 56, 58, 59, 61, 151n1
Dulce of Provence, 90
Duncalf, Frederic, 26
Dunn, Peter N., 63, 79
Dyer, Nancy Joe, 16, 33, 151n3

Eleanor of Aquitaine, 75
Elliott, Alison G., 116
Elpha, 107
Elvira, Cid's daughter in poem. *See* Daughters, Cid's
Elvira, daughter of Manrique Pérez de Lara, 95, 107
Elvira, daughter of Pedro González de Lara, 95
Elvira, possible daughter of Pedro de Molina, 95
Elvira, wife of lord of Fuentearmegil and San Esteban de Gormaz, 94–5
Enfurción, 56
Enrique I, 76
Enrique, Count, 124
Epic, 2, 20, 62, 133, 144, 147, 151n1; Yugoslavian, 131, 136, 155–6n6, 156n7
Epic prayer, 117–18, 120, 121, 154n2
Epithets: Babieca, 109; Campeador, 10; *campiator*, 128; *campidoctor*, 128; *campidoctus*, 128; el Castellano, 35; Cid Campeador, 16–17; Mio Cid, 7, 10, 128
Ermesinda, wife of Manrique de Lara, 85–6, 93, 95

"Ese buen Diego Laínez," 49–50
Estoria de España, 11, 16, 18, 33, 73, 127, 149n4, 151n1, 153–4n11
Eva, wife of Jimeno Pérez de Rada, 86, 98
Excommunication, 73
Exile, king's decision to impose, 17

Fame as correlative of wealth, 26
Fáriz, 22–3, 24, 25, 28, 60, 83, 99, 141
Fazañas, 65
Félez Muñoz, 59, 80, 96, 111, 153n4
Fernando I, king of Castile and Leon, 28, 53
Fernando II, king of Leon, 70, 135
Fernando III, king of Castile and Leon, 74, 75, 76, 88, 91, 153–4n11; heir to the castles of the dowry, 75, 91; illegitimacy, 74, 76–7; recognized as heir to throne of Leon, 74, 91; recognized by Pope as legitimate heir, 77
Fernando, son of Alfonso VIII, 72, 76, 88
Fernando, son of Alfonso IX and Teresa of Portugal, 74, 76
Fernando Díaz, 50
Fernando Muñoz, 96
Fernando Rodríguez de Castro, 43, 93
Fernando Ruiz de Azagra, 11
Feudalism, 19, 30, 150n7
Fierabras, 118
Financing: Cid's activities, 19, 22, 23, 37; First Crusade, 26
Fines, 31
First Crusade to the Holy Land, 26, 140
Fita, Fidel, 104
Fletcher, Richard, 62
Florence de Rome, 109–13, 122, 154n3
Foreros, 52, 65
Formulas, 121, 132, 154–5n2; composition by, 136; density, 136–9, 155–6n6
Fouque de Candie, 113
Fradejas Lebrero, José, 68
Fraga, battle of, 28
Francis, E.-A., 67
Fresno-Lavandera, treaty of, 70
Froila Díaz, 60, 124
Fuero juzgo, 41, 64, 125
Fuero real, 48, 67
Fuero viejo, 44, 52, 64

Index

Fuero viejo de Vizcaya, 152n2
Fueros, municipal: 22, 25, 43, 51–2, 54, 63–5, 128; *Fuero de Cuenca*, 64, 67; *Fuero de León*, 64; *Fuero de Madrid*, 126, 127; *Fuero de Molina de Aragón*, 52, 66; *Fuero de Navarra*, 117; *Fuero de Salamanca*, 52, 67; *Fuero de Soria*, 52, 67; *Fuero de Teruel*, 64; *Fuero de Viguera y Val de Funes*, 55; *Fuero de Zorita de los Canes*, 67

Gacto Fernández, Enrique, 45, 52
Galbert of Bruges, 147–8
Galicia, 40
Galind Garciaz, 90, 124
Galve, 22–3, 24, 25, 28, 60, 83, 99, 141
Ganelon, 115, 147
Gárate Córdoba, José M., 150n6
García Gallo, Alfonso, 52
García Luján, José Antonio, *Cartulario del monasterio de Santa María de Huerta*, 84, 85–7, 101, 153n8
García Ordóñez, 16–17, 26, 43, 45–6, 53, 60, 61, 92, 115, 119; historical figure, 124, 134
García Pérez de Lara of Molina, 86, 93, 99, 107
García Ramírez "el Restaurador," king of Navarre, 78, 90, 93; lord of Monzón, 93, 97–8
Garci-Gómez, Miguel, 150n6
Garin le Loherain, 19
Gascony, 75
Gautier Dalché, Jean, 64
Geary, John S., 132, 139, 155–6n6
Generation of 1898, 2–3, 5
Génin, François, 108
Geography: area that dominates poem, 52, 61–2, 82–100, 107; displacement, 129; exactness, 19
Gerli, E. Michael, 117
Gibraltar, Strait of, 71
Gift economy, 30–1; 34; 61, 146
Gifts: from Alfonso, 31, 151n4; *arras*, 37, 39, 80; *donadío*, 31; dowries, 39, 41; favors asked in connection with, 34; functions, 146; from Cid at *vistas*, 37; Cid never receives, 56, 146; from Cid to Alfonso, 23, 26, 33–5, 37, 83, 100, 146, 151n1; from Cid to Alvar Fáñez, 35–6; from Cid to Counts Anrrich and Remont, 56; from Cid to Infantes de Carrión, 39; from Cid to Jerónimo, 36; from Cid to Jimena's ladies, 36; from Cid to Rachel, 31; from Cid to Remont Verenguel, 35; from Cid to San Pedro de Cardeña, 32; from Cid to Santa María de Burgos, 32, 84, 103; from Cid to wedding guests, 37; from Rachel to Martín Antolínez, 31, 42; not required by law, 34; refusal of, 42; return of, 41; value of, 31, 33; of women, 147
Gil, Juan, 7
Girart de Roussillon, 19, 114, 116
Gombau, bishop of Lérida, 89
Gómez Peláyet, 49, 124
Gómez Pérez, 88
González, Julio, 68, 70, 71, 72, 73, 74, 75, 76, 77, 78, 87, 88, 89, 90, 91, 94, 98, 105, 106, 135
Gonzalo, bishop of Segovia, 88
Gonzalo Ansúrez, 124, 151n3
Gonzalo Núñez de Lara III, Count, 94
Gonzalo of Finojosa, bishop of Burgos, 153–4n11
Gonzalo Pérez de Lara, 86, 93–4, 98–9, 153n6
Gonzalo Rodríguez Girón, 88
Gormont et Isembart, 138
Gorosterratzu, Javier, 98
Gould, Stephen Jay, 144
Gran Conquista de Ultramar, 116
Grassotti, Hilda, 28, 79
Gregorio de Sant Angelo, Cardinal, 70
Guadalajara, 81, 84, 93, 99, 103, 106, 143
Guadalquivir, river, 71
Guglielmi, Nilda, 150nn6&7, 151n4
Guillem de Castellazol, 89
Guillermo González, 88
Guinevere, 67
Gutierre Díaz, 88
Gutierre Fernández, 88
Guy of Cîteaux, Abbot, 88

Háriz, 22, 60
Harney, Michael, 151n4
Harvey, L. P., 139, 156n7
Heers, Jacques, 144
Henares, river, 141; *see also* Campaigns, military
Henríquez Ureña, Pedro, 138
Herslund, Michael, 120–2

Index

Heubeck, Alfred, 133
Hidalgo, 11–12; *hidalguía*, 52–3
Hinojosa, Eduardo de, 7, 9, 12, 41
Hinojosa del Campo, 86
Historia Roderici, 60, 61, 82, 128
Historical elements, 4, 148; absence of expected, 60; appropriation by the poet, 58, 124, 131, 139, 144, 148; discrepancies in, 58–61; kernel of poem, 130; names of obscure figures, 124
Hofmann, Conrad, 49
Holland, Michael, 26
Homer, 62, 133, 145
Honorius III, Pope, 77
Hook, David, 59, 79, 112–13, 120, 121, 150n9, 152n5
Horrent, Jules, 13, 14, 43, 59, 79, 82, 91, 108, 121–2, 129, 131, 134, 140
Horses: as wealth, 20, 23, 26; evaluation of, 23–5, 33, 150n9; value of equipment, 33
Huber, Victor Aimé, 50
Huerta, 84–91, 93, 95–6, 98, 99, 100, 103, 104, 105, 106, 140, 141, 153n6, 153–4n11; abbots of, 101; occasions on which poem may have been performed there, 88, 90, 106, 143
Huerta del Rey, 99
Huesa, 10, 12
Huesca, 64; League of, 88
Huete, 85, 106; battle of, 43, 93
Hugo de Torreroja, 89
Huici Miranda, Ambrosio, 71–2, 96
Huntington, Archer M., 50, 151n3

Illegitimacy: accusation of against the Cid, 48–57, 61–2, 80, 130, 143; of Cid in popular literature, 50; legal effects, 44, 51–2, 76; offspring of Berenguela and Alfonso IX, 73–4, 76, 77, 80, 88, 91
Infamy, 48; causes of, 44–5; effects of, 44–6, 53
Infante of Aragon, 9, 78, 92; see also Marriages, Cid's daughters'
Infante of Navarre, 9, 78; see also Marriages, Cid's daughters'
Infantes de Carrión, 9, 31, 36, 37–8, 43, 51, 53–4, 59, 65, 96, 103, 109, 131, 147; Diego, 47, 54, 98, 99, 124, 130, 134; Fernando, 46–7, 54, 98, 124, 130;

choice as villains, 60, 80, 125; effect of *menosvaler* on, 44–5; failure to give gifts, 37–8, 41; fictional relation to Cid's daughters, 58; historical figures, 44; legal defense, 45–7, at lowest point, 56; misconceptions about values, 36, 39
Infantes de la Cerda, 80
Iñigo Jiménez, 59, 95, 124
Iniuria, 48
Innocent III, Pope, 73–5, 77, 78, 88, 89, 90, 130
Insults, legal status of, 51–2, 55
Interdiction, 73–4, 79, 89
Interest, 18, 31
Ira regia, 34
Irony, 39, 150n2, 151n4

Jacobo, bishop of Avila, 88
Jalón, river, 83, 141; valley of, 84, 107, 142, 143; see also Campaigns, military
Janko, Richard, 133
Jaume I, 153–4n11
Jerónimo, Bishop, 22, 36, 62, 79; historical figure Jérôme of Périgord, 104
Jimena, 32, 34, 36, 46, 54, 55, 58, 60, 100, 114, 116, 117–18, 124; historical figure, 60, 61, 77, 78; prayer, 117–18
Jimeno, abbot of Huerta, 88, 90, 101, 153n8
Jimeno Cornell, lord of Huesca, 89
Jimeno de Lusia, 89
Jimeno Pérez de Rada, 86, 89, 98, 107
Joan de Berax, 89
Jordán de Asso, Ignacio, 52
Jordán de Pedra Alta, 89
Jousse, Marcel, 136
Juan, bishop of Calahorra, 88
Juan Díaz, nephew of Martín Muñoz, 153–4n11
Judicial duels, 6, 98, 130, 135
Juglares, 11, 45, 53, 132
Julián, bishop of Cuenca, 88

Lacarra, José María, 11–12
Lacarra, María Eugenia, 4, 15, 17, 21, 22, 25, 31, 34, 35, 41, 43, 46, 47, 54, 62, 65, 66, 80, 93, 94, 134, 135, 150n4
Lalinde Abadía, Jesús, 63–4
Lambert of Ardre, 140, 144, 156n8
Lambert of Watrelos, 144

Index

Lancelot en prose, 67
Lanval, 152n5
Lapesa, Rafael, 10, 11, 12, 125, 126, 127, 129, 132, 133, 139, 151n1
Lara family of Molina, 43, 54, 71, 77, 79, 80, 93, 134, 143, 146, 153n4; counts "by the grace of God," 94; patrons of Huerta, 85, 93
Largess, 30–1, 36, 143; as a key to exemplary value, 42
Las Huelgas, 85, 87, 88, 94, 104
Las Navas de Tolosa, battle of, 29, 68, 69, 84, 85, 87, 88, 89, 91, 96, 105
Law: Castilian, 43; Cid's knowledge of, 27; customal, 63–4, 66, 67, 152n3; Germanic, 152n4; memorial transmission of, 63–4; poet's knowledge of, 62–3, 67; Roman, 65–7
Layna Serrano, Francisco, 103
Legal profession, 2, 63–7
Leon: anti-Leonese sentiment in poem, 60, 61; bishop of, 73; kingdom of, 11, 12, 40, 43, 70–1, 72, 73, 74, 75, 76, 87, 91, 94
Leonor, daughter of Alfonso IX and Berenguela, 74
Leonor, queen, 72, 75, 76, 79, 88, 102
Lévi-Strauss, Claude, 147
Liber feudorum, 97
Liber regum, 22
Libro de Apolonio, 155–6n6
Libro de los fueros de Castilla, 63
Libro del infante Epitus, 57
Linaje navarro del Cid, 10
Lindley Cintra, Luis Felipe, 50
Lineage, invention of, 147–8; of Rodrigo Díaz of Vivar, 43, 79, 90, 91, 93, 99, 105, 106–7, 134, 135, 143, 146, 151n2, 153n4; values of, 36–7, 39, 43, 45–7, 49, 51, 54, 61, 77, 78, 130, 146, 147–8
Linguistic traits, 7, 125–8, 132–3; archaisms, 8, 126, 127, 132–4, 139; French influence, 108, 111; Homeric, 133
Lion episode, 6, 37–8, 39, 46–7, 115–17, 154n4
Literary resemblance, nature of, 112–22, 152n5
Loans, 31, 150n5; from Rachel and Vidas to the Cid, 18, 22, 23, 32, 132
Localization, 4, 6

Lomax, Derek, 9, 10, 13
Longinus, 118
Lope de Valtierra, 89
Lope Sánchez, 88
López de Ayala, Pero: *Rimado de palacio*, 62–3
Lord, Albert B., 131, 137, 154–5n2, 155–6n6; *The Singer of Tales*, 136, 139
Luzón, river, 103

McMillan, Duncan, 19
Mafalda, mother of Gonzalo Pérez de Lara, 98, 107
Mafalda of Portugal, 76
Magi, 118
Magnotta, Michael, 14
Mahalda, wife of Ramon Berenguer II, 92
Malanda, 65–6, 104, 152n4
Mandates, royal, 62–3, 66; threat contained in, 63, 78–9; *see also* Seals
Manrique, Angel: *Annales Cistercienses*, 85, 87, 100, 101
Manrique Pérez de Lara, 43, 85–6, 93, 94, 95
Manuel y Rodríguez, Miguel de, 52
Manuscript of the poem, 3, 4, 9, 13–15, 16, 80, 106, 149n1, 151n3, 153n11; writing on folio, 74, 56–7; *see also* Colophon
Maquila, 48–9, 56
Marcos Marín, Francisco, 14, 125, 126, 127, 139
María Palacín, mother of Martín de Finojosa, 96
María Rodríguez. *See* Daughters, Cid's
Marie de France, 67, 152n5
Marquesa, wife of Muño Sánchez de Finojosa, 86
Marriage, legitimate, 45, 47, 49, 55, 78
Marriages, Cid's daughters', 146, 147, 152n6; historical, 58; to the Infantes de Carrión, 6, 7, 31, 34, 36–7, 45, 48, 58, 130; to the Infantes of Navarre and Aragon, 55, 58, 78, 79, 90, 130, 147; invitation, 37
Martín, abbot of Cardeña, 103
Martín, bishop of Burgos, 88
Martín, bishop of Osma, 88
Martín Antolínez, 17, 32, 36, 41, 47, 50, 51, 54, 98

Index

Martín de Finojosa, St., abbot of Huerta and bishop of Sigüenza, 86–8, 94, 95–7, 99, 100, 101, 102, 103, 105, 106, 107, 143, 153n8; buried at Huerta, 87
Martín López de Pisuerga, Archbishop, 71, 79, 88
Martín Muñoz, "el que mando a Mont Mayor," 96, 124
Martín, Muñoz, nephew of Martín de Finojosa, 96, 152–3n3, 153–4n11
Martín Pérez de Vilel, 89
Mass of the Holy Trinity, 87, 99–100
Mateu y Llopis, Felipe, 8–9
Mauss, Marcel, 30, 146, 153n5
Mayor, daughter of Pedro Ansúrez, 59
Medinaceli, 6, 10, 12, 22, 60, 61–2, 81, 82, 84, 85, 100, 102, 103, 125, 130, 132, 140, 141, 143
Menéndez Pidal, Gonzalo, 122
Menéndez Pidal, Ramón, 2, 4–15, 16, 18, 21, 22, 32, 33, 44, 47, 48, 53, 55, 57, 60, 65, 73, 82, 92–3, 94, 95, 99, 100, 108, 115, 117, 119, 122, 125–8, 129, 132, 137, 141, 149n3, 149n4, 150n9, 151n3, 154n1, 154n4; dating of the poem, 7–8, 125–7, 134; theory of two poets, 6–7, 61, 82, 93, 125, 130, 131–2, 140
Menosvaler, 36, 43–7, 54
Michael, Ian, 22, 32, 38, 83, 99, 100, 133, 151n2, 151n3
Michaëlis, Carolina, 49
Miguel de Lusia, 89
Miguel Muñoz of Hinojosa, 86, 96
Miletich, John, 155–6n6
Millares Carlo, Agustín, 102, 103
Minguella y Arnedo, Toribio, 86, 87
Miret y Sans, Joaquin, 85, 91
Mocedades de Rodrigo, 120, 139, 155–6n6
Models of poetic creation, 117, 131, 134, 139
Molina de Aragón, 54, 61–2, 66, 77, 85, 87, 93, 98–9, 103; *see also Fueros*, municipal
Money, 8–9, 18, 20, 24, 151n10; dinar, 28; *dinero*, 8; *maravedí*, 8; mark, 18, 24, 28, 150n3; *solidus*, 24, 28
Moneylenders, 61, 80
Moniage Guillaume, 138
Monk of St. Gall, 116
Monreal del Campo, 10

Monsalud, 100
Montalbán, 10, 12
Montes Claros, king of the, 8, 9, 129, 130
Montgomery, Thomas, 152n7
Monzón, 64, 97, 98
Moreta Velayos, Salustiano, 104
Morimond, 91, 102
Morocco, 8, 9, 91, 129
Motivation, 16, 37
Mudaffar, king of Córdoba, 16
Muño Gustioz, 40, 48–9, 51, 54, 55, 77; historical figure 40, 55, 60, 124
Muño Sánchez de Finojosa, 86, 87, 88, 96
Muret, battle of, 91
Muriel, 102
Murviedro, 59
Mutamid, king of Seville, 16–17, 32
Mutamin, king of Saragossa, 22, 59, 60

Naissance du chevalier au cygne, 112
Navarre, 7, 9, 25, 55, 69, 72, 89, 90
Nepaulsingh, Colbert I., 112
Njal's Saga, 152n4
Nota Emilianense, 122–3
Núño Alvarez, 53

Ojarra, 59, 127
Ondra, 37
Onís, Federico de, 52
Oral composition, 4, 117, 131, 132, 134, 136, 140, 144, 145, 149n1, 154–5n2, 155n4, 156n7
Ordenamiento de Nájera, 44
Order of Calatrava, 70, 99; Master of, 67, 71
Order of the Hospital, 91
Order of the Temple, 70
Ostentation and fame, 26–7
Otero Varela, Alfonso, 49
Ovid: *Metamorphoses*, 112
Ovila, 86, 102–3, 105, 106
"Oy los reyes d'España sos parientes son" (l. 3724), 6, 9, 12, 56, 77, 90–1

Palencia, 74, 106, 139; bishop of, 73; university of, 66
Paragogic -e, 125–6, 133
Parchment, 145–6
Pardo, Aristóbulo, 149n1
Parise de Duchesse, 117–18, 119

Index

Parmly, Ruth, 19
Parry, Milman, 136, 145, 155–6n6
Pastor de Togneri, Reyna, 24, 150n9
Patrons: of poet, 62, 68
Pattison, D. G., 11, 12, 83, 127–8, 153–4n11, 156n1
Payment in kind, 41, 49, 51
Pedro I, king of Aragon, 90
Pedro II, king of Aragon and count of Barcelona, 11, 69, 72, 78, 84, 88–9, 90, 91–3, 98, 99, 107; patron of Huerta, 85, 88; see also Debts
Pedro, abbot of Huerta, 101–2, 105, 106, 145
Pedro, abbot of Ovila, 102, 104, 105–6, 145
Pedro Abad, 153n6
Pedro Ansúrez, 59, 60
Pedro de Mediano, 89
Pedro de Molina, 85–6, 88, 93, 94, 98–9, 107
Pedro Fernández, 89
Pedro Fernández de Castro, 71–2, 74, 75, 80, 135
Pedro García de Lerma, 88
Pedro González de Lara, 95
Pedro González de Marañón, 88
Pedro, infante, 151n1
Pedro Jiménez de Orrea, 89
Pedro Ladrón, 89
Pedro Manrique de Lara. See Pedro de Molina
Pedro Ruiz de Azagra, 88
Pedro Tizón, governor of Estella, 98, 107
Pedro Tizón, lord of Monzón, 97–8, 107
Pèlerinage de Charlemagne, 138
Pellen, René, 125, 126, 155n3
Peñalcázar, 83, 141
Per Abbat, 3, 4, 11, 12, 13, 14, 15, 77, 95, 99, 112, 124, 139; identity of, 81, 101–2, see also Pedro Abad
Pérez de Urbel, Justo, 97, 100
Pérez-Prendes y Muñoz de Arracó, José Manuel, 44, 52, 63–5, 152n3; *Curso de historia del derecho español*, 67
Pero Vermúdez, 33, 38, 41, 46–7, 50, 51, 66, 98; historical figure, 124
Petronila, wife of Ramon Berenguer IV, 92
Pirenne, Henri, 150
Plasencia, 67
Poblet, 95

Poema de Almería, 7, 9–10, 12, 122, 128–9, 130, 134, 144
Poema de Fernán González, 117, 139, 155–6n6
Poet, 14, 17, 92; access to documents, 61, 62–3; choices reveal purpose, 58, 107; events invented by, 22, 79, 82; fatigue, 132; geographical milieu, 107, 152n2; *juglar*, 132, 140, 141, 143–4, 145, 148; knowledge, 62, 144, 152n5; literacy, 108, 139, 145, 149n1; places invented by, 83; single, 132; themes invented by, 130; see also Patrons
Portugal, 9, 88
Poyo, el, Poyo de mio Cid, 66, 82
Principal, 18, 23
Prise de Cordres et de Sebille, 114, 116
Prise d'Orange, 138
Profit, 38, 40
Propagandistic function, 68, 80, 143
Property: armor, 20, 23; houses, 24, 25; land, 19–20, 23, 24, 150n6; movable goods, 19–21, 25, 150n6; tents, 20, 33, see also Tent, king of Morocco's; wheat, 56; see also Horses
Pseudo-Ordenamiento de Nájera, 52
Puns, 35, 151n2

Quinea, calçada de, 152n2
Quiñoneros, 20

Rachel and Vidas, 17–18, 22, 32, 36, 61, 131, 150n6; episode of, 31; request gift, 42; see also Loans
Raimond V, count of Toulouse, 91
Raimundo, bishop of Saragossa, 89
Rainerio, Papal Legate, 73, 89
Rajna, Pio, 154n4
Ramiro II "el Monje," king of Aragon, 92, 98
Ramiro Sánchez, lord of Monzón and infante de Navarre, 58, 78, 97–8
Ramon Berenguer II "Cabeza de Estopa," count of Barcelona, 92
Ramon Berenguer III "el Grande," count of Barcelona, 7, 58, 78, 92, 97; married to María Rodríguez, 90, 151n1
Ramon Berenguer IV, prince of Aragon and count of Barcelona, 7, 92–3
Ramon de Castellvell, 89
Ramos Loscertales, José María, 55

Index

Raoul de Cambrai, 118, 138
Reception of Cid's legend, 4, 58, 146
Reception of poem: by earliest audiences, 4, 100; first documented, 57
Reconquest of Spain, 3, 20, 67, 68, 69, 80, 143, 146
Reilly, Bernard F., 95
Remont, Count, 56, 124, 152n4
Remont Verenguel. *See* Berenguer Ramon II
Resina, Juan Ramón, 149n2, 151n4
Riba, 86, 105
Riepto, 43–4, 55, 62
Riquer, Martín de, 108
Rodrigo, bishop of Sigüenza, 87, 88, 105
Rodrigo Alvárez, 53
Rodrigo Díaz of Vivar: choice as topic, 58; date of death, 61; descendance, 43, 79, 90, 93, 99, 107, 135, 143, 153n4; donation to Santo Domingo de Silos, 60; exiles, 58, 59, 79, 82, 91; historical figure, 5, 6, 7, 10, 11, 22, 31, 59, 95, 141; illegitimacy, 46, 55, 61, 77; illegitimacy in *romancero*, 49–50; independent ruler, 94; in *Poema de Almería*, 128; rise in status, 56, 62, 78, 80; tradition of songs, *see* Transmission of the Cid legend
Rodrigo Jiménez de Rada, bishop of Toledo, 86, 98–9, 152–3n3; buried at Huerta, 87; *De rebus Hispaniae*, 69, 72, 82, 86, 94, 97–8, 128
Rodríguez Fernández, Justiniano, 59
Rodríguez López, Amancio, 71, 94
Rodríguez Puertolas, Julio, 51, 150n6
Roland, 154n6
Roman d'Alexandre, 139
Romero, Agustín, 86, 87, 93, 96, 100, 152n1
Roncesvalles, 126
Russell, P. E., 9, 11, 62, 79, 83, 119, 120, 133, 149n3, 151–2n2
Rychner, Jean, 133, 136, 138, 155n5

Sabidores, 65–6, 104, 152n4
Sacedón, 100
Sagrajas, battle of, 115
St. Victor de Marseille, 104
Salamanca, bishop of, 73
Salazar y Castro, Luis, 94, 95, 98, 99, 153n6
San Esteban de Gormaz, 6, 16, 56, 61–2, 77, 81, 82, 85, 93, 96, 106, 107, 111, 132, 140–1, 143, 151–2n2, 152–n2
San Servando, 61, 104–5
Sancha, daughter of Alfonso IX, 76
Sancha, infanta, wife of Pedro de Molina, 85–6, 93, 95, 98–9, 107; buried at Huerta, 86, 107
Sancha, mother of Pedro II of Aragon, 72, 85, 88–9, 98
Sancha Gómez of Almazán, mother of Martín of Finojosa, 86, 87, 152n1
Sancha Gómez, wife of Gonzalo Pérez de Lara, 153n6
Sánchez, Galo, 52
Sánchez, Tomás Antonio, 6
Sancho I, king of Portugal, 70–1, 76
Sancho III "el Deseado," king of Castile, 7, 12, 15, 135
Sancho IV, king of Castile and Leon, 80
Sancho VII, king of Navarre, 71, 78, 91
Sancho, abbot of Cardeña, 32, 58, 61, 79, 125
Sancho, son of Alfonso VIII and Leonor, 76
Sancho García, count of Castile, 28
Sancho Izquierdo, Miguel, 66
Sanctioning function, 156n8
Santiago, pilgrimage route to, 123
Santo Domingo de Silos, 60, 61, 96, 153n10
Santos, Francisco: *La verdad en el potro y el Cid resucitado*, 50–2
Saragossa, kingdom of, 84
Scribes of the *Cid* manuscript: scribe of 1207, 14–15, 105, 107; fourteenth-century scribe, 9, 14, 153–4n11
Seals, royal, 11, 62–3
Sepúlveda, 64, 67, 95, 106
Serra Ruiz, Rafael, 48, 52, 53
Serrano, Luciano, 71, 72, 90
Severin, Dorothy, 57
Seville, 16, 71, 119
Siège de Barbastre, 138
Sigüenza: diocesis, 84, 97, 101, 102, 103, 105; *señorío*, 86
Sisebuto, Abbot, 58, 61, 125
Smith, Colin, 14, 32, 38, 43, 62, 66, 95, 111, 112–19, 122, 151n3, 152n6, 153n9, 153–4n11, 154nn1&2&3, 154n5, 156n9; *Estudios cidianos*, 117; *Making of the Poema de mio Cid*, 119, 124; *Poema de mio Cid*, 149n5

177

Index

Social mobility, 20, 39, 151n4
Sol, daughter of Cid. *See* Daughters, Cid's
Sol, wife of Domingo Martínez, 94
Sol, wife of Domingo Sánchez of Belena, 94
Spinaz de Can, 99
Spitzer, Leo, 2, 43
Suárez, Federico, 65
Sumption, Jonathan, 32

Tagus, river, 102, 104
Tamin, king of Valencia, 22, 59, 60, 79, 83
Tarazona, bishop of, 74, 85
Tello Téllez de Meneses, 66
Tent, king of Morocco's, 24, 33
Tercera crónica general, 50
Teresa, daughter of Sancho I of Portugal, 70–1, 76, 90, 135
Teresa, sister of Martín de Finojosa, 86, 93
Teresa Núñez, 50
Terrer, 83, 84, 86, 100, 141
Teruel, 11, 99
Teshufin, 129
Tévar, battle of, 21, 24, 91
Tierra de Campos, 72
Tizón, 14, 24, 25, 39, 40, 51, 97–8, 153–4n11
Toledo: archbishop of, 73, 74; cathedral of, 85, 104, 106; city, 61, 64, 71, 84, 85; court scene at, 16, 40–1, 43–9, 51–7, 58, 65, 104, 130, 152n4; diocese of, 94; kingdom of, 16–17, 82
Tordehumos, treaty of, 70–1
Transierra, 15, 22, 52, 77, 79, 100, 106, 126, 129, 130, 132, 142
Transmission of the Cid legend, 58, 79, 129, 134, 136, 137, 140, 148; process of change, 130
Tribute, 16, 27–9, 31, 33, 56, 119; paid to historical Cid, 28, 59, 79

Ubierna, river, 48–9
Ubieto Arteta, Antonio, 9–14, 58, 59, 60, 83, 91, 97–8, 99, 128, 135, 141, 151n1, 152n2, 156n9
Urban II, Pope, 26
Urraca, daughter of Alfonso VIII, 9, 135
Urraca, queen of Castile and Leon, 8, 9, 28, 95, 96, 104

Valdanzo, 97
Valencia, 10, 21, 28, 54, 60, 61, 79, 94, 96, 103, 105, 116, 129; historical battles after capture of, 58, 91; kingdom of, 83, 88; siege and capture of, 10, 23, 25, 32, 33, 37, 59, 69, 82, 90, 141; *see also* Campaigns, military
Valladolid, 72, 74
Vallerie, Josephine, 19
Versification, 131–2, 133, 137–8, 139, 140, 145–6, 156n7
Vicens Vives, Jaime, 23–*Vistas* on the Tagus, 37, 45, 55, 90
Vitoria, capture of, 78

Walker, Roger M., 108–13
Walsh, John K., 110, 112, 151n1
Waltman, Franklin M., 132
Wathelet-Willem, Jeanne, 133
Wax tablets, 145–6
Wealth, 5; acquisition of, 16–29, 54, 61, 80, 130, 146, 150n6; effective use of, 35; and honor, 26; instrument of loyalty, 36, 69; and marriageability, 36; surplus, 30; transmutation into other values, 37, 78, 130, 147; *see also* Booty
Webber, Ruth House, 145, 152n5, 155n4
Wolf, Ferdinand, 49, 92–3

Ya'qub al-Mansur ibn Yusuf, 71–2
Yseult, 67
Yusuf ibn Texufin, 21, 24, 25, 26, 33, 36, 37, 59, 79, 129; historical figure, 8

Zahareas, Anthony, 46
Zalaca, battle of, 28
Zamora, Florentino, 84, 86, 153–4n11
Zamora, bishop of, 73
Zorita, 103

UNIVERSITY LIBRARY